CHAPTER 1

Introduction

SCOTLAND, in the same latitude as southern Alaska and southern Sweden, and approximately twice the area of Switzerland, has a population of 5,196,600 (1962), almost identical to that of Switzerland. Like Switzerland, Scotland displays an extraordinary range of geographical facets within small compass and, although not as completely independent from England now as it was 500 years ago, it would be difficult to find another semi-autonomous region displaying to such a marked degree, without open revolt, so deep a sense of tradition, national heritage and individualism. Scotland is at once both a poor and a rich country, poor in natural resources but rich in human talent, otherwise little could have been made of what is largely a rather hostile environment of harsh climate, stony, acid soils and rugged relief.

In our appraisal of Scotland we hope to indicate some of the features of the varied physical background and the ways in which these features have contributed towards the present development of the most northerly part of Britain. No two human faces are identical, and likewise, in *The Face of Scotland* there is to be found a stamp of individuality which so distinguishes this particular country from any other. Although the outward appearance of the face of Scotland is not entirely carefree, recent indications of a resurgence in the shipyards, rationalization of some of the older industries and significant expansions in the new town sites, do give an air of confidence in continued growth. These matters will be treated more fully at a later stage as the initial introductory aim is to outline to what degree the physical forces of nature have conditioned a particular environmental response in Scotland.

THE NATURAL LANDSCAPE

Scotland's diminutive size is compensated for by the variety of its landscape: steep-sided fiorded incisions into the north-west coast contrast with the shallow, shelving bays of Fife and Galloway; plunging mountain torrents witht he stately meanders of the Earn and Forth across wide, open carse lands; the ice-smoothed humps of the Grampian massif with the jagged, weathered peaks of the Cuillins of Skye; and the host of islands of varying

1

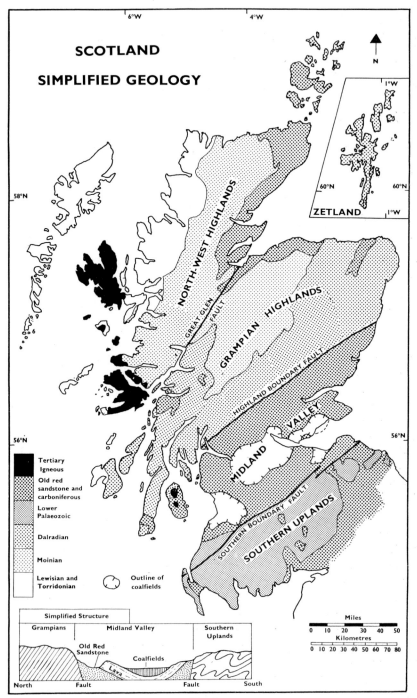

SCOTLAND

SIMPLIFIED GEOLOGY

Legend:
- Tertiary Igneous
- Old red sandstone and carboniferous
- Lower Palaeozoic
- Dalradian
- Moinian
- Lewisian and Torridonian
- Outline of coalfields

Map labels: NORTH-WEST HIGHLANDS, GREAT GLEN FAULT, GRAMPIAN HIGHLANDS, HIGHLAND BOUNDARY FAULT, MIDLAND VALLEY, SOUTHERN BOUNDARY FAULT, SOUTHERN UPLANDS, ZETLAND

6°W   4°W   1°W

N

58°N   60°N   60°N

56°N   56°N

Simplified Structure

Grampians	Midland Valley	Southern Uplands
	Old Red Sandstone	
	Lava Coalfields	
North Fault	Fault	South

Miles
0 10 20 30 40 50

Kilometres
0 10 20 30 40 50 60 70 80

Fig. 1.

After H.M. Geol. Survey

2

THE COMMONWEALTH AND INTERNATIONAL LIBRARY

Joint Chairmen of the Honorary Editorial Advisory Board

SIR ROBERT ROBINSON, O.M., F.R.S., LONDON
DEAN ATHELSTAN SPILHAUS, MINNESOTA

PERGAMON OXFORD GEOGRAPHIES

General Editor: W. B. FISHER

The Face of Scotland

Second Edition

The Face of Scotland

by

I. G. McINTOSH, M.A.

and

C. B. MARSHALL, M.A.

SECOND EDITION

PERGAMON PRESS

Oxford · New York

Toronto · Sydney · Braunschweig

Pergamon Press Ltd., Headington Hill Hall, Oxford

Pergamon Press Inc., Maxwell House, Fairview Park, Elmsford, New York 10523

Pergamon of Canada Ltd., 207 Queen's Quay West, Toronto 1

Pergamon Press (Aust.) Pty. Ltd., 19a Boundary Street,
Rushcutters Bay, N.S.W. 2011, Australia

Vieweg & Sohn GmbH, Burgplatz 1, Braunschweig

First edition 1966
Second edition 1970

Library of Congress Catalog Card No. 75–104119

Printed in Great Britain by A. Wheaton & Co., Exeter

08 015549 9 (flexicover)
08 015550 2 (hard cover)

Contents

LIST OF ILLUSTRATIONS   vii

PREFACE   xi

ACKNOWLEDGEMENTS   xiii

1   Introduction   1

2   Scotland's Natural Resources   16

3   Population   34

4   The Central Lowlands: Introduction   41

5   The Straths and Coastlands of the Lower Tay Region   47

6   The Fife Peninsula   59

7   Edinburgh and the Lothians   73

8   The Middle Forth Region   90

9   The Middle and Lower Clyde Region   97

10   Ayrshire   122

11   The Southern Uplands   133

12   The Central Highlands (Grampians)   145

13   The Coastal Lowlands of the North-east   159

14   The Crofting Counties   175

15   Trends in Scottish Industrial Development   187

BIBLIOGRAPHY   197

GLOSSARY OF THE MORE UNUSUAL TERMS   199

INDEX   201

List of Illustrations

Fig.	1. Scotland: simplified geology	2
Fig.	2. The Great Glen, looking north-eastwards	4
Fig.	3. The ice-moulded landscape of South Harris	5
Fig.	4. Scotland: drainage	7
Fig.	5. Strath Conon (Ross-shire), showing typical U-shaped valley caused by the passage of a glacier	8
Fig.	6. Climate graphs for selected stations	10
Fig.	7. Incidence of snow	12
Fig.	8. Rainfall and relief	13
Fig.	9. Typical Podzol profile	18
Fig.	10. Number of hill sheep-farms	20
Fig.	11. Agricultural units in Scotland	22
Fig.	12. Arable/livestock rearing farms	23
Fig.	13. Beef and dairy cattle	24
Fig.	14. Crop comparisons	24
Fig.	15. Major forest areas	26
Fig.	16. Early-morning fish landings at Ullapool, Wester Ross	28
Fig.	17. Electricity in Scotland	30
Fig.	18. Sources of electricity generation in the Highlands	32
Fig.	19. The population drain	35
Fig.	20. Scottish population changes	36
Fig.	21. Population decline in the Hebrides (Isle of Barra)	37
Fig.	22. Major settlements in Scotland	38
Fig.	23. Scotland: population density	39
Fig.	24. The Central Lowlands: subdivisions and general features	41
Fig.	25. Scotland's coalfields	42
Fig.	26. Scottish coalfields—1968	43
Fig.	27. Central Scotland: some important new developments	44
Fig.	28. The straths and coastlands of the Lower Tay Region	48
Fig.	29. Strathmore seen from the north-western slopes of the Sidlaw Hills	49
Fig.	30. The Lower Tay Region: occupations and industries	50
Fig.	31. View along the Carse of Gowrie	51
Fig.	32. Strathmore and the Tay: land utilization	51
Fig.	33. Dundee, seen from the south-east	54

Fig. 34. The growth of Dundee   55
Fig. 35. Arbroath   57
Fig. 36. Fife peninsula: relief and routes   60
Fig. 37. Fife peninsula: occupations and towns   61
Fig. 38. An aerial view of Crail   62
Fig. 39. Fife: physical features and land utilization   62
Fig. 40. The Lomond Hills   64
Fig. 41. Seafield Colliery   66
Fig. 42. The Longannet Scheme   67
Fig. 43. Glenrothes from the air   70
Fig. 44. Glenrothes: map of the new town   71
Fig. 45. Edinburgh and the Lothians: relief and routes   74
Fig. 46. East Lothian: physical features and farming   75
Fig. 47. Edinburgh and the Lothians: occupations and industries   76
Fig. 48. Section through the Midlothian coal basin   78
Fig. 49. The Kinneil Colliery   79
Fig. 50. Edinburgh from the air   81
Fig. 51. Central Edinburgh: the old and the new town   82
Fig. 52. The Scottish paper industry   83
Fig. 53. Lothian landscape: bings of spent shale   84
Fig. 54. Livingston New Town   86
Fig. 55. The Forth Bridges: twin arteries to the North   87
Fig. 56. Middle Forth region: relief and routes   91
Fig. 57. Stirling   92
Fig. 58. Middle Forth region: employment diagram   93
Fig. 59. The growth of Grangemouth   94
Fig. 60. A Norwegian tanker discharging crude oil at Finnart on Loch Long   95
Fig. 61. Middle and Lower Clyde region: relief routes and towns   98
Fig. 62. Glasgow (and Hillington): occupations   99
Fig. 63. Middle and Lower Clyde region: occupations   99
Fig. 64. Iron and steel industry: statistics   101
Fig. 65. Central Scotland: the iron and steel industry   102
Fig. 66. The steel mills at Ravenscraig, Motherwell   104
Fig. 67. Shipbuilding on Clydeside   105
Fig. 68. Clydebank   109
Fig. 69. The growth of Glasgow   110
Fig. 70. Glasgow Docks   112
Fig. 71. Hillington Industrial Estate   114
Fig. 72. The Lower Clyde region: built-up areas   116
Fig. 73. Glasgow: redevelopment areas   117
Fig. 74. The "new" Gorbals   118

FIG. 75. Ayrshire: relief and routes 123
FIG. 76. Ayrshire: occupations and industries 124
FIG. 77. Ayrshire: milk output 125
FIG. 78. Killoch Colliery 127
FIG. 79. Ayrshire: occupations diagram 128
FIG. 80. Ayrshire ports 131
FIG. 81. Southern Scotland 134
FIG. 82. Land utilization in the Urr valley 137
FIG. 83. Drumlin, near Castle Douglas 137
FIG. 84. The Galloway Hydro-electric Scheme 139
FIG. 85. Peeblesshire valley sketch 142
FIG. 86. Loch Einich (Grampians) 146
FIG. 87. Sketch, looking west along Glen Lyon 149
FIG. 88. Pitlochry dam, looking upstream 151
FIG. 89. Hydro-electricity 153
FIG. 90. Aluminium in the Highlands 154
FIG. 91. British Aluminium Lochaber Works 155
FIG. 92. Electrically operated ski-lift in the Cairngorms 156
FIG. 93. North East Scotland 161
FIG. 94. Paper mill at Mugiemoss, near Aberdeen 164
FIG. 95. Twin fishing ports on the Banffshire coast 167
FIG. 96. Firth lowlands: land use in Elgin Parish 167
FIG. 97. The Dounreay Experimental Reactor Establishment 170
FIG. 98. The erosive power of the sea on the northernmost coast of the mainland of Britain 173
FIG. 99. Lake delta formation on the north shore of Loch Broom, Wester Ross 177
FIG. 100. Small crofting township on the west coast of Lewis 177
FIG. 101. Crofting on the south shore of Loch Broom, Wester Ross 178
FIG. 102. The main and only road from Ullapool to Inverness 180
FIG. 103. Industrial employment 188
FIG. 104. Scottish port trade, 1961 189
FIG. 105. Rootes (Scotland) Limited—Linwood plant 190
FIG. 106. Unemployment in Scottish counties, December 1962 191
FIG. 107. Rail and sea routes, 1969 192
FIG. 108. Scottish airfields and air routes 194

Preface

The Face of Scotland is but one volume in the Geography Section of the International Library, and it is therefore intended for use, not only in Scotland, but also in many other lands. Conscious of this, the authors have endeavoured to present this study in a manner acceptable to a wide public and not merely as a school textbook.

Any contemporary geography must emphasize many aspects. For instance, striking relationships between physical and human geography abound in Scotland, as do the complex and varied economic and social problems of our modern society, ranging from those of the isolated crofter to those of the redundant shipyard worker in Britain's overcrowded third city.

Multitudes of facts (and fancies) present themselves, but in selecting and arranging what is relevant little attempt has been made to delve deeply into subjects that are better studied from other sources. The Glossary of the More Unusual Terms is not an apology for this, but is intended to offer readers without specialist training sufficient enlargement where necessary.

Above all, the authors are aware that the 1960s evinced a period of significant and lasting change for Scotland. They try to describe frankly, and to interpret where possible, the forces at work in the changing economy and society. Such is the pace of change that a revised edition has already become necessary.

The book is illustrated with a wide range of maps, diagrams, sketches and photographs. The choice of these has been determined by the need to amplify points in the text, but it is hoped that the variety of subjects and techniques used may prove to be stimulating as well as instructive to the reader, who is urged, as ever, to read in conjunction with a good atlas. Population figures, based on the 1961 census, are given to the nearest thousand and are amplified, where necessary, by reference to the 1966 sample census.

From the list of acknowledgements it will be seen that many people have given freely of their time, interest and advice. To these people the authors are much indebted, as they are to their respective wives for unending patience, forbearance and encouragement during the research and preparation of the work.

I.G.M. and C.B.M.

Acknowledgements

IN ADDITION to information from numerous town clerks, clerks to county councils, various planning authorities and sundry firms and organizations, the authors would like to acknowledge, in particular, valuable assistance from the following:

The Scottish Council (Development and Industry).
C. Davidson & Sons, Aberdeen.
Mr. Napier, Roxburgh County Council.
Dr. A. B. Stewart, Macaulay Institute for Soil Research, Aberdeen.
Mr. W. C. Wright, Town Clerk and Chamberlain, Dornoch.
Mr. N. D. Couper, County Planning Officer, Elgin.
Col. R. Armstrong, Dumfries and Galloway Development Association.
Col. Webber, Director of Publicity, Aberdeen Corporation.
Mr. G. D. Banks, Information Officer, North of Scotland Hydro-electric Board.
The British Aluminium Co. Ltd., London.
Clyde Port Authority.
British Association for Advancement of Science.
Department of Agriculture and Fisheries.
Industrial Estates Management Corporation.
British Iron and Steel Corporation.
Mr. A. B. Adamson, of the N.C.B. (Scotland).
Meteorological Office.
Scottish Oils Ltd.
Ministry of Labour, Scottish H.Q., Edinburgh.
Colvilles Ltd.
Mr. W. Bryce Johnston, Town Clerk, Grangemouth.
Edinburgh and East of Scotland College of Agriculture.
West of Scotland Agricultural College.
The Shipbuilding Conference.
Milk Marketing Board.
British Jute Trade Federal Council.
Flax Spinners and Manufacturers Association.
Board of Trade, London (statistics relating to aircraft movements in Britain).

size in the west and north-west with the regular isle-free east coast. A double series of discontinuous fault lines runs across the "waist" of central Scotland, from south-west to north-east, dividing the country geologically and economically into three distinct regions:

(1) the Highlands
(2) the Central Lowlands ⎫ (Fig. 1).
(3) the Southern Uplands ⎭

The Highlands

North of the Highland Boundary Fault, from Helensburgh to Stonehaven, extends nearly two-thirds of the total area of Scotland, comprising the highest, most barren and least-populated part of Britain. Composed largely of crystalline and metamorphosed rocks, rising in parts to over 4000 ft, the Highland massif is one of considerable geological complexity. Being such an ancient and complicated area in the geological sense, most of the Highlands present merely the stumps or roots of former mountain systems created aeons ago under an enormous burden of rock now largely removed. The Torridonian Sandstones of the north-west, mute evidence of a vastly different desert type of climate obtaining hundreds of millions of years ago, represent some of the oldest-known rocks of Europe, and at the other end of the geological scale are the lavas and intrusions of the Inner Hebrides, belonging to Tertiary times—a span of 525 million years. To these we might well add, a mere million years ago (which is comparatively recent, geologically speaking), glacial depositional formations, fragments of which are to be found in the great troughs or glens. An earth history in miniature is thus traceable through the Highland landscape with the effects of wind, water and ice on these surfaces present for all to see.

Firstly, about 300 million years ago, the ancient pre-Cambrian strata, having been subjected to much wearing down by normal sub-aerial denudation processes, suffered intensive folding and faulting during the early Caledonian mountain building period, leaving as present-day evidence the north-east to south-west rupture of the Great Glen (Fig. 2), together with a characteristic north-east to south-west "grain" of the rocks in many areas. Tear faults, as along the edges of the Highlands and of the Southern Uplands, bear witness to a succeeding pressure activity during Hercynian times, but the most easily recognizable features of the landscape today result from the later Alpine mountain building period, which in reality was only felt as an outer ripple from the centre of the movements in the Alps and Mediterranean region. Faulting in Scotland during these times brought up lavas and other igneous material, with a honeycombed mass of dyke swarms in the west, radiating from the extremely active volcanic centre on Mull. Effects of these

Fig. 2. The Great Glen, looking north-eastwards. The chain of lochs can be seen occupying the fault-guided trough. This photograph is best studied in conjunction with 1 in. O.S. Sheet No. 36. (Photo: Aerofilms & Aero Pictorial Ltd.)

outpourings range from the tabular basalts of Skye and the Antrim plateau in Ulster to the hexagonal basalt columns of Staffa (Fingal's Cave immortalized by Mendelssohn) and the groyne-like dykes of the south coast of Arran jutting out into the Firth of Clyde. Attacked by the elements, the great mountain masses of Scotland became worn down into a plateau, tilted generally eastwards, with rivers and glaciers gouging out their valleys and isolated summits of uniform level remaining.

Separating the Central Highlands (Grampians, Monadliath Mountains, etc.) from the North West Highlands and Islands is one of the world's great topographical schisms (see Fig. 2), the Glen More or Great Glen Fault, occupied now by a series of long, narrow, deep lochs, stretching over 50

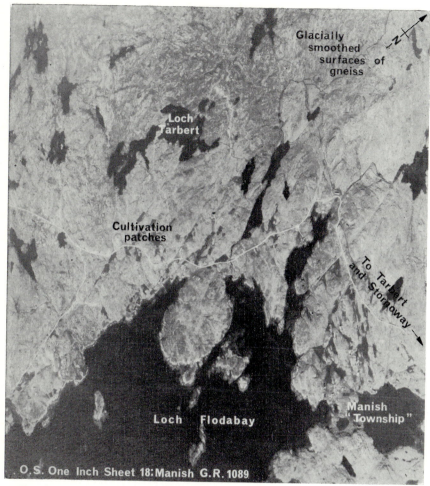

Fig. 3. The ice-moulded landscape of South Harris. (Photo: Air Ministry. Crown Copyright Reserved.)

miles from Inverness to Fort William in a north-east to south-west direction, in full sympathy with the Caledonian trend. Included within this area are the very ancient Lewisian Gneiss, Torridonian Sandstone, much-altered Moine Schists, Old Red Sandstone and Tertiary Basalts.

From a distance the tough, durable Lewisian Gneiss is easily recognized as bare, barren, elongated domes and ridges, giving a hummocky appearance to the landscape (Fig. 3). An inextricable labyrinth of low hills and valleys and the absence of prominent peaks and crags suggest an age-old land surface, much reduced in stature by the processes of normal erosion and that of ice also, as indicated by the polished and striated rock surfaces. An indication of quite different climates to those of present days is given by the plum-coloured Torridonian Sandstones of the north-west. Sun cracking and ripple-marks suggesting desert conditions are clearly seen on the many fine exposures of this rock in Wester Ross. In contrast to the barren, unproductive Torridonian or Lewisian formations, some of the most productive areas of Scotland are to be found where Old Red Sandstones form the base. These rocks, formed by the deposition of sediments, have been proved to be over 10,000 ft thick in places, and the original Caledonian Mountains from which the sediments were derived must have been enormous to yield such a depth of deposit. When mixed with fluvio-glacial deposits the easily weathered Old Red Sandstone forms a good soil base, as is evidenced by the productive farms of the "Black Isle" of Easter Ross.

South-east of the Great Glen rift valley the main bulk of the Grampian highlands, forming a highly resistant rampart of metamorphic and crystalline rocks, stands out as the Cairngorms and Monadliath Mountains, the former group with several summits over 4000 ft. This area is treated in more detail in Chapter 12, but it is important to note here that in contrast to the short, swift streams flowing to the Atlantic, north of the Great Glen, most of Scotland's longest rivers have their sources in the Grampians (Tay, Don, Dee, Spey, etc., see Fig. 4) and here also are to be found some of the largest inland lochs, often several miles in length (e.g. Tay, Earn, Ericht).

Although all Scotland was completely covered by ice-sheets, with the main dispersal areas radiating outwards from the highest ground, evidence of ice action is most easily recognized in the Highlands. Inexorable ice-sheets have smoothed and polished the surfaces of the Outer Hebridean rocks, removing all protuberances and leaving the present landscape as a bespotted, lake-pitted surface (Fig. 3). As the continental ice-sheet receded from lowland Britain with the onset of warmer conditions, small ice-caps remained on the higher parts of the country, Wales, the Lake District, the Southern Uplands and, of course, the Highlands. From these isolated areas fingers of ice, mostly following pre-cut valleys, gouged their way along, over deepening parts of the floors, subsequently to become water-filled as inland rock basin lochs, or sea lochs of the fiord type, smoothing off spurs along the sides and generally forming the characteristic U-section glaciated trough (Fig. 5). So lasting have the effects of valley glaciation been, that it is possible in many of the larger glens of Scotland to trace the whole course of a glacier from its corrie origin to the terminal bands of recessional moraines athwart the lower reaches.

All of the land north of the Highland Boundary Fault is not majestic mountain landscape as several significant expanses of lowland occur, all on the eastern side. These low tracts, which comprise the undulating Buchan

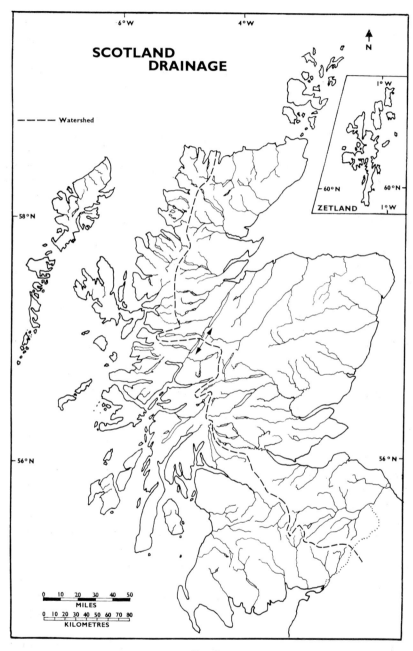

FIG. 4.

FIG. 5. Strath Conon (Ross-shire), showing typical U-shaped valley caused by the passage of a glacier. (Photo: H.M. Geol. Survey. Crown Copyright Reserved.)

peninsula, the Moray Firth coastlands, the plain of Caithness and the low tableland of the Orkneys contrast sharply with the rest of Highland Scotland and are treated separately in Chapter 13.

The Central Lowlands

In contrast to the resistant masses of igneous and metamorphic rocks comprising the bulk of the Highlands, wherein the erosional effects of water and ice are most pronounced, the Central Lowlands consist largely of relatively recent sedimentary strata, interrupted sporadically by volcanic intrusions and masked in many places by a generous covering of marine, fluvial and glacial material to give a much more hospitable landscape.

With a lower surface than areas to north and south, more varied soils and a more favourable climate, this is the economic heart of Scotland, collected neatly in a downfaulted trough bounded by faults following the original north-east to south-west Caledonian trend. Being interrupted by low lines of volcanic hills like the Sidlaws, Ochils, Campsie Fells and isolated volcanic residuals, the Lomond Hills and Cleish Hills, the valley, in relation to the regions north and south of the fault lines, is really a number of lowlands separated by areas of higher ground, and these lowlands are given distinctive names: Strathmore, Strathallan, Vale of Mentieth, Howe Fife and Carse of Gowrie. Of greater significance to the economic development are the three large estuarine incisions, Tay, Forth and Clyde, and it is around these estuaries, particularly the latter two, that the industrial and commercial growth of Scotland has taken place with easy shipment to and from Europe and the Atlantic routes.

The Southern Uplands

Nowhere in excess of 3000 ft, the Southern Uplands present a more subdued form of relief than do the Highlands but, nevertheless, act as a hilly division between the densely populated Central Lowlands and northern England. The main hill masses are the Cheviots, rising to 2600 ft in the south-east, Merrick at 2700 ft in Galloway, and the Hartfell–Broadlaw group at 2700 ft at the meeting-points of the shires of Lanark, Selkirk, Peebles and Dumfries. Three lower ranges, the Lammermuirs, Moorfoots and Pentlands, again following the north-east to south-west Caledonian trend, form an arc south of Edinburgh, and the capital city itself actually extends as far as the foothills of the Pentlands.

Drainage in the Southern Uplands, which, unlike the Highlands, have few large lochs, is more balanced than that of the north of Scotland, with large rivers finding outlets on three distinct sides: the Clyde to the north-west and Firth of Clyde, the Tweed eastwards to the North Sea, and the Nith, with several other parallel Galloway rivers, southwards to the Solway Firth. Use of several of these river valleys is made by the main through routes from England, all of which, except the east coast route from Berwick to Edinburgh, have to climb to considerable height in forging their way by means of the dales cut through the smooth-topped moorlands. In the case of the main Carlisle to Edinburgh/Glasgow railway route up Annandale, the addition of a second locomotive is necessary in order to negotiate Beattock Summit.

CLIMATE

British weather is renowned for its variability, or, as some would prefer, its changeability. Nowhere in Britain is this seen to greater effect than in Scotland, and when long-term averages are taken, upon which climate considerations are based, several variations in climate within relatively small areas can be seen. A comparison of selected stations on the basis of total annual rainfall, mean monthly temperatures and the duration of snow cover indicates these contrasts quite clearly (Fig. 6).

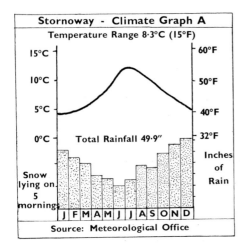

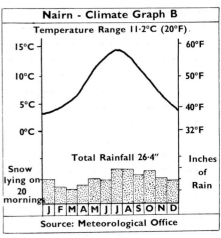

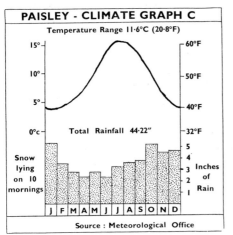

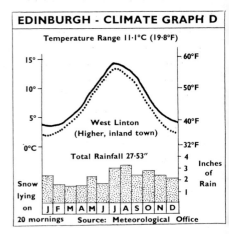

Fig. 6. Climate graphs for selected stations. Note the basic contrasts between west and east situations.

Temperature

Scotland, including the Shetlands, extends between approximately 55 and 60°N., and these are the latitudes which exhibit the highest frequency of depressions over Europe. Most of these depressions proceed along the path, and are an integral part, of the moisture-laden south-west airstream coming across the Atlantic Ocean. As this airstream passes over the North Atlantic Drift, a body of warm water originating in the Gulf of Mexico and moving constantly northwards between Iceland and north-west Scotland, it is relatively easy to understand why the crofters of South Uist enjoy a January temperature of 6° C (42° F), several degrees above that of south-east Scotland or, for that matter, south-east England, which comes under cold continental influences at this time. Particularly in the west of Britain, the winter isotherms trend north to south, emphasizing the predominant influence of the Atlantic Ocean as a source of relative warmth.

Although summer temperatures are lower in the north than in the south of Scotland or England, the crofter is aided in his work by the longer hours of summer daylight, a feature of high latitudes. Increasing summer warmth becomes apparent on moving southwards into central Scotland, where successful ripening of wheat, barley and fruit is accomplished. Along the milder but wetter western coastlands, oats, early potatoes and grass for dairy cows are the chief responses.

Except where actual surface temperatures are specified, isotherm maps usually indicate temperatures reduced to mean sea level, hence it should be borne in mind that much of Highland Scotland, during April to November, experiences in reality temperatures which are little above the critical plant growth limit of 6° C (42° F). Pronounced elevation causes considerable changes in temperature and rainfall and, with parts of the Highlands over 4000 ft and the Border Hills rising over 2500 ft, it is hardly surprising to notice that the January average on Ben Nevis is −5° C (23° F), as opposed to Fort William with 4° C (39° F) nearly 4400 ft below at the foot of the mountain. The result of this is to produce a misty landscape ("Scotch mist") with hills often cloud-capped, even in summer. Sour, acid soil due to excessive moisture, low temperatures and consequently low evaporation, and generally poor drainage are conducive only to the growth of peat and heather moor relieved only by patches of poor grass development.

Precipitation

The use of this term, in place of the more common "rainfall", is deliberate as rainfall incidence and amount do not tell, by any means, the whole story in relation to Scotland. Britain's first snows of the winter are, almost without exception, experienced in the Highlands of Scotland and the main roads of this area are usually the first to be hampered, or closed, by drifting. The reasons for this are interacting and include the northerly latitude and the vast expanse of high ground constantly exposed to the mositure-laden winds from the Atlantic. It should be noted that only on high ground (above 1500 ft) in the interior are falls likely to be excessive as snow never lies more than a few days on the low coastal tracts of the Hebrides and Wester Ross exposed to the mild airstream, which areas escaped almost completely the record-breaking winter of 1962–3 when some parts of Lowland Britain suffered snow on the ground for 10 weeks (Fig. 7). Although prolonged snow coverage is harmful to human activities in general, it must not be overlooked that it

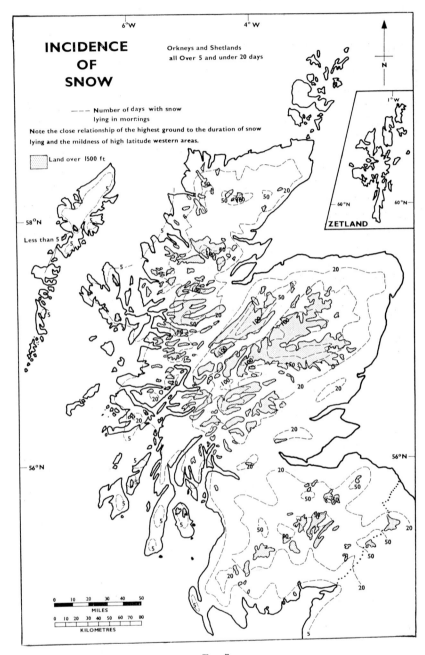

FIG. 7.

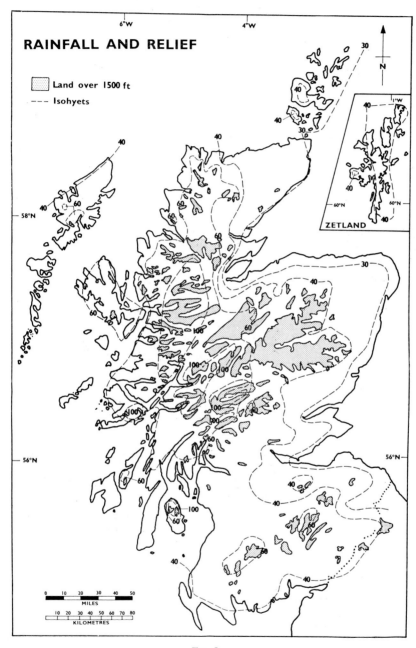

FIG. 8.

can act beneficially by trapping air between the flakes and forming an anti-frost blanket. This, however, is small recompense to hill sheep farmers who incur heavy annual losses of sheep in the snowdrifts of the average winter of Highland Britain.

From the combined rainfall–relief map (Fig. 8) the relationship between the bulwark of high ground on the western parts of the Grampians, Wester Ross and Inverness-shire and the south-westerly winds coming from the open Atlantic, charged with moisture, is clearly apparent, with these areas receiving, on their highest parts, over 100 in. rainfall every year. The Southern Uplands are neither so high as the Highlands, nor do the south-westerlies have a completely uninterrupted approach, as some of their moisture is released in ascending the mountains of Donegal and Ulster, which lie in their path. Notwithstanding this, a considerable part of upland Galloway receives over 60 in. Eastern Scotland, in a distinct rain-shadow, shows a marked contrast with the west, with East Lothian and the southern shores of the Moray Firth having less than 25 in. It is a fortunate accident of geology that the productive coastal lowlands of Scotland, enjoying a more favourable climate, are much more extensive in the east, rendering large-scale intensive farming possible. Seasonal incidence of rainfall does not appear to vary greatly except that most places in the east appear to have most of their rain during the second half of the year, whereas westerly stations record their highest amounts between October and March.

THE SCOTS

Few attempts are made to correlate directly the physical features of a country with its characteristic development, including the history and temperament of its inhabitants. Scotland portrays an excellent example of this close interrelationship. From each of the aspects of the physical geography of Scotland so far considered a marked degree of variation emerges. This might help to explain the fiercely independent nature of the real Scot, in spite of the fact that his people are but a fractional part of the British nation, as well as his resource and "dour" determination to succeed in the face of long odds as instanced by a ceaseless toil with little reward against what is really rather a hostile environment.

The geological break between the Highlands and the Central Lowlands has exerted considerable influence in the past on the grouping of quite different peoples. North of this break, until well into the eighteenth century, the Gaelic population, by virtue of its isolation in a mountain fastness, was able to enjoy a comparative freedom from outside influences, both Roman and English, who preferred punitive expeditions and could see little point in attempting colonization and permanent settlement. Due to the difficulty of access to his lands, the true Highlander, or Gaelic Scot, was able to maintain a degree of independence and individuality comparable to that of the various Swiss groups in their secluded, mountain-girt valleys. Thus the survival of the clan system until the mid-eighteenth century could also be attributed to the physique of Highland Scotland, which lent itself into separation by "glen" units, with large tracts of divisional no man's land, comprising peat bog, heather moor and craggy mountain slopes, effecting segregation of the clans, who usually met to exchange views only on the field of battle!

Variability in all the facets of nature is the keynote in this small country. There is present a variation in structure, relief, drainage and climate to a considerable degree and, when linked with the sense of individualism inbred in the Scot, it is not the least remarkable to notice similar variations in the human response to the natural resources outlined in the ensuing pages.

CHAPTER 2

Scotland's Natural Resources

SCOTLAND's natural resources are not difficult to assess due to their relative inadequacy and they may be broadly grouped as follows:

(1) Economic Minerals.
(2) Soils.
(3) Agricultural Resources.

(4) Forestry.
(5) Fishing.
(6) Power Resources.

Economic Minerals

Many of Scotland's minerals are considered to be uneconomic due to inaccessibility or dispersal over a wide area with insufficient concentration to cover working overheads. Whilst this is true of the minerals which are igneous in origin, it is not in regard to those occurring in sedimentary strata.

Minerals of sedimentary origin. Chief amongst these are the coal deposits, all of which, excluding the small privately worked Jurassic "brown coals" of Brora (Sutherland), are of the Carboniferous Age and are located in the Central Lowlands. Products of bygone thick forest and swamp vegetation, these coals are mostly bituminous with some good coking varieties and are dealt with in detail in Chapters 4–10.

Large reserves of clayband and backband ironstone still remain in the coalfield regions of central Scotland, where their occurrence in conjunction with the coal was fortuitous for the early iron industries, but these deposits are not competitive with the high iron content of foreign ores as, in most cases, the percentage of iron is between 25 and 35 in thin seams a mere foot or two wide. Seams of Jurassic iron ore do occur in 8 ft thicknesses on the island of Raasay, between Skye and the mainland, and, although worked in the past, the phosphoric content is too high to warrant heavy charges for freight shipment and subsequent purifying.

At one time, before the great oilfield discoveries in Pennsylvania and Texas, Scotland was the leading world producer of oil derived from the shale deposits of West Lothian. Once again modern competition proved too much as it is cheaper to import crude oil from the Middle East than to extract 12 tons of shale to obtain 1 ton of oil, hence production from shale has ceased.

Igneous minerals. Few igneous minerals have been worked in Scotland but certain deposit indicators might, in the future, be worth a more thorough investigation. Lead has been intermittently worked at Leadhills and Wanlockhead, near to the small Sanquhar coalfield in northern Dumfriesshire, but the progressive exploitation of the veins suffered from fluctuations in the free market metal prices, as well as from flooding of the workings. Other random vein minerals, often associated with dykes or sills, are lead and zinc in Strathspey; silver and copper pyrites have been worked up until the late nineteenth century in the small glens of the Ochils north of Tillicoultry and Alva, and lead, zinc and pure quartz occur in wide veins along the Tyndrum fault, west of Loch Tay in Perthshire. The bulk of Scottish talc, which occurs amongst the larger igneous masses of the Highlands and Shetlands, is too impure for use as a cosmetic base but, if transport costs were not too high, it could be useful for furnace lining, ceramic ware and firebricks. Small outcrops of chromite at Unst in Shetland are incidental signs of what may lie at depth, but generally, as far as is known, economic minerals, with the notable exception of coal, are conspicuous by their absence in Scotland.

Soils

Nearly two-thirds of Scotland's 30,000 square miles consists of land above 1000 ft around which level cultivation ceases. The climate is cool and moist and the resultant natural vegetation cover is one of open coniferous forest on the more favourable hill slopes below the acid moorlands, and at lower altitudes where temperatures are higher and soils richer in plant nutrients broad-leaved deciduous forest is predominant, as in Perthshire or the Border counties.

A well-drained soil usually develops under coniferous forest showing 3 or 4 inches of decaying organic material, known as the A horizon, below which is a grey layer called the A_2 horizon. Organic acids caused by the activity of microbes in the A horizon are washed down by rainwater and in their turn wash away the iron and aluminium compounds from the grey layer, which is left rich in silica. These iron and aluminium compounds are subsequently deposited in the underlying B horizon, which is yellow brown in colour. The underlying parent material, known as the C horizon, is usually little affected by these processes and the complete ABC profile is called a Podzol (Fig. 9), named by the Russians who pioneered soil studies and were the first to relate climate with soils.

At lower levels, formerly covered in deciduous forest but now mainly put down to arable farming, the horizon differences are less easy to spot, but several characteristic types do emerge. Those with relatively uniform brown layers and little humus in the A horizon are known as Brown Forest Soils, some are derived from the Podzol, outlined above, and others, in areas of poor drainage, showing a mottled grey and blue-grey appearance are termed Gley Soils. In basin-like depressions receiving heavy rainfall, peat may form with its arrested decomposition of the plant remains and the soil below the peat, often waterlogged, is known as a Peaty Gley Soil.

Often associated with peat is a development of the Podzol called the Peaty Podzol Soil, decidedly wet and acid and supporting little but moorland vegetation. Reasons for this are fairly simple as below the peat layer, usually

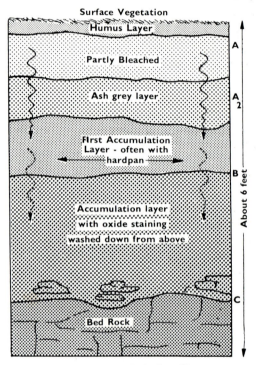

Fig. 9. Typical Podzol profile.

6–12 in. thick, is an A_2 horizon similar to the ordinary Podzol and below this in turn is a thin band called the iron pan forming a continuous barrier to the downwash of oxides, etc., from the A to the B horizon. With the B and C horizons thus sealed off, the top layer, A and A_2, becomes saturated with water for long periods, and the accumulation of this water-saturated organic matter leads to the ultimate formation of hill peat, which may be as much as 8 ft thick.

To date, a soil survey of Scotland has not been completed although work in this direction by the Macaulay Institute for Soil Research, in Aberdeen, is proceeding apace. As the survey progresses the greatest benefits to agriculture and land use in general must accrue, by means of recommendations for the application of certain fertilizers in certain areas to compensate for particular soil deficiencies. Scotland suffers an abundance of rainfall, which leaches nutrients out of the soil, and the application of suitable manures and fertilizers, based on the findings of the soil-survey scientist, must serve to increase the yield in crops.

Agricultural Resources

Although farming in Scotland is highly diversified, there is a decided emphasis on livestock, due largely to the poverty of the soil and harshness of the climate. A total labour force of 66,000 decreasing annually by 2 per cent return a yearly output of £168 million, 80 per cent of which is derived from livestock and livestock products, of which milk, beef, mutton, eggs and pigs are the most important.

Much of the land surface of Scotland consists of mountain and moorland, relieved only occasionally by sea and hill-girt undulating lowlands, consequently it is hardly surprising to note that agriculture is difficult. Contrasts in land use do appear, however, when we consider that some 3 million acres of admittedly poor land in the Grampians and North West Highlands is alienated in unproductive "deer forest" for the select few, sufficiently wealthy to pay several hundred pounds for a few days of highly "dubious" sport. On the other hand, the sheltered Tweed, Forth and Tay lowlands of the east coast can boast some of the most productive arable land in the whole of Britain.

Excessive rainfall, a large proportion of land over 1000 ft and a glacially denuded landscape combine to render much of the Highlands unproductive and, from Fig. 10, it is clear that hill sheep farms abound in this area. Much of the land is incapable of providing winter feed for both cattle and sheep and reared cattle are often fattened when 2 years old on the arable farms of the east and south-east. The low plateau areas of Orkney, Caithness, Aberdeen and Banff are extensively ploughed, but distance from the main consumption regions restricts the production of saleable (cash) crops and the concentration upon roots, oats and ley grass is largely intended for the feeding of beef cattle.

Crofting is the basic agricultural practice in the Islands and Highlands north of the Great Glen and this system, involving the tenure of small patches of improved land to farm on a near-subsistence level, is treated more fully in Chapter 14. It should be noted here, however, in this overall survey of Scottish agriculture that all is not well in the crofting communities, where family income has to be supplemented by fishing, spinning and weaving, and catering for holiday-makers. To maintain his staunch individualism and love of complete freedom the crofter's life is a constant struggle in comparative isolation against an unremitting climate and poverty of resources. Many of the uneconomic land units need reapportionment, as instanced by recent Crofters' Commission reports. Progressive reseeding of pastures is imperative and, in spite of heavy subsidies of up to 85 per cent grants for land improvement and equipment and even low-interest loans to purchase livestock, the crofters' economy is still a precarious one.

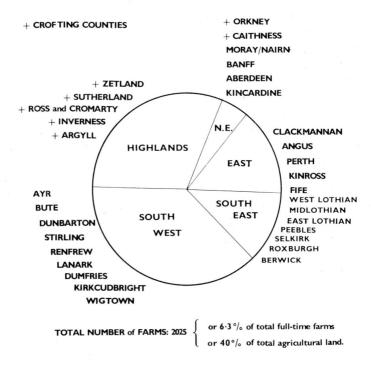

Fig. 10. Number of hill sheep farms. (Based on Dept. of Agric. for Scotland figures, H.M.S.O.)

In fine contrast to the dismal northern picture, milder winters, more succulent pastures and proximity to large urban markets have made large-scale dairy farming a profitable activity in the south-west of Scotland, where arable cropping is mainly directed towards feeding herds of Ayrshire, Friesian and Jersey cows, which supply the numerous creameries of the south of Scotland. A notable specialism is the production of high-quality seed potatoes in Ayrshire and Wigtownshire, which, together with Angus, Strathmore and the Lothians, supply England, South Africa and Spain with a potato free from disease and suitable for propagation in warmer climes.

Further specialized farming takes place in lowland eastern Scotland, which enjoys a comparatively low rainfall, prolonged sunshine and a relative freedom from late spring frosts. These factors, when allied to a generous admixture of productive soils, good transport facilities and a reasonable supply of casual labour for harvesting, help to explain the concentration of soft fruit (i.e. raspberries, blackcurrants and strawberries) and market garden products (tomatoes, peas and carrots, chiefly) in Strathmore, the Carse of Gowrie, the middle Clyde valley and the Lothians. Yet another specialism in eastern Scotland is the rearing of pedigree livestock: Aberdeen–Angus and Shorthorn cattle, some of which have been sold latterly to the U.S.S.R. (a new market altogether), Blackface and Cheviot sheep. This activity is undertaken on selective farms, often owned by large companies, and animals sold at the annual bull sales in Perth, fetching upwards of 30,000 guineas each, may be subsequently introduced to a Texas herd or a Bovril estancia on the Pampas of the Argentine.

Research by the North of Scotland College of Agriculture has revealed an alarming state of farm economics in that part of the country. Working on a basis that a successful farm should show a minimum profit equal to a farm worker's average wage of £550 per annum, plus interest at 5 per cent on the capital invested in the farm, it was found that in a sample study of 326 farms more than half of the farmers would have been better off working for someone other than themselves (Fig. 11). It would seem that farmers here must be content with rewards other than financial ones for being their own masters.

The small size of the holdings often mitigates against the farmer making economic returns and there is a tendency for small farmers to adopt cropping and livestock policies better suited to larger establishments. For instance, too much milk is produced on these small farms, due to the understandable temptation of the regular cheque, and many such farms, in order to maintain a regular contribution, invest heavily in machinery and equipment, which must be kept in use if value for capital expenditure is to be gained. Additionally, many farms are too inflexible in their management, preferring to follow crop rotations practised by generations of forefathers rather than alter procedures to conform with price changes. Similar resistance to change has to be overcome in crofting areas where only now are the application of chemical fertilizer, progressive reseeding of grazings and the introduction of artificial insemination becoming accepted without scepticism and scorn. In contrast to this, schemes with sound financial backing, such as the Canadian-style ranch in the Great Glen, with cattle being rounded up by men on horseback in Wild West style, or the great beef herds of Lord Lovat, near Beauly, have proved to be measurable successes and point the way to increasing Britain's home beef production by widespread ranching methods not previously adopted.

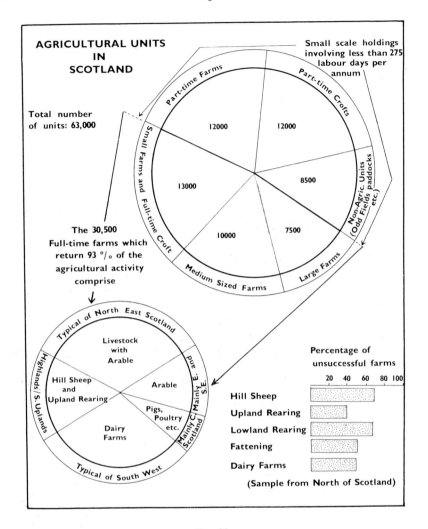

FIG. 11.

Forestry

The main agency of forestry development in Scotland is the Forestry Commission, established in 1919 to promote the interests of forestry, afforestation and the production of timber in Great Britain. Land is acquired by the Commission, the largest landowner in Scotland, through purchase and gift, and it is the agency through which encouragement and assistance are given to the restoration of privately owned woodlands. Now in control of over 1½ million acres of Scottish forest land, the Commission hopes to have

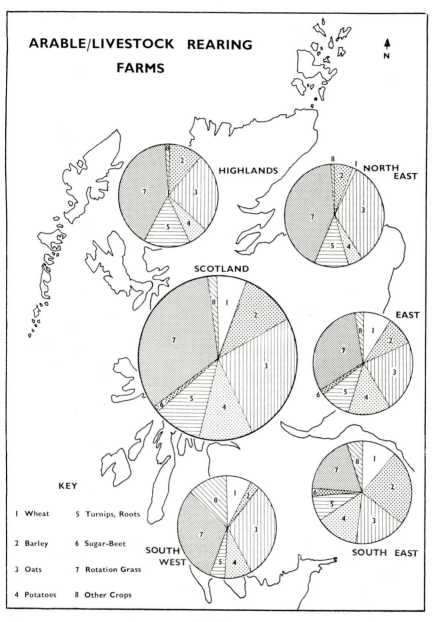

ARABLE/LIVESTOCK REARING FARMS

HIGHLANDS

NORTH EAST

SCOTLAND

EAST

SOUTH WEST

SOUTH EAST

KEY

1 Wheat   5 Turnips, Roots

2 Barley   6 Sugar-Beet

3 Oats   7 Rotation Grass

4 Potatoes   8 Other Crops

Fig. 12.

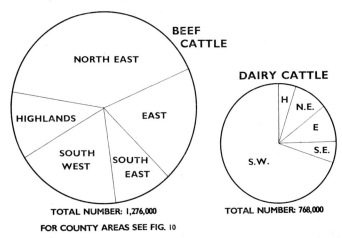

FIG. 13. Beef and dairy cattle. (Based on Dept. of Agric. for Scotland figures, H.M.S.O.)

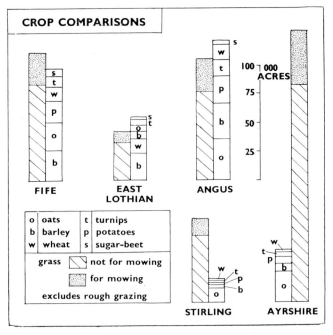

FIG. 14.

established, by the end of this century, through the extension of both state and private operations, over 5 million acres of well-managed woodland throughout Britain.

Of the several roles which a forest can play, the most obvious and important is the provision of commercial timber and the installation of the £20 million pulp and paper mill at Corpach, near Fort William, as well as bringing a reprieve to the Beeching-doomed railway, has provided a ready market for Scots-grown timber within a radius of nearly 100 miles. At Strachur, a saw-mill produces boxes and planking from the Argyll forests and, at Aberdeen on the opposite coast, there is a constant demand for timber for fishboxes manufactured in the city, but the reduced uses of thinned timber for pit-props (partly due to the increasing use of steel arches) means that a constant search is in progress for new timber outlets.

Less obvious functions of the Forestry Commission properties are the contributions made to the social structure and well-being of the country. The building of forest villages, begun since 1945, has already seen the establishment of three communities at Ae (Dumfriesshire), Glentrool (Galloway) and Dalavich (Loch Awe, Argyll). With afforestation employing ten times as many workers as hill sheep farming does, these measures are healthily indicative of a slowing down of decay and depression and, for this reason, the Crofters' Commission has long advocated the crucial part afforestation could play in reviving the crofting townships of the western and north-western seaboards. The recreational use of forests is another possible contribution which, as yet, has not been extensively developed in Britain. To date, only the National Forest Parks in Glenmore, Glentrool, Cowal (Argyll) and the Loch Achray–Loch Lomond area (Fig. 15) provide facilities for camping and other transient visitors, and the affording of facilities similar to those in the American and Canadian National Parks could bring nothing but benefit to the community.

Indigenous to Scotland, the Scots pine is the most important of the forest conifers, although the Sitka spruce, originating in North America, is more frequently planted by the Commission now. Thriving on heavy rainfall, peaty soils and turned turf, the spruce grows rapidly and can be used for fencing, poles, constructional timber, pit-props and pulp and is thereby adaptable to changing demands.

Certain side benefits are to be gained from afforestation, in addition to providing direct employment, a useful commodity, and recreational facilities, for the trees themselves provide valuable shelter to cropland otherwise exposed to the full rigours of a harsh climate. Additionally, soil erosion is arrested by the binding action of tree roots, and humus development takes place. Much weight is being given to increasing the forest resources of Scotland, which, in alliance with further development of hydro-electric

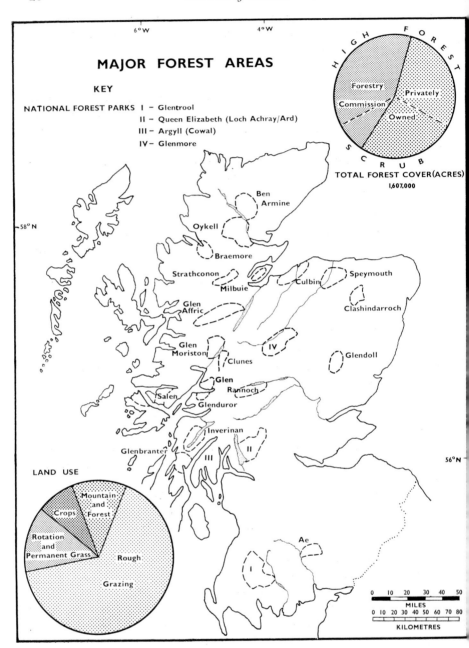

MAJOR FOREST AREAS

KEY

NATIONAL FOREST PARKS I – Glentrool
II – Queen Elizabeth (Loch Achray/Ard)
III – Argyll (Cowal)
IV – Glenmore

HIGH FOREST

Forestry Commission
Privately Owned

SCRUB

TOTAL FOREST COVER (ACRES)
1,607,000

58° N

Ben Armine

Oykell

Braemore

Strathconon
Milbuie
Culbin
Speymouth

Clashindarroch

Glen Affric

Glen Moriston
Clunes
IV
Glendoll

Glen Rannoch

Salen
Glenduror

Inverinan
II

Glenbranter
III

56° N

LAND USE

Mountain and Forest
Crops
Rotation and Permanent Grass
Rough Grazing

Ae

I

0 10 20 30 40 50
MILES
0 10 20 30 40 50 60 70 80
KILOMETRES

Fig. 15.

power, could form a firm foundation for more progressive development of the Highlands and the pleas for further pulp mills to be sited at Inverness and in Galloway could well be just ones.

Fishing

Scotland has long been renowned as a fishing centre both from the sporting viewpoint, in particular freshwater Tay, Spey and Tweed salmon and trout from the innumerable lochs and streams, and from the commercial "farming" of the deep-sea and inshore fish harvest.

Giving employment to over 10,000 fishermen, as well as a host of shore-based workers, the bulk of commercial fishing is concentrated along the east coast. This is due to:

(*a*) the relative nearness of the rich North Sea grounds,

(*b*) better transport, due to construction of railways to serve better situated ports which, in themselves, are capable of improving facilities to take progressively larger vessels,

(*c*) several European countries using the North Sea grounds, thereby giving the stimulus of competition,

(*d*) larger numbers of full-time fishermen existing on the east coast as opposed to the crofter–fishermen of the west coast.

Emphasis on this concentration can be laid by the author's experience in the summer of 1962, observing early-morning landings at Ullapool (Wester Ross) where it was noted that of the 26 boats unloading (Fig. 16) no fewer than 18 were vessels belonging to the east coast ports. Although line-baiting for white fish (haddock, whiting, plaice, etc.) is a major activity from small boats, particularly inshore on sea lochs on the west coast, deep-sea trawlers, often with refrigerated holds, working from Aberdeen and Leith as far afield as the Arctic and White Sea return by far the majority of the white fish catch. In fact, almost as many fishermen are employed in Aberdeen alone as on the whole of the west coast from Stornoway to Ayr.

Due to restrictions imposed by the Faroese Government with a further extension of the fishing limits to 12 miles which took place in March 1964, the days of the middle water fishing trawlers, which are too small for all-the-year-round operation around Iceland and other distant waters, appear to be numbered. The pattern is already discernible. Two types of trawler will be commissioned, examples of these types being already in operation. Fishing over the stern, with a 20-ton capacity trawl net (instead of the otter boards over the side), from a £500,000 vessel like the all-refrigerated *Junella* on trips to Greenland lasting up to one month indicates the future pattern of the "go anywhere factory ships". Those Scottish companies unable to afford a £500,000 trawler will probably invest in the 100-ft stern trawler of the *Ross Daring* type, which, being highly automated, needs only a skipper and four deckhands.

Herring can be kippered, canned, salted, deep-frozen, pickled and converted into oil and poultry meal, but, in spite of this versatility of use, the demand for this fish has gradually decreased, due largely to the loss of Continental markets. Shoals of herring are fished progressively southwards by boats operating from Lerwick in May to Lowestoft-based fleets in late October. The importance of the newer dual-purpose seine-net boats must

FIG. 16. Early-morning fish landings at Ullapool, Wester Ross.

not be overlooked in these times of recession in the fishing industry, as their size permits continuance of the tradition of ownership or co-ownership and suits the small harbours of the north-east and west coasts, into which they congregate in scores during the height of the season. These boats can be used for either seine-netting for demersal white-fish or quickly adapted to drift-net work to take the surface-swimming herring and mackerel, moving from port to port as they follow the herring shoals. Ancillary to the actual fishing are the labours of shore-based workers engaged in the gutting, smoking (kippers), salting, canning and quick-freezing activities of the various processing plants sited at the major herring ports.

The most significant aspect in the development of the Scottish fishing industry has been the vigorous growth of the seine-net fleet at the expense of the herring drifter. Decline in the herring industry, always subject to considerable fluctuations, has been offset by progression in white-fish, principally haddock. This activity is shared by seine-net boats, working in home waters up to 40 miles offshore and trawlers engaged on the more distant fishing grounds. With Britain importing £20 million worth of fish-meal annually, there should be scope for expansion within the herring sector but the danger of causing a glut on the market is ever present. Paradoxically expansion could be adversely affected also by "lean harvests" of herring, shoals of which are neither so reliable nor so predictable as are the white-fish.

Efforts are at present being made by the Crofters' Commission to encourage developments in the shellfish industry and it is interesting to note that the Crofter–Fishermen Limited, which was established as a co-operative society in 1962, paid £90,000 to west coast crofter–fishermen for 250,000 lb of lobsters and sundry other shellfish. As a further stimulus, a new freezing and cold storage plant was opened in 1963 at Oban to cater for expected heavier fish landings. All along the west coast, the crofter–fisherman is actively engaged in catching lobster, crab and shrimp, but the saleability is dependent upon the live state of the lobsters. Limited transport facilities render this difficult, but at £1 per lb weight it has been proved to be profitable to fly consignments of these fish from Orkney and the Hebrides to the gourmets in London and Paris. Rapid charter flights are essential as lobsters in particular have a high mortality rate in transit.

Although recent years have seen a decline in the relative importance of the fishing economy to Scotland as a whole, the traditional fishing burghs of the north-east are still heavily dependent upon it. Almost exclusive dependence is shown in the islands of Burra and Whalsay (Zetland) and Scalpay (Harris), with Zetland's economy being markedly related to the prosperity of fishing.

Power Resources

With an estimated potential electricity power development in the region of 10,000 million units, it can hardly be said that Scotland's power is dependent upon the coalfields of the Central Lowlands. Furthermore, the coal reserves are likely to be exhausted long before the more permanent high annual rainfall in the mountain districts. Power in Scotland is derived from five main sources:

(1) coal-burning thermal electric stations—all located in the Central Lowlands (see Chapters 5–10),
(2) diesel-electric stations—invariably sited on the coast for ease of import of oil (Fig. 17),

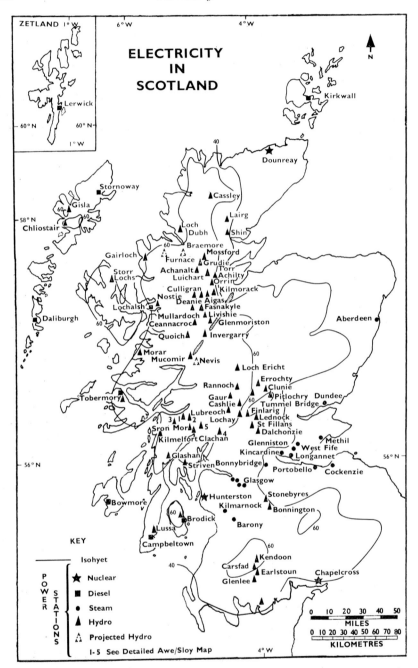

ZETLAND 1° W

ELECTRICITY
IN
SCOTLAND

Lerwick

60° N
60° N
1° W

6° W
4° W

N

Kirkwall

Dounreay

Stornoway

Gisla

Chliostair

Cassley

Lairg

Loch
Dubh

Shin

58° N

Braemore

Gairloch

Mossford

Furnace

Grudie

Torr

Achanalt

Achilty

Luichart

Orrin

Kilmorack

Storr
Lochs

Culligran

Nostie

Deanie Aigas

Aberdeen

Lochalsh

Fasnakyle

Mullardoch

Livishie

Daliburgh

Ceannacroc

Glenmoriston

Quoich

Invergarry

Morar

Mucomir

Nevis

Loch Ericht

Errochty

Rannoch

Clunie

Gaur

Pitlochry

Dundee

Cashlie

Tummel Bridge

Lubreoch

Finlarig

3

2

Lochay

Lednock

Sron Mor

5

St Fillans

Kilmelfort

Clachan

4

Dalchonzie

Glenniston

Methil

Kincardine

West Fife

Glennison

Longannet

Glashan

Bonnybridge

Portobello

Striven

Cockenzie

Glasgow

Bowmore

Hunterston

Stonebyres

Kilmarnock

Bonnington

Lussa

Brodick

Barony

Campbeltown

Kendoon

KEY

Carsfad

Earlstoun

Chapelcross

Glenlee

Isohyet

P
O
W
E
R

S
T
A
T
I
O
N
S

Nuclear

Diesel

Steam

Hydro

Projected Hydro

1-5 See Detailed Awe/Sloy Map

Tobermory

56° N

56° N

0 10 20 30 40 50
MILES
0 10 20 30 40 50 60 70 80
KILOMETRES

4° W

Fig. 17.

(3) hydro-electric stations—predominantly in the Highlands but with one large scheme, the Galloway Power Scheme (see Fig. 84), in the Southern Uplands,

(4) peat which, unlike in Eire and in the U.S.S.R., is almost wholly confined to domestic fuel,

(5) nuclear power from generating stations at Chapelcross (see Chapter 11), Hunterston (Chapter 10) and Dounreay (Thurso), the first successful nuclear power station for non-military purposes (Fig. 97).

Hydro-electric power. Prior to World War I there had been much opposition to the development of power schemes in the Highlands of Scotland (see Chapter 12). The North of Scotland Hydro-electric Board was created by Act of Parliament in 1943 and, since then, this body has been engaged actively in surveying, promoting and building hydro-electric schemes and, indeed, has been intimately concerned with overall development of the Highlands. The Board's work is of great importance to the depopulated northern counties in the provision of much-needed and increasing stimulus to life in the Highlands, which includes the establishing of over 200 new industries using electricity and giving employment to about 15,000 people. During 1967/8, over 4700 million units of electricity were generated by the Board, of which total hydro-electricity contributed 3200 million units (Fig. 18).

The extension of electricity supplies to the remoter parts of Scotland presents considerable problems. The west coast is deeply indented by long sea lochs and there are hundreds of islands, few of which have water power resources, and most of which are too far from the mainland and too sparsely populated to justify laying a submarine cable. These cables have already been laid to supply Jura, Skye, Raasay, Scalpay, Bute and, most recently, Islay, but it must be recorded that although 92 per cent of the farms and crofts are now connected (1 croft in 100 had electricity in 1948), supplying these remote rural customers involves the Board in a loss of £1,700,000 annually. Even on the mainland tracts the population is very scattered, but the value of electricity supply cannot be measured in pounds sterling alone as it is of vital importance in agriculture, new industry and, perhaps most of all, in amenity provision by helping to minimize some of the social causes of the drift of population away from the Highland counties.

Peat. Cutting of peat for fuel is a time-honoured occupation in the Highlands and Islands of Scotland and the neatly stacked peats beside the white-washed cottages are a feature of the rural scene. So heavy are the freight charges for coal haulage to the remoter districts that the traditional use of peat as a domestic fuel is an economic necessity, and so extensive are the reserves of peat that there will never be a shortage. Thus the likelihood of it

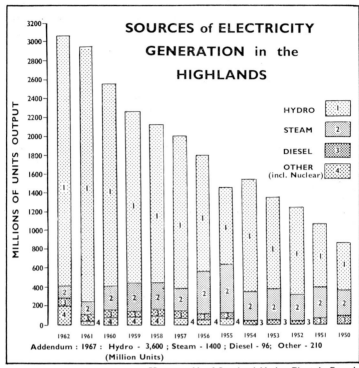

[Source : N. of Scotland Hydro-Electric Board
Annual Report 1967]

FIG. 18.

being completely supplanted by coal, oil or electricity as a domestic fuel is very remote. In recent years, stimulated by the knowledge of successful peat-burning power stations in operation in the U.S.S.R., and also in Eire, consideration has been given to its wider operation as a source of power. The Scottish Peat Committee, appointed by the Secretary of State for Scotland, has estimated the total workable deposits of peat to be in the region of 600 million tons, roughly equivalent to 500 million tons of coal. An additional advantage is that when land is cleared of peat, development of agriculture or forestry is made possible, but such an enterprise, involving the exploitation of these vast reserves in the remotest parts of Britain, really demands national action with government backing.

Nuclear power. Although technically not a "natural resource", the generation of electricity from nuclear power in Scotland is becoming increasingly important in its contribution to the National Grid which supplies both industrial and domestic consumers. Consideration that nuclear power stations be kept as remote as possible from dense urban populations, in case of accidental escape of harmful radioactive materials, has been uppermost in the siting of Dounreay in scantily peopled Caithness—the most northerly part of mainland Britain, Hunterston at an isolated point on the Firth of Clyde, and Chapelcross on the little-frequented Solway Firth. Location on the coast enables sea water to be used for cooling purposes and for the dubious expedient of disposing of atomic waste. Dounreay has a capacity of 60 million units of electricity per annum, and is already producing 30 million units, Chapelcross with its four Calder Hall type reactors has been contributing 1000 million units to the National Grid since 1959, and Hunterston, whose first reactor "went critical" in September 1963, produced enough electricity in 1964 to supply a town as large as Aberdeen or Dundee.

Although Scotland's natural resources appear to be superficially scant, progressive developments such as the increasing use of hydro-electric and atomic power could help immeasurably to make fullest use of her greatest resource—skilful and hardworking people.

CHAPTER 3

Population

CYNICS contend that Scotland's greatest natural resource is its population and that much of this "exports" itself across the Border to England or overseas. Admittedly, Scots are not hard to find in key posts in education, commerce, the Civil and Foreign Services and in the many branches of industry scattered throughout England. Corby, a steel town in the English Midlands, has over 70 per cent Scots by birth or parentage in its 45,000 population. The Registrar-General for Scotland has estimated the present annual rate of outward movement of population from Scotland to be 29,500 (1962). Also clear from the returns of the Registrar-General is the depressing fact that Scotland is acquiring an aged population (Figs. 20, 21), which again reflects the drain away from the country of younger people likely to maintain or increase population growth. This is particularly true in the Highland and crofting counties examined in Chapters 12 and 14.

With nearly four-fifths of the 5,196,000 population (1962 estimate) concentrated in the Central Lowlands, between the boundary faults, the influence of the physical landscape would appear to be paramount in the distribution of population. Underlying this concentration within these limits it can also be seen that nearly all the largest burghs, with a population of over 25,000, of Scotland are within 10 miles of the coast or, as in the case of Glasgow, have direct access to the open sea (Fig. 22). Salient differences between the three major regions emerge when the county population densities are compared:

Region	County	Persons per square mile
Highland	Sutherland	6
Central Lowlands	Renfrew	1408
	Lanark	1844
Southern Uplands	Kirkcudbright	32

(Fig. 23)

Emphasis to these differences may be given by a consideration of population growth and movement within the country. In common with

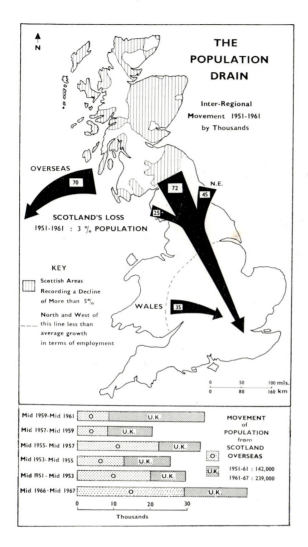

THE
POPULATION
DRAIN

Inter-Regional
Movement 1951-1961
by Thousands

OVERSEAS

70

SCOTLAND'S LOSS
1951-1961 : 3 % POPULATION

72   N.E.   **45**

25

KEY

Scottish Areas
Recording a Decline
of More than 5%

North and West of
this line less than
average growth
in terms of employment

WALES   **35**

0   50   100 mls.
0   80   160 km

Mid 1959-Mid 1961	O	U.K.
Mid 1957-Mid 1959	O	U.K.
Mid 1955-Mid 1957	O	U.K.
Mid 1953-Mid 1955	O	U.K.
Mid 1951-Mid 1953	O	U.K.
Mid 1966-Mid 1967	O	U.K.

MOVEMENT
of
POPULATION
from
SCOTLAND
O   OVERSEAS

1951-61 : 142,000
1961-67 : 239,000

0   10   20   30
Thousands

Fig. 19.

progressive countries like the United States, the U.S.S.R., Germany,
Canada and Australia, we find drift to, or concentration in, towns proceeding
apace. Between 1901 and 1951, Scotland's population increased by 14 per
cent, but the percentage increase of urban population was exactly double
this figure. All three areas of Scotland have shared in the growth of urban
population, which, as might well be expected, is most pronounced in the

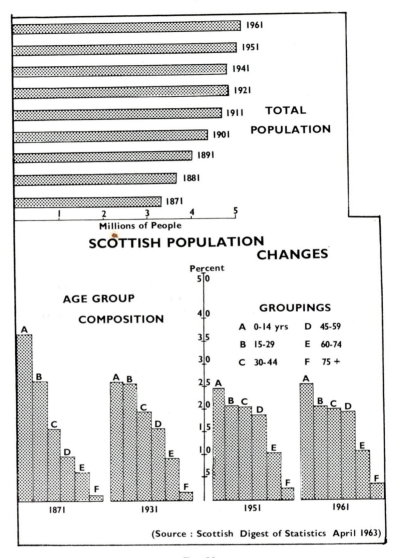

Fig. 20.

Central Lowlands, where over 90 per cent of the people are now town-dwellers.

Since 1871 the northern part of Scotland has lost 60 per cent of its population by migration to the Central Lowlands, England, or overseas and, even in central Scotland, between 25 and 30 per cent have moved out of the country during the past 90 years. Consequently, it is clear from the age-structure pyramids (Figs. 20, 21) that stagnation of population in the rural areas has now been passed and retrogression, with an ever-decreasing Net Reproduction Rate (N.R.R.), is developing due to the ageing population. Root causes of and possible remedial measures against this decay are considered in the relevant regional chapters.

Efforts to redistribute Glasgow's massed populations, where virtually 1 in 5 Scots live, are being made by designating existing towns "overspill for Glasgow" and establishing new towns like Cumbernauld and East Kilbride,

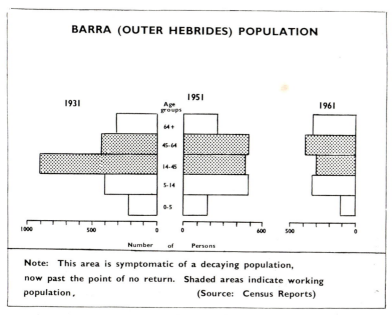

Fig. 21. Population decline in the Hebrides (Isle of Barra). (Source: Census Reports.)

with target populations of 70,000 and 100,000 respectively. It remains a sober fact, however, that 35 per cent of the total population crowds the central Clyde-side conurbation, where densities can be in excess of 5000 per square mile and where many are now being adversely affected by the recession in the world-famous Clyde shipbuilding industry.

Much of Highland Scotland has little inducement to offer for increasing the population densities, although towns as far removed as Inverness have been rather optimistically designated "Glasgow overspill reception area". On the west coast, the steep-sided fiords and bare, polished gneiss surfaces (Fig. 3) afford scant opportunity to wring a living from the soil, except by the age-old crofting tenures and techniques, utilizing small patches of improved

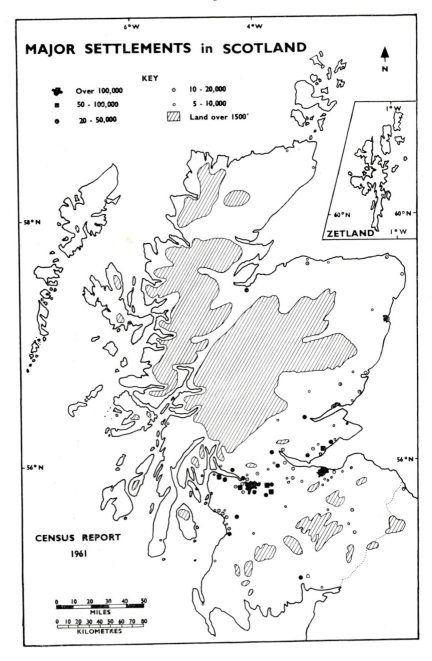

Fig. 22.

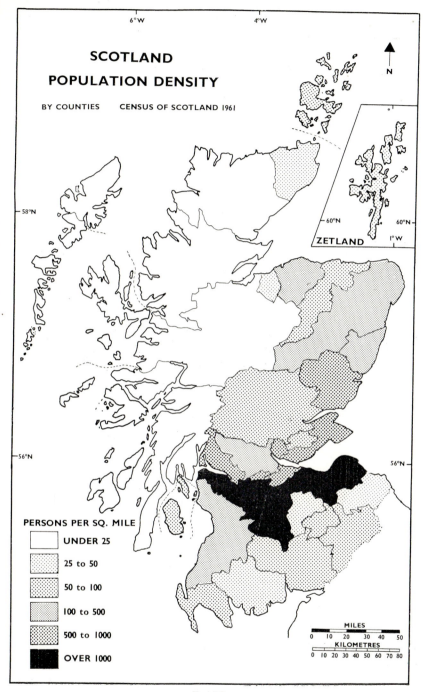

SCOTLAND
POPULATION DENSITY

BY COUNTIES   CENSUS OF SCOTLAND 1961

ZETLAND

PERSONS PER SQ. MILE

UNDER 25

25 to 50

50 to 100

100 to 500

500 to 1000

OVER 1000

MILES
0 10 20 30 40 50
KILOMETRES
0 10 20 30 40 50 60 70 80

Fig. 23.

39

land and sharing common grazings. A heavy annual rainfall of between 60 and 100 in. and soils containing little plant food, weathered from hard, crystalline rocks, are conditions hardly conducive to dense agricultural settlement, and much of the land not suitable for crofting tillage forms hill sheep grazings, or even more uneconomic deer forest. Remoteness, rugged relief, poor transport facilities and a scarcity of economic minerals preclude industrial development, as on the scale of central Scotland, in both the Highlands and Southern Uplands and, consequently, only in the sheltered, favoured lowlands of the Merse of Berwickshire (Fig. 81), or the north-east coast from the Beauly Firth to Kincardine, is there any appreciable density of settlement.

It would seem that the concentration of workpeople in the Central Lowlands is due to the following:

(1) Mineral resources, chiefly coal, bearing in mind that, in some areas, particularly in Lanarkshire, this is becoming economically unworkable.

(2) The development of heavy industries, based originally upon the presence of coking coal and iron ore in the blackband seams (see Chapter 9).

(3) Early trade connections of Glasgow with the New World (see Chapter 9).

(4) Clydeside's rise to the forefront of the world's shipbuilding areas (see Chapter 9).

(5) The commercial and cultural momentum of Glasgow and Edinburgh, providing as magnetic an appeal to the Scots as does London to the English.

(6) Facility of communications by road and rail within the region and with England.

In setting the above considerations against the meagre opportunities nature has to offer outside the Central Lowlands, it is not difficult to see why the population of Scotland is unbalanced in several ways and why the condition is likely to continue to deteriorate under the present economic circumstances. Climatic considerations and the accidents of geology are the agents chiefly responsible for the unbalanced nature of the distribution of population in Scotland, the narrow "waist" of which, with but 24 miles separating the Forth and Clyde estuaries, is seen to be crammed with people to the detriment of the rest of the country. Add to this the alarming fact that, during 1951–61, the population of Scotland showed a net increase of 82,000 against an estimated loss by migration of 142,000 over the same period and it is not difficult to conclude that many Scottish counties are now showing a Net Reproduction Rate which is below unity—a decidedly unhealthy state of affairs!

CHAPTER 4

The Central Lowlands:
Introduction

OVER 75 per cent of Scotland's people live in the Central Lowlands on only
one-seventh of the country's area, and here are found the main agricultural,
industrial and commercial developments. The reasons for this great concentration, particularly around the lower Clyde, are numerous and changing:
lower altitudes and the productive soils have encouraged varied farming;
large coal resources and iron ore provided the base for heavy industries;

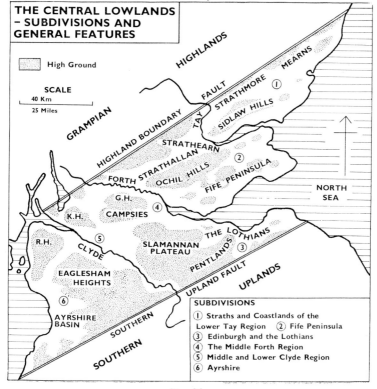

FIG. 24.

penetration by long estuaries gives access to shipping; centuries of effort and adaptation have created industrial skills and traditions.

On account of the lower relief, the Central Lowlands has a more favourable climate than have the Highlands or Southern Uplands—summers and winters are warmer and rainfall is less. However, western areas are noticeably milder than eastern areas in winter and have more rain. Besides this west–east contrast, relief differences give rise to other variations. A combination of suitable soil and climatic conditions supports varied farming activities. In general, the drier eastern areas are more important for arable and mixed farming, in contrast to the moist western districts where dairying predominates. In certain favoured parts more specialized farming is superimposed on the general pattern: such areas include the Ayrshire coast, the Middle Clyde valley, Midlothian and the Carse of Gowrie. On the other hand, the hill ranges, with their poor soils and harsh climates, can only support sheep.

Important though agriculture is, it is on the basis of industrial development that the majority of the population depends. The main development of heavy industry took place in the Glasgow and Lower Clyde area, and we shall see how natural advantages, such as coal and the associated ironstones, were exploited, and how the development of the Clyde estuary as a major port led to the growth of a large and varied trade with related industries. Iron and steel, shipbuilding and engineering are dominant. The pace and scale of these developments created problems in the Glasgow region: an over-dependence on shipbuilding and heavy metallurgical industries, which

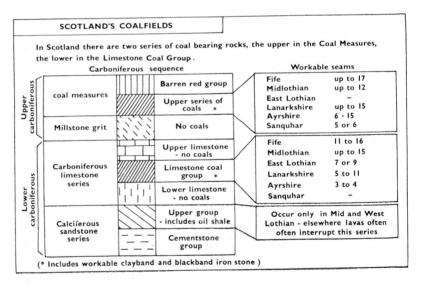

Fig. 25.

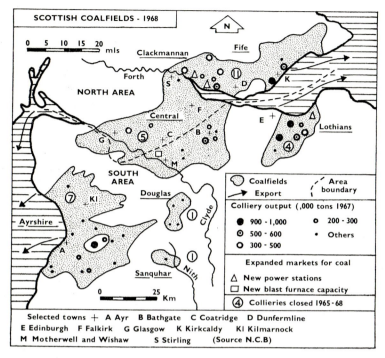

FIG. 26.

have undergone contraction and reorganization since the war, and congestion in the ill-planned urban areas. As the traditional industries decline in importance, one notes not only the reorganization and modernization of these industries, but also the growth of new light industries in industrial estates and new towns, of which Scotland has five (see table below): these industries vary greatly but comprise mainly the dynamic growth industries, such as vehicles, consumer goods, electronics, instruments and chemicals.

Just as the traditional pattern of industries in the Glasgow area is fast changing, so the programme of urban renewal and overspill to new towns

SCOTLAND'S NEW TOWNS

Town	Date of designation	Population (1968)	Target population
Glenrothes	1946	25,000	70,000
East Kilbride	1947	57,000	100,000
Cumbernauld	1956	25,000	70,000
Livingston	1962	7,000	100,000
Irvine New Town	1966	38,400	100,000

and widespread reception areas is alleviating problems inherited from the industrial revolution and changing the social geography of the area.

Elsewhere in the Central Lowlands industrial development has been, until recently, on a much smaller scale than in the Clyde region. But the initial advantages enjoyed by that region have diminished, and this,

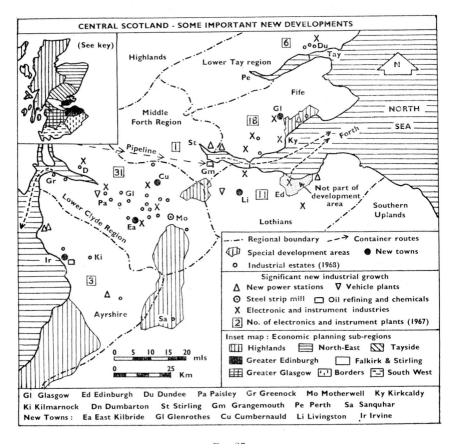

FIG. 27.

together with transport developments and advances in the production and distribution of energy, has given new industries greater freedom in their choice of locations—the less-congested areas and the new towns are often preferred. In this way, new growth points and industrial concentrations are developing.

In Ayrshire, in addition to mining, agriculture and the long-established textile industries, the range of engineering trades is ever widening, as is the concentration on chemicals and man-made fibres. Edinburgh remains predominantly an administrative centre but, in the Lothians as a whole, the contraction of employment in the coal and oil shale industries has led to the growth of significant new industries (commercial vehicles, electronics, etc.) to add to the longer-established ones, such as paper. Here, Livingston New Town is becoming a focus for population growth and industrial expansion, as Glenrothes is in Fife and Irvine in Ayrshire. Fife, with its traditional dependence on agriculture, fishing, mining, textiles and paper, is also undergoing significant change, due largely to the closure of many collieries; this has necessitated the establishment of industrial estates and new growth industries, most noticeably in West Fife. The contraction of the coal industry in Fife and the Lothians has not been so severe as in Lanarkshire, and the collieries remaining open in 1968 are, for the most part, modern and efficient,

THE SCOTTISH COAL INDUSTRY IN 1968

	North area	South area	Total
Number of collieries open	12	32	44
Number of collieries closed 1967/8	7	9	16
Saleable output 1967/8 (million tons)	5·5	8·2	13·7
50% of output comes from	4 collieries	7 collieries	—
Manpower (June 1968)	12,923	19,590	32,513
Manpower (December 1967)	—	—	37,740

with large reserves and have assured markets in the huge new thermal power stations at Cockenzie and Longannet; nevertheless, the markets for coal are very limited.

The long-continued decline of the coal industry is well known, production having fallen to 13·7 million tons in 1967/8, scarcely 30 per cent of the maximum output in 1913, and a drop of 4 million tons since 1962. What is striking, however, is the greatly increased efficiency of the remaining collieries and the increase in the scale of enterprise: there are already four pits near the 1 million tons a year mark, one in Ayrshire and three in the Lothians–Fife area—the accompanying table outlines the present structure of the industry.

The completion of the Forth and Tay road bridges has made the movement of labour, raw materials and manufactured goods to and from Fife and the Dundee region much easier and has brought these areas into closer contact with markets. Dundee has a long connection with textile manufacture, an industry that is widespread in Angus and Perthshire, but here too there is a widening range of new light industries on industrial estates.

Transitional between these eastern areas and the Glasgow region, the middle Forth area forms a compact and increasingly important industrial district centred on Falkirk and Grangemouth. The traditional metal and textile industries have been dwarfed by the great petro-chemical complex at Grangemouth, and Falkirk is envisaged as the pivot of a greatly expanded urban area.

Throughout the entire region a long-established pattern of industries is discernible and the contrast between west and east remains pronounced. However, with the growth of new industries (often as a result of considerable foreign investment) in widely scattered areas, the contrast is breaking down. In other words, the balance of locational advantage is no longer solely in favour of the lower Clyde area. The continued growth of new towns and the programme of overspill from Glasgow mean that the excessive concentration of population in the Glasgow area is also becoming less marked.

Thus, the degree to which Central Scotland is identified with coal, ships and heavy metal industries is declining, while the manufacture of consumer products, vehicles, office machinery, electronics and instruments is firmly established and rapidly expanding.

EMPLOYMENT IN INDUSTRIES ESTABLISHED WITH NON-SCOTTISH CAPITAL (1966)

	% of total employed in manufacturing	% increase 1964/6	Exports £ million	% change in exports (1964/6)
North American	8·5	17	118	+57
U.K. firms	5·0	6	32	− 3
European	0·5	0	2	−33
Total	14·0 (i.e. 102,000)12		152 (i.e. 30% of Scotland's manufactured exports)	

EMPLOYMENT IN ELECTRONICS INDUSTRIES

		Scotland		Great Britain	
Scotland's share	Year	Total	Index	Total	Index
3·6%	1959	7,400	100	214,000	100
5·7%	1965	16,500	214	290,000	136
6·5%	1967	20,800	270	320,000	150

The Straths and Coastlands of the Lower Tay Region

BETWEEN the Highland Front and the North Sea, and corresponding broadly to the counties of Perthshire, Angus and Kincardineshire, lies a varied region of wide lowlands and rounded hills, drained for the most part by the Tay and its tributaries. With the exception of Dundee, which is a major industrial centre, this region is not one noted for industrial development.

Physical Features

Extending south-west from Stonehaven, the Highland Front forms a pronounced scarp, diminished in places by foothills, overlooking the wide fringing vale of Strathmore ("the great valley"). Strathmore extends north and south into the Howe of the Mearns and Strathearn respectively; this strategic corridor has an average width of 6 miles and an average height of 200 ft. The surface is varied by glacial deposits and the alluvial flood plains of the Earn, Tay, Isla and the North and South Esk—thus the underlying Old Red Sandstone is masked by recent deposits, giving generally productive soils.

Throughout its length, Strathmore is walled to the south-east by the Garvock Hills, Sidlaw Hills and Ochil Hills. The rounded Sidlaws, composed of volcanic rock, rise to 1492 ft in Auchterhouse Hill, and dip gently towards Strathmore. This contrasts with the steep, often precipitous slopes overlooking the Firth of Tay. Extending north-eastwards from the Sidlaws, lower ridges and plateaux, cut by wide valleys such as the Lunan, link the main range to the Garvock Hills, which are generally below 900 ft.

The River Tay breaks out from Strathmore between the Sidlaws and the Ochil Hills—Perth occupies this important gap at the head of navigation.

The coastal lowland, masked by glacial deposits, is widest in the south, near Arbroath, and rises gently inland to the ridges and plateaux already mentioned. Rounded ridges reach the coast to form cliffed headlands which alternate with sandy bays containing raised beaches and wind-blown sands.

Between the Sidlaw scarp and the Tay estuary, the Carse of Gowrie is a narrow plain of rich marine soil reclaimed from peat marsh.

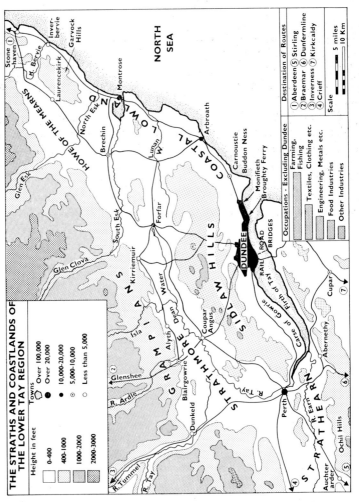

THE STRATHS AND COASTLANDS OF
THE LOWER TAY REGION

Height in feet

0-400
400-1000
1000-2000
2000-3000

Towns

◯ Over 100,000
● Over 20,000
◉ 10,000-20,000
⊙ 5,000-10,000
○ Less than 5,000

Occupations - Excluding Dundee

Farming, Fishing
Textiles, Clothing etc.
Engineering, Metals etc.
Food Industries
Other Industries

Destination of Routes

①Aberdeen ⑤Stirling
②Braemar ⑥Dunfermline
③Inverness ⑦Kirkcaldy
④Crieff

Scale

5 miles
10 Km

NORTH SEA

Fig. 28.

Fig. 29. Seen from the north-western slopes of the Sidlaw Hills, Strathmore is a wide, fertile valley. Beyond the Strath, foothills give way abruptly to the Highland front. (By courtesy of *Scots Magazine*.)

Climate

Sheltered by the Highlands, Strathmore has less than 30 in. of rainfall, while the east coastlands often have less than 25 in. This comparative dryness, coupled with fairly warm summers 15° C (59° F) and high sunshine totals, favours the practice of arable and mixed farming. Winters are cooler in Strathmore, 3° C (37° F) compared with 4° C (39° F) on the coast.

Agriculture

Apart from the Sidlaw tops and some ill-drained plateaux such as Rossie, the soils of the region favour a full development of agriculture, for which the district is noted.

With 10,000 workers, farming is the region's main occupation. Strathmore is renowned for rich and often specialized agriculture. Mixed farming is the rule, and on an average farm of 150–200 acres, two-sevenths of the land is in rotation grass, the remainder is used for oats, wheat, barley, potatoes and roots such as turnips and perhaps sugar-beet. While sugar-beet, malting barley, wheat and seed potatoes are cash crops, rotation grass, oats and turnips are fodder crops, for fattening beef cattle and lambs. Young store cattle and lambs often come from the upland farms of the region. Just as

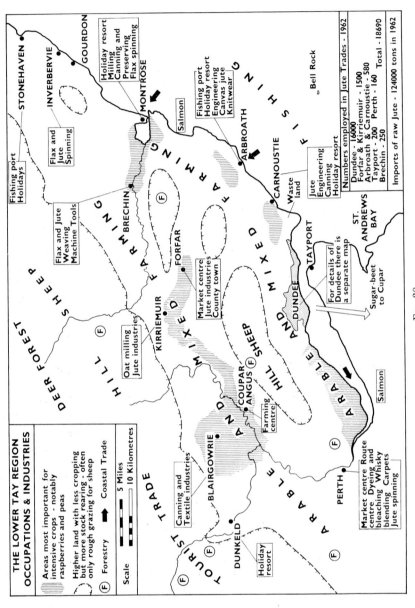

THE LOWER TAY REGION
OCCUPATIONS & INDUSTRIES

Areas most important for intensive crops - notably raspberries and peas

Higher land with less cropping but more stock rearing - often only rough grazing for sheep

(F) Forestry   Coastal Trade

Scale

5 Miles

10 Kilometres

Fishing port
Holidays

Flax and Jute
Spinning

Flax and Jute
Weaving
Machine Tools

Oat milling
Jute industries

Canning and
Textile industries

Holiday resort

Market centre Route
centre. Dyeing and
bleaching. Whisky
blending. Carpets
Jute spinning

Farming
centre

For details of
Dundee there is
a separate map

Sugar-beet
to Cupar

Jute
Engineering
Canning
Holiday resort

Waste
land

Fishing port
Holiday resort
Engineering
Canvas jute
Knitwear

Salmon

Holiday resort
Milling
Canning and
Preserving
Flax spinning

Market centre
Jute industries
County town

Salmon

Bell Rock

STONEHAVEN

GOURDON

INVERBERVIE

MONTROSE

BRECHIN

FORFAR

KIRRIEMUIR

COUPAR
ANGUS

BLAIRGOWRIE

DUNKELD

PERTH

DUNDEE

TAYPORT

CARNOUSTIE

ARBROATH

ST.
ANDREWS
BAY

DEER FOREST

HILL SHEEP

ARABLE AND MIXED

HILL AND MIXED

HILL SHEEP

ARABLE

ARABLE AND MIXED

TOURIST TRADE

FISHING FARMING

FISHING

Numbers employed in Jute Trades - 1962
Dundee - 16000
Forfar & Kirriemuir - 1500
Arbroath & Carnoustie - 580
Tayport - 200   Perth - 160   Total - 18690
Brechin - 250

Imports of raw Jute - 124000 tons in 1962

FIG. 30.

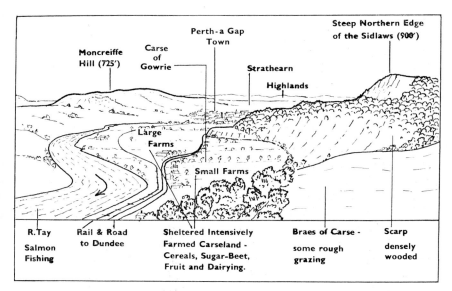

FIG. 31. This view along the Carse of Gowrie emphasizes the sheltered position of this intensively farmed lowland strip.

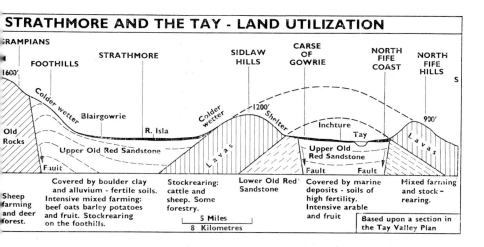

FIG. 32.

Angus and Perth are famed for their fine seed potatoes (exported to England, Spain, Cyprus and South Africa), they are renowned for their beef cattle.

Similar farming, with an emphasis on potatoes, oats and beef, extends into the Mearns and Strathearn.

While the soils of Strathmore are normally fertile, reddish loams, areas of infertile sands and gravel remain as heath or forest. Alluvial areas along the river support permanent pasture.

The coastal districts, from Dundee to Stonehaven, are also mixed farming areas. A 7-year rotation is used, whilst farms, particularly in southern coastal areas, may be larger than in Strathmore. Seed potatoes and beef cattle are again prominent, but, on the lighter coastal soils, barley replaces oats as the major cereal, and sugar-beet is much more important. Some coastal areas of sand, such as Buddon Ness, are agriculturally useless. Dairy and pig farming assume more importance in coastal areas, near the larger towns.

The Carse of Gowrie, in a sheltered position, with a southerly aspect, is an area of rich farming. The fertile soils (heavy towards the Tay) often carry dairy pastures, but it is for crop farming, particularly wheat, barley, sugar-beet and beans, together with the intensive production of soft fruits (raspberries and strawberries) and peas, that the Carse is best known. Inland, the Braes of Carse, with lighter soils, are mainly cultivated, with some rough grazing. From Bridge of Ern to the river mouth, the Carse of Earn, with heavy soils, is similar to Gowrie, but carries rather more grassland.

The production of soft fruits and peas extends far beyond the Carse of Gowrie into Strathmore and coastal districts. Nine-tenths of Scotland's raspberry acreage is in these areas, annual production reaching 10,000 tons. Low rainfall, prolonged sunshine, freedom from late spring frosts, and light soils favour the crop. The main production is in the Blairgowrie, Coupar Angus and Alyth areas in Strathmore, and the coastal areas around Montrose and Carnoustie. Part-time workers harvest the crop, 90 per cent of which goes to canneries or jam factories in Dundee, Blairgowrie, Forfar, Montrose, Carnoustie and Arbroath. These industries prompted the growing of green peas for canning and freezing.

The hills and plateaux are less favourable for farming; in these marginal areas, fewer crops are grown and the breeding and rearing of beef cattle and lambs is important. While mixed farming often extends up to 1000 ft, large areas of the Sidlaws support only sheep, forest or heath.

Fishing

The coastline provided numerous havens from which fishing became important. Although some small harbours are disused, and the numbers of men and boats now employed are less, the more localized and efficient industry of today is very important. The main centres are Arbroath and

Gourdon. Stonehaven, Montrose and Johnshaven are smaller centres. From Arbroath, thirty-four vessels (150 men) engage in inshore fishing, using seine-nets in summer and lines in winter, catching haddock, codling, plaice and whiting from banks in St. Andrews Bay and near Bell Rock. Lobsters are caught close inshore. Gourdon is similarly engaged. From these ports there is an export of fresh fish, but also from Arbroath of the traditional "smokies".

The importance of this industry is not to be measured by the few hundred people employed full time—many others are involved, in smoking fish, marketing and baiting lines. In a town such as Arbroath, the fisher folk form a closely knit community with distinctive customs.

A growing problem facing the industry is that of over-fishing, particularly serious in the inshore ground; this is due in part to indiscriminate fishing by foreign vessels.

Industry and Towns

Most of the region's industries are concentrated in Dundee, Scotland's fourth city; 75 per cent of the area's manufacturing population are in Dundee. Perth, Arbroath, Forfar and Brechin account for most of the remainder.

Dundee began as a small fishing hamlet, developed into a medieval trading burgh, and eventually into an industrial city with 180,000 people. Early industrial life was based upon a small textile industry using local flax wool. Later, flax imported from the Baltic lands supported the coarse linen industry of the eighteenth century. The linen industry reached its peak in the 1860s, but a drop in the demand for sailcloth as the era of the sailing ships waned led to a decline. The contraction of the whaling industry, and the fear of interruption of overseas flax supplies encouraged the establishment of the jute industry, using the coarse fibre imported from Bengal. Thus the manufacture of jute and hessian, from jute first imported in 1840, grew to eclipse the flax industry. However, 2000 people are still engaged in the manufacture of an increasing range of flax products.

Dundee gradually became a one-industry town—at one time over half the workers were employed in the jute trades. The city maintains a virtual monopoly of the industry in Britain. However, competition from cloth made in Bengal (with the help of Dundee men and machines!) and from other fibres led to a decline in the relative importance of the industry; compared with 40,210 employed in 1924, only 16,000 are employed today (this is 20 per cent of the city's workers). Still Dundee's main employer, the efficient modern industry produces a widening range of products, notably backing for carpets and linoleum, and sacking.

The manufacture of textile machinery is prominent among Dundee's varied engineering industries.

Fig. 33. Dundee, seen from the south-east, is an important industrial city, controlling routes along and across the Tay Estuary. Since this photograph was taken the Tay Road Bridge has been completed. (Photo: Aerofilms and Aero-Pictorial Ltd.)

The extent to which jute dominated the industrial scene made Dundee vulnerable to depression. As the numbers employed in the textile industries has dropped, a variety of modern, light industries has sprung up, mainly in two industrial estates employing over 6000 people. Most of these workers are engaged in the manufacture of cash registers, watches, refrigerators, batteries, radio and radar components. Clearly Dundee is acquiring an increasingly varied industrial basis.

Some famous traditional industries include the preserving and canning industry (which often uses locally grown fruit), the printing and publishing industries, baking and confectionery.

The annual trade of the port of Dundee does not exceed 500,000 tons and comprises largely imported jute, flax, crude oil and timber. Exports include jute products, potatoes and linoleum. Several important industries are associated with the dock area. Foremost is the shipbuilding industry: though less important than during the whaling era, the industry is the largest on the east coast. The manufacture of bitumen, road materials, roofing and fertilizers and timber working are other dock industries.

Dundee also serves as a major route centre, with the rail and road bridges carrying routes south. The Tay Road Bridge (1966) not only connects Dundee and its hinterland more quickly with Fife and Edinburgh but also makes possible the expansion of residential settlement on to the south side of the estuary in preference to a continued sprawl along the north shore.

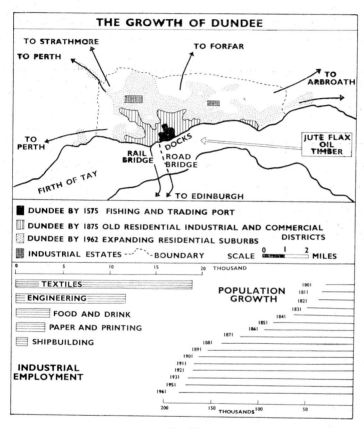

Fig. 34.

As Dundee now has a large sector of rapidly growing modern industry, and is physically well adapted to expansion, the Tayside region is clearly capable of considerable growth. The Tayside Study Report is devising a phased development programme based upon a projected population increase of perhaps 175,000–300,000 in the region by the end of the century. The region being considered includes not only Angus and Perth, but also the predominantly agricultural areas of North and East Fife.

There is undoubtedly a need to diversify employment in some of the inland areas of the Lower Tay region, where there is excessive dependence on agriculture—this lack of employment is seen in the static or declining population in many landward areas. Thus, any proposals must make provision for the expansion and diversification of employment potential in Dundee's hinterland.

POPULATION CHANGE IN ANGUS AND PERTHSHIRE 1951–66

	1951	1961	1966[1]	Change %
Angus (excluding Dundee and Arbroath)	78,015	75,878	75,560	−3·5
Perthshire (excluding Perth)	87,525	85,819	84,320	−3·1
Large Burghs and City Dundee	177,340	182,959	184,870	+4
Perth	40,504	41,199	41,910	+3·3
Arbroath	19,521	19,533	21,370	+8·6

[1] 1966 Sample Census.

Industries Outside Dundee

From as far afield as Arbroath and Coupar Angus people travel daily to Dundee for work but, despite this, and the agricultural nature of the hinterland, manufacturing is locally important. As in Dundee, locally produced flax initiated widespread textile industries in the area. Most of Scotland's coarse linens still come from this region.

Arbroath (20,000), an ancient abbey town and fishing port, presents two faces. First, exploiting its fine coastal position and sunny summers, it is a holiday resort. Secondly, it is an industrial town, similar in many respects to Dundee—the main industries are engineering (textile machinery, machine tools), textiles (canvas, jute, knitwear), iron founding, roofing felt and boat building. New industries on an industrial estate include the making of cans used in the local canning industry.

Montrose (11,000), a coastal resort, has fewer industries, reflecting the local agriculture—flour milling, fruit canning and preserving. Flax spinning is also important.

Stonehaven (4000) and Gourdon are both fishing and holiday centres, while Inverbervie has a flax and jute spinning industry. Carnoustie and Monifieth function partly as small engineering and jute working towns, but also as holiday resorts and dormitory towns for Dundee.

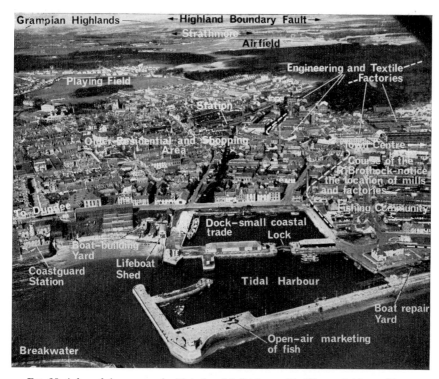

FIG. 35. Arbroath is concerned with industrial, fishing and holiday activities and has a rich agricultural interland. Beyond the town Strathmore and the Grampians are visible. (Photo: Scotsman Publications Ltd.)

In Strathmore, **Forfar** and **Brechin** are the largest towns. Forfar (10,000), the county town, is a market and agricultural centre. Apart from Dundee, it is the main jute manufacturing centre. Brechin has flax and jute weaving industries and a large machine tool industry. Kirriemuir, with oatmilling and jute industries, is an agricultural centre, as is true of many small towns, such as Laurencekirk, Alyth and Coupar Angus. The widespread canning industries focus on **Blairgowrie** (5000), which also has textile industries.

In Strathearn the main towns are Crieff, a holiday resort, and Auchterarder, with wool spinning and hosiery industries.

Perth (41,000) owed its historical importance (it was once the Scottish capital) to its strategic position. It is at the head of navigation, and is an important bridging point. The new Tay Road Bridge will detract little from its nodality. Occupying as it does a river gap, opposite the point where the Tay breaches the Highlands at Dunkeld, Perth is the "gateway to the Highlands" and is a natural route centre. It has become an important market town, serving Strathmore and Strathearn, and is famous as the hub of the beef cattle trade. Aberdeen–Angus and Shorthorn cattle are sold to many overseas buyers, fetching prices approaching six figures. The tourist industry takes second place to agriculture, but there is a surprising array of manufacturers recalling names like Bells and Dewars. The soft Tay waters support dyeing and bleaching industries (Pullars) while whisky blending is equally important. Other industries include jute spinning, carpets, glassware and footwear.

CHAPTER 6

The Fife Peninsula

SITUATED between the Tay and the Forth estuaries, the Fife peninsula shows great variety in its physical and human geography. The county was for long isolated, and only the "golden fringe" was developed, but land improvement, the growth of mining and access by rail and road made the peninsula a prosperous farming, mining and industrial region. The decline of the coal industry is being accompanied by significant changes in the economic and social geography of Fife.

Physical Features

Bordering the Tay, a narrow coastal lowland has rich raised beach deposits. East of Tayport, Tents Muir extends south to the Eden mouth—the 25-ft raised beach is covered by wind-blown sands, supporting coniferous plantations.

South of this coastal strip, lavas (similar to those of the Sidlaws) form rounded hills between 600 and 1000 ft. They form no barrier to communications, but continue south-west to become the more formidable Ochil Hills. This massive dissected plateau of volcanic rocks rises from Strathallan and Strathearn and is highest in the south (Bencleuch, 2363 ft), where the range towers over the Devon valley in a great fault scarp. Valleys, such as Glendevon and Glenfarg, which penetrate this barrier, carry major north–south routes.

The hills of north Fife give way southwards to a discontinuous furrow of lowland, comprising three main parts: the Kinross basin is framed by the Ochils, the Cleish Hills, the Lomond Hills and Benarty Hill; to the northeast the Howe of Fife lies between the northern hills, the Lomonds and the East Neuk plateau. The Howe has heavy but productive soils; it has been reclaimed from marsh and indeed some areas are still waterlogged. Leaving the Howe, the Eden follows a wide, fertile valley (Stratheden) to the tidal flats beyond Guardbridge.

South of these lowlands is a second line of uplands. The Cleish Hills and Benarty Hill both exceed 1000 ft, while the lava-capped Lomond Hills rise abruptly to 1812 ft and are separated from Benarty by the Leven valley. East of the Lomonds, much of south-east Fife (the East Neuk) is occupied by a plateau (500–700 ft) with ill-drained clay in places. Fringing this plateau from St. Andrews to Leven, the coastal lowland has raised beaches, alternating with cliffed or rocky sections.

Beyond the Leven and Ore valleys in south-west Fife, a low, undulating and often ill-drained plateau rises towards the Cleish Hills. The rocks of this plateau contain coal measures. To the south-west, the plateau merges with the raised beach lowland bordering the Forth estuary.

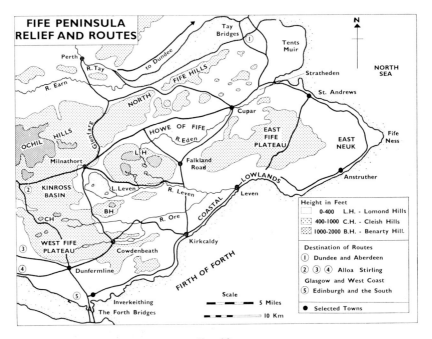

FIG. 36.

The Fife peninsula has therefore a fringe of lowland, normally of high fertility. The inland areas, the former "beggar's mantle", have been reclaimed and improved to become very productive, the only exception being the high hill ranges.

Climate

The easterly position of the region ensures a relatively dry climate, similar to that of Angus. Winters are cool, January with 3–4° C (37–39° F), but the summers are relatively warm at 15° C (58–59° F) with 4 months over 10° C (50° F). In common with other east coast districts, cold easterly "haars" are frequent in winter and spring.

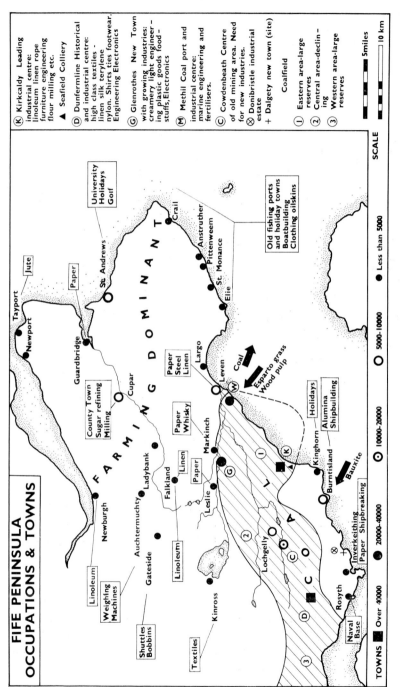

FIG. 37

Fig. 38. An aerial view of Crail, an old fishing port on Fife's "golden fringe". In the background the East Neuk is intensively cultivated. (Crown Copyright Reserved.)

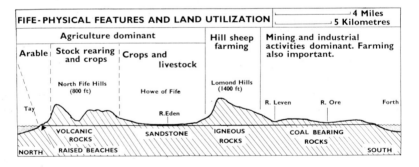

Fig. 39.

The lowlands of Fife have light, well-distributed rainfall: eastern areas have less than 30 in., but further west rainfall is heavier and exceeds 30 in. (Dunfermline 32·5 in.). In hill areas, annual rainfall often exceeds 40 in.

Agriculture

The combination of fertile lowlands and a favourable climate makes agriculture very important. The number of people employed on farms in 1966 was 3400, compared with 5400 in 1956—this, compared with the greatly increased productivity in this period, is a measure of the increased intensity and mechanization of agriculture. The new road bridges, giving greater accessibility to markets for high value, perishable crops, may be expected to effect some changes. For example, farms in North Fife have easy access now to the canning and preserving plants north of the Tay.

The East Neuk, the Howe, the north coastal strip and the Leven and Ore valleys with their light rain and fertility are suited to the growing of barley, wheat and oats, as well as sugar-beet. Barley, in great demand for malting and stock feed, and also more suitable for mechanized harvesting, has dramatically ousted oats as the major cereal. Almost 40 per cent of Scotland's sugar-beet is grown in these areas, because of the existence of Scotland's only sugar-beet refinery at Cupar.

Beef cattle are fattened on most farms, where in the 7- or 8-year rotation fodder crops such as oats and turnips are included, and rotation grass provides silage and hay as well as grazing. In addition to beef cattle, farms in the East Neuk, and especially the Howe of Fife, may also fatten store lambs in winter on roots and sugar-beet tops. A typical farm in these areas, one of 300 acres, employing five workers, may have only 60 acres of grassland, yet as many as seventy beef cattle may be fattened. Yields compare favourably with those of East Lothian. Soil fertility is maintained by manure from winter court feeding of beef cattle.

On the high, less fertile plateau of the East Neuk, cropping declines slightly in favour of stock rearing. Also many farms on the productive north coastal strip have a hinterland of rough grazing for sheep and cattle. The higher ranges, e.g. the Lomonds, are used for stock rearing.

Framed by hills, the Kinross basin, with alluvial and boulder clay soils, is an intensive mixed farming region: dairying, cash cropping and livestock fattening are important.

West Fife has heavier rainfall, so that south and west of the Ore valley considerable differences are evident. More land is devoted to grass, and less to cropping: oats and potatoes replace wheat, barley and sugar-beet as the main crops. A farm of 250 acres might have 135 acres of rotation grass, 40 acres of oats and 20 acres of potatoes; there may be some permanent grass, particularly where mining subsidence or heavy clay soils cause poor drainage.

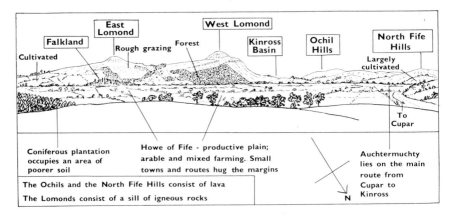

FIG. 40. South of the productive Howe of Fife, the Lomond Hills rise sharply and form a central feature in the relief of Fife.

The emphasis on grass and fodder crops presupposes important pastoral activities. Indeed, dairying is dominant, and an average farm might support forty-five milking cows, but also fifty store lambs. The presence of a large mining and industrial population creates a large demand for milk in west Fife.

Farming is thus especially important in central and east Fife. Only 24 per cent of the agricultural workers are in west Fife: this reflects on the one hand the more favourable conditions in East Fife, and on the other the importance of mining and industry in western areas.

Fishing

Fishing is concentrated on the south-east coast, in Anstruther, Pittenweem, Crail, St. Monance and Leven. These ancient burghs of the "golden fringe" grew as ports trading with the Baltic and the Mediterranean. This function has ceased until only Methil retains substantial trade. Unfortunately, the traditional herring and white fishing industry of the Forth has also declined and now employs fewer than 400 people. Anstruther and Pittenweem are the main centres, but, whereas 50 years ago these old harbours were full of fishing boats, fewer than forty vessels are now operating. Before the last war, Anstruther alone harboured forty-six steam drifters. In addition to the inshore seine-net industry, crabs and lobsters are caught: Crail is foremost in this activity.

Certain industries are attached to these old ports, perhaps the most striking being boatbuilding at St. Monance, an industry established for over 200 years. Others include the manufacture of sailcloth and waterproofed wear at Anstruther.

Holiday Industry

The isolated but colourful coastal burghs have developed as holiday resorts. The picturesque harbours and sheltered beaches alternating with rocky headlands attract large numbers of holiday-makers from Edinburgh and Glasgow: Elie, Earlsferry, Crail, Anstruther and Pittenweem are all concerned.

The varied coastal scenery, dry summers and proximity to a large urban population make the holiday industry important all round the coast. St. Andrews, an ancient university city and golfing centre, is a major resort. Other resorts include Largo, Aberdour and Kinghorn.

Mining

Although many collieries have closed in recent years and employment in mining has dwindled, coal mining remains a major industry in the county, which accounted for over 25 per cent of Scotland's mine workers and coal output in 1967–8. Records of mining in Fife date to the thirteenth century, but the main development of the coalfield took place in the nineteenth century. Peak production of over 10 million tons was reached in 1913, when 30,000 men were employed. The rapid evolution of the industry was mirrored in the upsurge of population in the mining areas and in the growth of new towns; perhaps most striking was the growth of Cowdenbeath, whose population increased from 127 in 1841 to 7,467 in 1901. The mining areas grew much more rapidly than other parts of the county:

	1755	1801	1851	1901	1951
Mining parishes					
Auchterderran	1143	1045	3210	8626	17,599
Ballingry	464	277	568	4156	13,831
Beath	1099	613	1252	15,812	22,643
Rural parishes					
Kemback	420	626	956	412	464
Saline	1285	945	1792	1012	1413

The coalfields comprise three areas: the western field of Valleyfield, Blairhall and Comrie; the central field in the Cowdenbeath–Lochgelly area; the eastern section in the Kirkcaldy district. With the closure in 1967 of the last pit (excluding Westfield opencast site) in the central area, output now comes from a handful of collieries in east Fife and four in west Fife—output from eleven Fife pits in 1967–8 was almost 4 million tons; this is only slightly less than was produced by twenty-one pits in 1961. This, of course, implies the closure of uneconomic pits, and the expansion of output from new or reconstructed collieries which have a long life, particularly those such as Seafield and Valleyfield tapping the large reserves of coal in the strata dipping under the Forth—these constitute the main resources for the future. Already, Seafield Colliery, a new sinking at Kirkcaldy, is producing almost 1 million tons a year.

Thus, although production has dropped over a long period, Fife's importance as a coal-producing region is assured and, in fact, is increasing. As the Lanarkshire field declines, Fife's share of the national output rises.

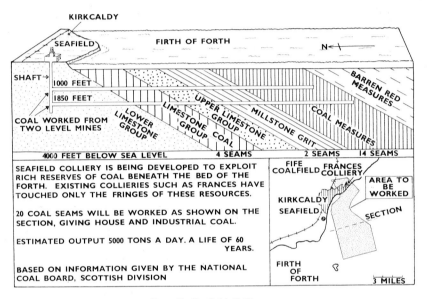

Fig. 41. Seafield Colliery.

Fife supplies household and industrial coal to much of Scotland, but the export of coal from Methil is now negligible compared with the 3 million tons exported in 1913. An increasing proportion of the coal produced is being used in new thermal power stations at Methil (using slurry—colliery waste) and the much larger station at Kincardine. The shrinkage of markets for coal and the increasing dependence on the electricity industry as the major consumer is more marked with the completion of the Longannet project. This scheme is explained in Fig. 42, and, when in full production, in 1972, the 2400 MW station will produce 50 per cent of the projected Scottish electricity demand.

The 6 million tons of coal consumed annually by Longannet is coming largely from new collieries, such as Seafield, and from the four drift mines linked to the power station.

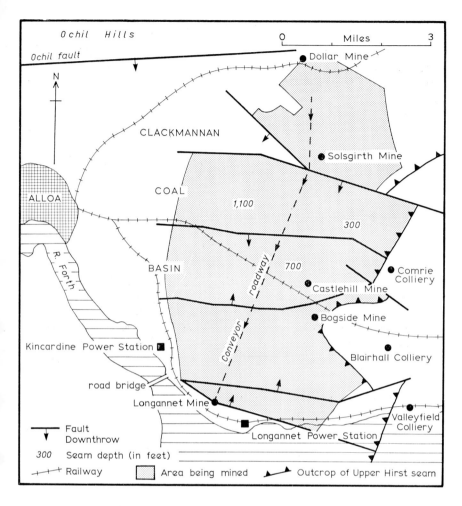

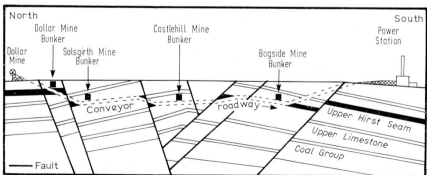

Fig. 42. The Longannet Scheme. (Reproduced from *Geography*, Vol. 53, No. 241, November 1968, by permission of the Geographical Association.)

Therefore, despite a contraction in coal output, the industry remains of great importance. After over a century of coal extraction large areas of the county have been left badly scarred. Reclamation schemes are transforming such areas (for example, near Lochgelly) and rehabilitating the land for agricultural, building and recreational use.

Industries and Towns

Manufacturing industries are varied, and some, like textiles, rival agriculture as Fife's oldest industry, while others such as paper-making and engineering are more recent and followed the development of the coalfield. Still more recent is the rapidly expanding group of electronic and instrument industries. The major concentration of population and industry is in the south-western part of the county with Kirkcaldy and Dunfermline the major centres—it is notable that all the larger burghs are located in this area, with the exception of St. Andrews and Cupar.

TOWNS IN FIFE—POPULATION GROWTH

	1851	1901	1951	1961	1966 (Sample census)
County	154,000	219,000	307,000	321,000	(314,000)
Burghs:					
Kirkcaldy	6,700	37,600	49,000	52,400	(49,800)
Dunfermline	8,600	25,300	44,700	47,200	(46,800)
Buckhaven–Methil	2,800[a]	7,500	13,200	12,000	(10,800)
St. Andrews	4,700	7,600	9,500	9,900	(10,500)
Lochgelly	1,600[a]	5,500	9,100	9,100	(7,900)
Leven	2,100	5,600	8,900	8,900	(8,300)

[a] 1861.

The origins of the linen and related industries are found in a very old domestic industry using locally grown flax, and their distribution is widespread. The rivers of Fife were vital to this early growth, providing power. Later, competition from other fabrics halted the expansion of the industry but it remains important.

Dunfermline (47,000), a former capital of Scotland and a centre of great historical interest, is noted for its textile industries. The weaving of fine linens and damasks has been surpassed, however, by silk, rayon and Terylene industries and the manufacture of footwear and clothing. The town also has engineering and electrical industries.

Elsewhere in Fife the linen industry survives at Kirkcaldy, Leven, Cupar, Falkland and Strathmiglo. The leading products are domestic linen, damasks and sheeting. The Fife industry thus concentrates on finer cloth, in contrast to the coarser products of Dundee and Angus. As in the Dundee region, the industry has contracted with small centres, such as Ladybank, closing down. Of Scotland's total linen and canvas output, a quarter comes from Fife.

Other textile industries include knitwear (Auchtermuchty and Cellardykes) and woollen goods (Kinross, Glenrothes and Markinch).

In **Kirkcaldy** (52,000) linen was the staple manufacture of the early nineteenth century. Flax and hemp spinning, linen weaving and dyeing are still important, but have been eclipsed by the remarkable growth of the linoleum industry. Using jute backing from Dundee, linoleum manufacture began in 1847, as a venture by Michael Nairn, and has expanded until Kirkcaldy is now the world's leading producer. Linoleum is also made in Falkland and Newburgh.

Apart from linoleum, "the lang toon's" many industries include carpets, furniture, rope, flour milling and a wide range of engineering and foundry work. Recent developments on an industrial estate include telephone equipment and projectors.

The paper industry is widespread and grew during the nineteenth century. Its development was encouraged by adequate supplies of water from rivers such as the Eden and Leven, access to coalfields and the ease of importing esparto grass and wood pulp through Methil and Burntisland. Fifty thousand tons a year is produced, much of it for export, in mills at Inverkeithing, Guardbridge, Markinch, Leslie and Leven. The wide range of products emphasizes the importance of the industry, employing over 3000 people: a long list includes writing paper, photographic paper, boards, paper bags, etc.

Shipbuilding and engineering industries are fairly widespread. One of the main shipbuilding centres on the east coast is Burntisland; among the ships built there are bauxite carriers. Bauxite, the ore from which aluminium is obtained, is imported from Ghana to Burntisland, where alumina is extracted and sent for refining to the Highlands (see Chapter 12). Methil has marine engineering industries, and Inverkeithing a shipbreaking yard, while Rosyth maintains its role as a major naval base. Numerous other centres house a variety of metal industries, from steel works at Leven to weighing machines at Auchtermuchty.

With the decline of employment in traditional industries, notably coal mining and agriculture, efforts to attract new growth industries have been intensified, and since the early 1960s, have borne fruit with the establishment of a significant and diverse concentration of light and electronic industries, which are showing all the signs of rapid growth. These industries are located chiefly on new industrial estates and in advance factories in the Kirkcaldy–Glenrothes–Dunfermline triangle, including such centres as Cowdenbeath, Inverkeithing and Donibristle. It is significant that it is in this area that pit closures have been most numerous; the great diversity of these new industries—radio, telecommunications equipment, computer components, etc.—should protect the region from the worst effects of the alternating boom and slump conditions prevalent in many other industries. Apart from the availability of land (some of it reclaimed from mining dereliction), labour and good educational facilities for retraining labour, the most significant factors in attracting these high value industries to Fife have probably been the provision of factories and the financial inducements associated with Development Areas, and the opening of the Forth Road Bridge, which not only removed the region's insularity but put Edinburgh Airport, with regular flights to London, within easy reach.

The natural tendency to growth that these industries possess, together with the further provision of industrial premises and transport developments,

Fig. 43. This aerial view shows the growing new town of Glenrothes; this is best studied in conjunction with Fig. 44. (Photo: Glenrothes Development Corporation.)

seems to ensure continued rapid and self-generating growth beyond all expectations of a few years ago.

The pace at which the new town of **Glenrothes** has developed is symptomatic of the nature of the changes taking place in Fife. A mere village in 1948, Glenrothes' population is now 25,000, and is expected to reach its planned target of 55,000 by 1975, and eventually 70,000.

Fig. 44. To be studied in conjunction with the aerial photograph of Glenrothes—Fig. 43.

GLENROTHES: SOURCES OF POPULATION

Fife	Elsewhere in Scotland	Elsewhere in United Kingdom	Overseas
56%	34%	6%	4%

The new town was planned originally as a cornerstone in the post-war expansion of the coal industry, but the life of the new Rothes Colliery was indeed very short! Besides the long-established whisky, paper and blanket industries at Markinch, industries are multiplying rapidly in the new town's industrial estates, and range from computers and electronic components to mining machinery, clothing, foodstuffs and plastics as well as many others. By mid-1968, some fifty firms were established in the new town, which has become the self-styled "capital of the British electronics industry".

The influx of new technological industries to Fife is transforming the industrial scene—so, also, urban renewal, new housing projects such as that at Dalgety Bay, the removal of pit bings and the draining of areas affected by mining subsidence are changing the face of south-west Fife.

In marked contrast, the towns of **north and east Fife** are primarily agricultural centres or holiday resorts, although we have noted the scattering of textile, engineering and paper industries. Consequently, no towns here rival Dunfermline, Kirkcaldy or Methil in size—in fact, only two, Cupar and St. Andrews, exceed 5000 in population. The greater accessibility granted to north Fife by the Tay Road Bridge, and the projected expansion of Dundee, may, in the long term, alter this picture.

Cupar, the county town and the main agricultural centre, is on the edge of the productive Howe of Fife. It serves as a grain and livestock market, and its industries reflect its farming hinterland: acrigultural engineering, tanning, oat milling and sugar refining. Scotland's only sugar-beet refinery is at Cupar, and produces over 25,000 tons of sugar a year. Cupar's role as a road and rail centre is vital to its markets and industries. Routes along Stratheden lead on the one hand to St. Andrews, and on the other to the Tay Rail Bridge and the new road bridge; south-westwards, a route skirts the Howe of Fife and gives access to Kirkcaldy and the important coastal route; from Cupar, the road west to Auchtermuchty links the Howe to the Kinross basin, and to the passes leading through the Ochils.

CHAPTER 7

Edinburgh and the Lothians

THE ancient province of Lothian, between the Forth and the Southern Uplands, comprises three counties: West Lothian, Midlothian and East Lothian. Dominating the region, as it has throughout history, is Edinburgh, Scotland's capital and second city. Edinburgh's hinterland is a productive agricultural and mining region, but not one noted for great industrial developments, though, as elsewhere in Scotland, changes are taking place with the influx of new industries, particularly to areas in West Lothian.

Physical Features

The Pentlands, dividing the region into two parts, consist of old lavas and sedimentary rocks and rise to over 1800 ft. They are widest in the south where they are less dissected, and they provide recreation areas for the city dwellers.

The relief of **West Lothian** is complicated. To the west and south-west a moorland plateau separates the Forth and Clyde valleys. From the Slamannan Plateau (700 ft) the moorland extends south to meet the Pentlands and rises to over 1000 ft; this area is often ill drained, due in part to mining subsidence. The River Avon cuts a deep valley between the Slamannan Plateau and the Torphichen Hills, with the latter igneous ridge exceeding 1000 ft. The broad Almond lowlands are linked by a coastal furrow to the middle Forth carse; between this furrow and the estuary is a low plateau.

The hilly defile occupied by Edinburgh connects West Lothian to East Lothian. To the east of the Pentlands, the **Midlothian basin,** framed by the Pentlands, Moorfoots and the Camp Ridge, is drained by the North and South Esk, flowing in incised valleys. Within the basin. there is a north/south contrast: the northern part is low-lying and fertile with raised beach and glacial deposits; the south rises to over 1000 ft. and is often badly drained moorland.

East of the rounded Camp Ridge, the central feature of **East Lothian** is a plateau extending east from the Camp Ridge and highest in the Garleton Hills (590 ft.). To the north of the plateau the coastal plains have a mantle of fertile raised beach and glacial deposits, and are only interrupted by igneous crags, such as North Berwick Law.

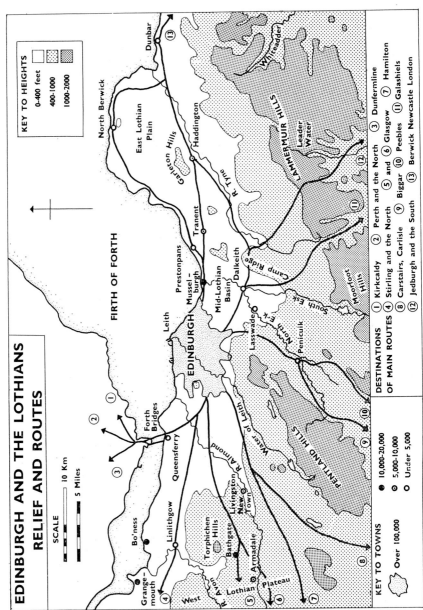

Fig. 45.

South of the Garleton Hills, the Tyne valley widens between Pathead and East Linton. Between the Tyne and the Lammermuirs, a higher bench (700 ft) is deeply cut by streams and hugs the fault scarp.

Climate

With a sheltered, easterly situation, the lowlands have light rainfall with less than 25 in. on the coast. Rainfall increases to the west and may exceed 40 in. on the hills. Summers are warm (14° C, 58° F), the growing season is long and, despite cold east winds (countered by shelter belts), the risk of ground frosts is diminished by westerly air streams. January temperatures of 4° C (39° F) near the coast contrast, however, with colder conditions on the higher inland areas, such as West Linton, 2° C (35° F).

Agriculture

With a long history of farming enterprise, the Lothians are in the fore-front of Scottish agriculture and are noted for high yields of grain and root crops. Extensive and fertile lowlands and a dry climate combine to make this the most important arable farming region in Scotland. The dry springs favour early sowing and the sunny summers quicken ripening.

It is on the deep loams of the **East Lothian plain** that arable farming is most intensive. Farms here are large, a typical one being 350 acres. The rotation is the old East Lothian six with only one year of rotation grass: on a 350-acre farm with six workers, there might be 200 acres of grain, 50 of potatoes, 30 of swedes, 20 of sugar-beet and 50 of grass. The amount of grain grown is increasing and malting barley (for the brewing industry) occupies over half the grain acreage. Potatoes are often grown in coastal areas (Dunbar area) as an early crop, and are widely used for seed. Sugar-beet is much less important than in Fife.

In addition to these cash crops, fodder crops such as grass (for hay and silage), swedes and beet tops make beef cattle fattening important in winter:

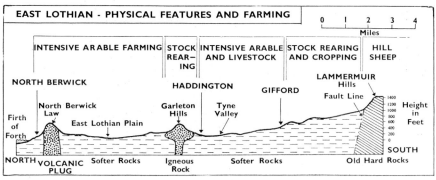

Fig. 46.

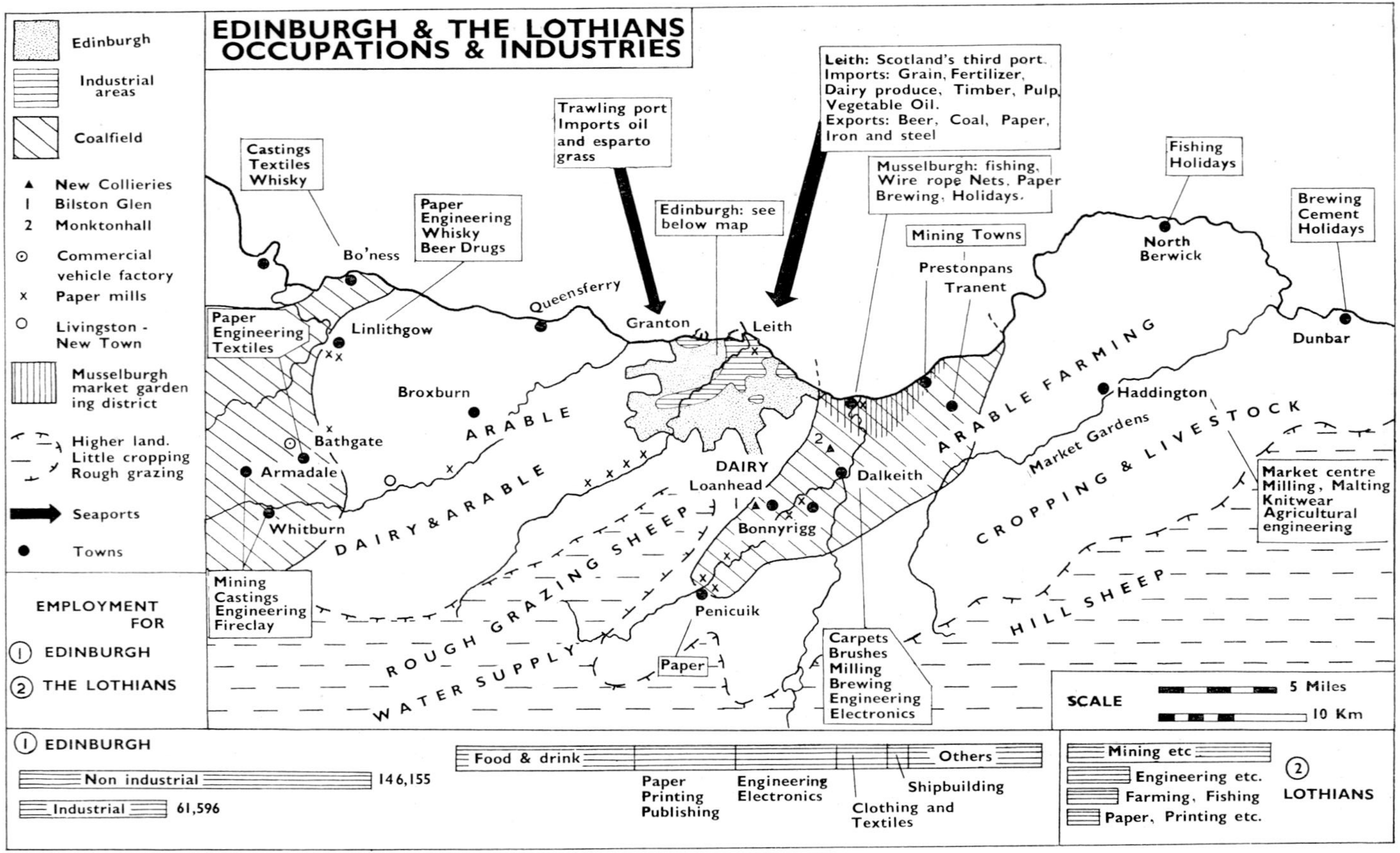

EDINBURGH & THE LOTHIANS
OCCUPATIONS & INDUSTRIES

Leith: Scotland's third port. Imports: Grain, Fertilizer, Dairy produce, Timber, Pulp, Vegetable Oil, Exports: Beer, Coal, Paper, Iron and steel

Musselburgh: fishing, Wire rope Nets, Paper Brewing, Holidays.

Mining Towns

Prestonpans

Tranent

Carpets
Brushes
Milling
Brewing
Engineering
Electronics

Dalkeith

Bonnyrigg

DAIRY

Loanhead

Penicuik

Paper

Edinburgh: see below map

Leith

Granton

Queensferry

Trawling port Imports oil and esparto grass

Paper
Engineering
Whisky
Beer Drugs

Bo'ness

Linlithgow

Broxburn

ARABLE

Castings
Textiles
Whisky

Bathgate

Armadale

Whitburn

Paper
Engineering
Textiles

Mining
Castings
Engineering
Fireclay

DAIRY & ARABLE

Brewing
Cement
Holidays

Dunbar

Fishing
Holidays

North
Berwick

Haddington

Market centre
Milling, Malting
Knitwear
Agricultural
engineering

Market Gardens

CROPPING & LIVESTOCK

ARABLE FARMING

HILL SHEEP

MINING GRAZING SHEEP

ROUGH GRAZING

WATER SUPPLY

Legend

- Edinburgh
- Industrial areas
- Coalfield

New Collieries
1 Bilston Glen
2 Monktonhall
⊙ Commercial vehicle factory
× Paper mills
○ Livingston - New Town

Musselburgh market garden ing district

Higher land. Little cropping Rough grazing

Seaports
Towns

EMPLOYMENT FOR
① EDINBURGH
② THE LOTHIANS

① EDINBURGH

Non industrial 146,155
Industrial 61,596

Food & drink

Paper
Printing
Publishing

Engineering
Electronics

Shipbuilding

Clothing and Textiles

Mining etc
Engineering etc.
Farming, Fishing
Paper, Printing etc.

② LOTHIANS

Others

SCALE
5 Miles
10 Km

FIG. 47

on a typical farm, seventy cattle are fattened and some sheep may be wintered.

Farming is similar in the Tyne valley, although rather more grass is grown, and cattle fattening is more prominent. On the higher ground towards the hills, half the acreage may be grass, and while grains are still important, fodder crops for rearing young beef cattle and sheep are more in evidence. Farms on the Lammermuir slopes veer even more towards grassland, and a large proportion of rough grazing makes sheep rearing the main concern.

The increase of small holdings has led to the growth of intensive crops such as strawberries and vegetables—this is well seen in the Tyne valley west of Haddington.

Farming in **Midlothian** is similar in some ways to East Lothian, with arable crops prominent. The demand Edinburgh makes for milk has made dairying more important: to support this, many farms in the lower areas of Midlothian have rotation grass as the main crop, though wheat, barley and roots remain important. The less fertile southern half of the basin is not important for wheat and barley, and much more rotation grass and oats make the rearing of sheep and cattle important. Large areas remain as unreclaimed bog or peat land.

At the northern end of the basin, Musselburgh is the centre of a market gardening area accounting for half of Scotland's vegetable acreage and 60 per cent of its production. This is made possible by rich soils based upon a light surface layer overlying gravelly subsoil mixed with shells; thin soils heat quickly in spring. Light rainfall and shelter provided by the East Lothian coast are further favourable factors. The larger market gardens extend to 200 acres, and produce leeks, peas, rhubarb, savoys, cauliflowers and soft fruits; smaller farms (1–3 acres) concentrate on early vegetables, tomatoes and flowers. There is a large market, locally and further afield, for these products.

West of the Pentlands, the pattern of farming is different from that of East Lothian. While the coastal areas and the Almond valley are predominantly arable, there is rather more rotation grass, and less barley and sugar-beet. Wetter conditions in the west and heavier soils make dairying a widespread activity, particularly in the higher southern and western areas. Farms are smaller, and one of 140 acres would have 80 acres of grassland, 40 of grain (mostly oats) and 20 of roots. In the least favourable areas, the plateau is waterlogged, and poor permanent grazing remains.

Fishing

Like the Fife coast, the south side of the Forth also saw the growth of numerous small fishing havens, concerned initially with herring and oyster fishing. Inevitably, too, the Lothian fishing industry. It is still important at Cockenzie and Fisherrow, where some forty small vessels combine herring fishing with winter seine-net fishing for white-fish, Dunbar and Newhaven participating on a small scale. Distinct from the inshore fisheries is the trawling industry centred on Granton; about twenty modern trawlers are based here and fish in distant ground for haddock, whiting and cod.

Among activities related to fishing, special mention may be made of Musselburgh's large net industry, based upon cotton spinning.

Mining

The earliest records of coal mining in the Lothians date back to 1200, when monks from Holyrood and Newbattle worked coal in the region.

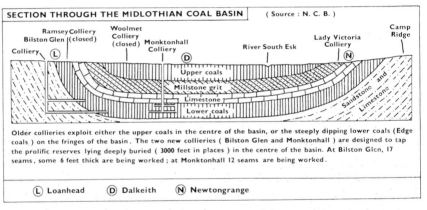

Fig. 48.

East of the Pentlands, coal-bearing rocks dip steeply under the **Midlothian basin** and re-emerge in the Camp Ridge, beyond which they sink eastwards in East Lothian. The lower coals outcrop along the fringes of the basin, and, with the upper measures in the centre, have been well worked from mines in small towns such as Loanhead, Bonnyrigg and Newtongrange. Coal has also been won from opencast sites on the Camp Ridge.

Very large reserves remain deeply buried in the centre of the basin and extend north under the Forth. To exploit these resources, mines have been reconstructed, and two new ones sunk at **Bilston Glen** (Loanhead) and **Monktonhall** (near Dalkeith); each of these collieries is producing over 1 million tons of coal annually, and they jointly employ almost 4000 men. As a result of these developments, the Midlothian field is the only Scottish one to have significantly increased output in recent years, to $3\frac{1}{2}$ million tons in

1967/8. In the Lothians as a whole, mining with over 12,000 employees in mid-1968 remains a major industry. The two new pits have combined reserves of over 100 million tons, and high levels of efficiency have been achieved.

As in the case of Fife, the output from the Lothian pits is increasingly directed towards the electricity industry, namely the new thermal power station (1200 MW capacity) completed in 1968 at Cockenzie. Together with Kincardine (760 MW) and its larger brother at Longannet (2400 MW), the Cockenzie site offered many advantages, including nearby coal resources, ample cooling water and facilities for dumping ash. The bulk of Cockenzie's annual $2\frac{1}{2}$ million tons of coal is being supplied by the new "merry-go-round" train system from Monktonhall and Bilston Glen. The overall demand for power station coal in Scotland will reach a peak in 1971/2 when it should comprise 50 per cent of the output (i.e. 8 million tons); thereafter, as nuclear and oil-fired stations gradually replace the coal ones, the markets for Scottish coal will be seriously curtailed.

FIG. 49. On the site of the old Furnace Yard Pit, the new Kinneil Colliery has workings reaching out under the Forth to tap huge reserves of coking, house and steam coals. This photograph, looking north-east, shows the colliery under construction. (Photo: National Coal Board.)

In West Lothian the coal seams are an eastward extension of the central coalfield, and mining is still a major activity south and west of Bathgate. Armadale, Fauldhouse and Whitburn are mining towns: at the latter, Polkemmet Colliery is one of Scotland's largest and an important source of coking coal. A fireclay industry, producing refractory bricks and tiles, is also found in this area.

While coal output from this western area has decreased, and is less than half of that of the Midlothian field, notice the new Kinneil Colliery at Bo'ness—this sinking is now linked under the Forth to Valleyfield Colliery, and taps prolific reserves of coking coal under the estuary.

Bo'ness used to share with Leith a large export trade; Leith's pre-war export of some 2 million tons a year has dwindled to 40,000 tons.

To the west of the Pentlands, **oil shales** have been worked since the 1850s and many settlements owe their existence to the industry. The main mining centres were Broxburn, Uphall and the Calders, and workings extended under the Forth. Production reached a peak in 1913, and in 1919 stood at 2,750,000 tons of shale (250,000 tons of oil), and 9000 men were employed. In face of increasing competition from imported oil, mines, retorts and refineries have progressively closed down, until the industry ceased in 1962. All that remained was Pumpherston refinery, where English crude oil was processed. Abandoned mines and huge tabular bings of spent shale are striking features of the landscape.

The death of the shale industry has left a large gap in the economy, a gap which, accentuated by a contraction in coal mining, is being filled by the development of new industries.

Industry and Towns

Although the Lothians do not form an industrial region on the same scale as the Glasgow region, there are numerous, important industries.

Edinburgh houses a surprising array of industries, many of which have their origins in the growth and functions of the capital and its hinterland.

The city originated as a tiny "burgh" on the impregnable castle rock, and was certainly a home for Malcolm Canmore in the tenth century. The town grew slowly on the protected tail, and extended during the reign of David I to meet the new Canongate burgh with Holyrood Abbey. Protected by the Castle and the Nor' Loch, the town had great strategic value in commanding the coastal route, and gradually became accepted as the capital, "a town where princes, magnates and other nobles were in frequent concourse". Edinburgh survived English occupation, protected by the Flodden Wall, and reached out to the port of Leith for trade.

Remaining a small, walled burgh until the mid-eighteenth century, it at last broke out of the cramped defensive site it had held for over 600 years. The valley to the north of the old town was drained and communication was made with the handsome "new town", with its rectangular plan based upon Princes Street. Many famous names (Adam, Boswell and Scott) are associated with this period, during which the city added literary and cultural activities to its government and legal functions.

Further growth followed in the nineteenth century, and the twentieth century has seen even greater expansion until the city covers over 50 square miles. This rapid growth is reflected in population increases: 1750—30,000, 1850—160,000, 1961—468,378.

Within the extensive modern city, the contrast between the "old town" and the "new town", separated by a picturesque valley, remains the most striking feature of the capital. The familiar picture of Edinburgh is one of the Royal Mile, the Castle, Holyrood, the University, colleges and churches, and not least Princes Street with its gardens, art galleries, hotels and shops.

Fig. 50. The contrast between the "old town" and the "new town" is a striking feature of Edinburgh. The early fortress, with its impregnable position, commanded the coastal defile. (Photo: Scotsman Publications Ltd.)

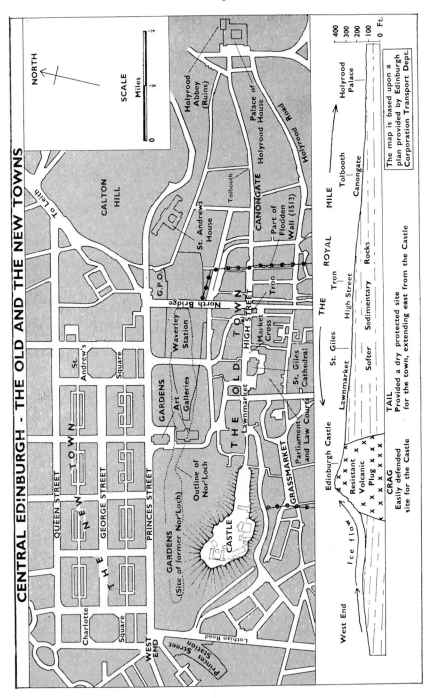

CENTRAL EDINBURGH - THE OLD AND THE NEW TOWNS

FIG. 51.

The map is based upon a plan provided by Edinburgh Corporation Transport Dept.

As the capital, Edinburgh is a centre of administration, law and education: over 100,000 people are engaged in professional and scientific services, administration, insurance, banking, etc. For long, historical associations and the "new town" have attracted visitors to Edinburgh; the tourist industry has been strengthened by the Edinburgh Festival.

The **industries of Edinburgh** are sufficiently far removed from the centre as to preserve its beauty. Three of the principal industries are paper-making, printing and publishing: local suitable water, and pulp and esparto grass imported through Leith and Granton support the old paper industries—mills in the Edinburgh area produce 20 per cent of Britain's fine papers. Just as the local demand encouraged paper-making, so also printing and publishing grew, and indeed date from 1507. Many of the world's finest books are published here; in addition, educational publishing and carto-graphy are specialities. The manufacture of paper-making machinery cartons and ink is also important.

The brewing industry rivals the latter in fame. From the days when ale brewed by the monks of Holyrood was renowned, local pure water and malting barley from the Lothians have established the industry's importance throughout the world. It supplies over 70 per cent of Scotland's beer. Whisky distilling and blending are also important.

The milling of oats was an early food industry to which many more have been added. Home-produced grain, supplemented by grain imported through Leith, support a large flour milling industry, and baking, chocolate and confectionery industries have grown.

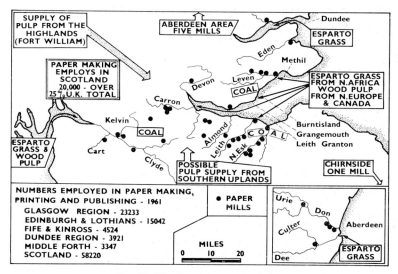

Fig. 52. The Scottish paper industry.

T.F.S.—D

While some industries have grown for obvious reasons, the large rubber industry landed here by chance: a wide range of products includes footwear, tyres, floor covering and golf balls.

Many engineering industries are established, ranging from marine engineering and shipbuilding activities in Leith, to electrical engineering, electronics and a variety of light products.

Other manufactures include hosiery, knitwear, fine chemicals, crystal glass and furniture.

Some of the city's industries depend upon raw materials imported through **Leith.** The milling, fertilizer and paper industries maintain the largest imports. The fertilizer industry is rapidly growing in the port and augments the established milling, food and engineering industries. Leith's exports are led by coal, beer, iron and steel and paper. It is Scotland's third port, and a major development programme, due for completion in 1969, is opening the port to vessels of 45,000 tons, including not only large tankers and bulk cargo carriers, but also passenger liners and cruise ships. Recent years have also seen the reclamation of land for industrial development in the dock area—this houses large oil depots and a greatly expanded fertilizer industry.

Mining remains dominant in Midlothian although there are some old-established industries, while, in West Lothian, the decline of mining and the collapse of the oil shale industry have led to an influx of new industries to join the older ones. On the whole, the region is not one noted for heavy industries.

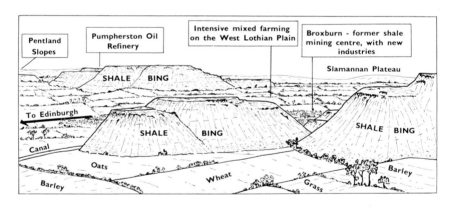

Fig. 53. The enormous bings of spent shale are a common feature of the Lothian landscape and bear mute evidence to the former importance of the shale industry.

The paper industry is widespread on both sides of the Pentlands, and is located at numerous centres on the Avon, Almond, Water of Leith and North

Esk, which supply the necessary water. Other factors that favoured this concentration of the industry were the large local demand for paper in Edinburgh, and the ease of importing raw materials through Granton and Leith; important centres include Penicuik, Musselburgh and Bathgate.

In **West Lothian** metal industries are important with foundries and castings industries in **Bathgate** (13,000), **Bo'ness** (10,000), Broxburn and Armadale. Bathgate is also a centre for electrical and general engineering industries. Textile industries, though less important, are nevertheless widespread, including hosiery and knitwear in Bo'ness, Bathgate, Linlithgow and Armadale.

Various other long-established industries include whisky distilling at Bo'ness and Linlithgow and whisky blending at South Queensferry.

The end of the shale industry and the run-down of coal mining affected West Lothian particularly, and created serious unemployment. The need therefore arose to attract new industries to the region and already many have arrived, and new growth points are discernible. The factors that have led to this industrial revival are numerous, and, while they include the advantages offered to firms by Development Area policy and the availability of labour, special importance is attached to local initiative in establishing industrial estates, the establishment of Livingston New Town, the new road bridge and West Lothian's central position astride the major west to east lines of communication. This latter factor enables it to attract not only planned overspill from Glasgow but also the unplanned overspill of some Edinburgh industry. Between 1964 and 1968 twenty firms have moved out to West Lothian from Edinburgh.

The population of Scotland's fourth new town, **Livingston** (designated in 1962), had grown to 7000 by 1968, and is planned to reach 70,000 by 1985 and subsequently 100,000 by natural growth; it is expected that 80 per cent of the population will come from Glasgow under the overspill arrangements. Livingston is becoming a major growth point and already many industries are established, showing the variety characteristic of new towns—foodstuffs, clothing, locks, gas appliances, etc. Service industries are also growing.

Close to Livingston is another major development, the British Leyland truck and tractor plant at Bathgate, which employs over 5000 and is being expanded. Although few ancillary vehicle component industries have been established, a new plant in Livingston is producing advanced metal forgings for the aircraft and vehicle industries, and further growth in this field seems likely, with Livingston as a focus. Side effects of the growth of the Bathgate plant also include an influx of vehicle collection and distribution firms and the manufacture of packing cases.

In addition to these developments, the industrial scene is being further transformed by the revitalization of towns formerly dependent on mining. This is being achieved by the formation of industrial estates and the attraction of new industry: Broxburn now has electrical, chemical and thread industries, while new estates at Whitburn have already attracted new industries, including electronics. The concentration of electronics industries noted in South Fife extends across the new bridge to South Queensferry, which has, since it was stripped of its ferry, expanded as a tourist and residential centre, attractive to a number of companies decentralized from

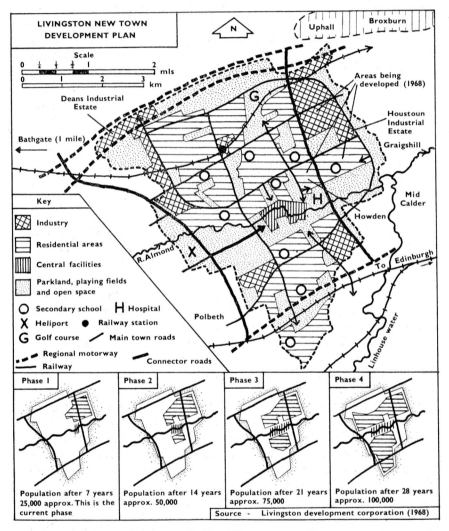

Fig. 54.

Lomond Hills

M90 to
Perth &
Highlands

Inverkeithing

Shipbreaking
Basin

FIFE

Ship

Railway
Bridge

Ship

E →

Former North
Shore Road
Ferry Terminal

Suspension
Cables

Former Road
Ferry Jetty

Road Bridge
(Note bend
at centre)

Naval
Anchorage

Cable
Anchorage
Points

South
Queensferry

Edinburgh

Fig. 55. Twin arteries linking the capital and the Highlands should help economic expansion north of the Forth. By permission of Lilywhite Limited.

87

Edinburgh. Easy access to airports, ports and a developing road system are aiding the industrial rebirth of West Lothian.

In contrast, **Mid and East Lothian** show comparatively little industrial change, this fact being attributable to the greater stability of the indigenous industries which are dominated by coal mining and paper-making. These and others centre on Musselburgh, Dalkeith and adjacent towns. **Musselburgh** (17,000) originated as a Roman settlement at a bridging point at the mouth of the Esk. Already mentioned for its fishing and horticultural activities, it has important industries, notably the making of wire ropes (including suspension wires for the Forth Road Bridge), fishing nets, twine, paper and beer. Proximity to Edinburgh and its historical interest make the "honest town" a seaside resort.

Dalkeith (9000), a bridging point on the North Esk, is the centre of a prosperous farming area. Once Scotland's largest grain market, it is now a mining centre with important and developing industries. The carpet industry is the largest and is accompanied by upholstery and brush-making. Oat and flour milling reflect the agricultural importance of the area. Other industries include brewing, printing, paper-making machinery and a new electronics industry.

Bonnyrigg, Lasswade and Roslin add the manufacture of carpets to their interests in coal and paper; Loanhead has hydraulic engineering and ferti-lizer industries.

East Lothian is primarily concerned with agriculture and shows little industrial development. Tranent and Prestonpans, the latter once famous for salt panning, brewing and soap manufacture, combine agricultural and mining activities. At Macmerry a small industrial estate has a precision engineering industry.

Coastal settlements take advantage of their nearness to Edinburgh, their dry, sunny summers and attractive locations, and act as holiday resorts—Aberlady, Gullane, North Berwick and Dunbar. North Berwick has a small fishing industry and is a dormitory town for Edinburgh. Dunbar, historically important as the gateway to the Lothians, has a brewing industry, and new cement works using local limestone.

Inland settlements are, for the most part, small farming centres, although light engineering and structural industries are developing. In the Tyne valley, East Linton (a road and rail bridging point) and Haddington (the county town) are the main settlements. **Haddington** (6000), strategically placed where routes cross the Tyne, preserves features of historical interest. It is the main market centre for East Lothian and has malting, flour milling, agricultural engineering, tweed and knitwear industries.

Communications

From Bathgate and Linlithgow in the west, Dunbar in the east, and now from Fife also, Edinburgh attracts many workers, and is the focus of local communications. Besides this, and important overseas connections through its port, the capital is a nodal centre by virtue of its control over the coastal defile carrying routes from England. The main routes and their physical controls are shown in Fig. 45. The Forth Road Bridge (1964) has replaced the centuries-old Queen's Ferry, and provides more rapid communications with Fife and beyond.

CHAPTER 8

The Middle Forth Region

A NARROW zone on either side of the Forth, between the Ochil Hills and
the Gargunnock and Kilsyth Hills, extends westwards and forms the premier
crossroads of Scotland. Pronounced nodality, distinctive agriculture and
striking industrial developments give this compact region a unique character,
although in some respects this central node may be regarded as transitional
between Fife and the Lothians, and the Clyde region.

Physical Features and Routes

   The region is framed by hills. South of the estuary the coastal plain rises
inland to the Slamannan plateau (700 ft). This plateau is separated from the
lava hills to the north-west by the corridor carrying routes from the Forth
to the Clyde valley. North of this gap, the rounded Kilsyth Hills and the
Campsie Fells rise to over 1800 ft and merge northwards with the Gargunnock Hills. The latter overlook the Forth valley with a precipitous slope.
   The northern boundary of the region extends from the Mentieth Hills
in the west to the fault scarp of the Ochils and the hills of south-west Fife
in the east. Several important routeways pierce this barrier: Callander in
the Teith valley controls entry to the Highlands; Strathallan carries the
main route to Perth and the north; Glendevon provides a passage through
the Ochils.
   Within these hilly confines lies a narrow lowland. South of the Ochil
scarp, the Devon valley is separated from the Forth by a triangular area of
low, hilly ground. The meandering Forth flows over an extensive, flat carse
of heavy clay soils. This is a raised beach left by the retreating sea. The
Carse of Forth reaches west to the Lake of Menteith, and extends along the
shores of the estuary beyond Kincardine and Grangemouth. The carselands
were formerly peat covered, and indeed some unreclaimed areas form wooded
"mosses".
   Routes enter this lowland through gaps in the hilly border, and along the
fringes of the estuary. Great significance has for long been attached to the
focus of these routes at **Stirling.** Stirling Castle, situated (like Edinburgh
Castle) on an igneous crag, has a commanding position overlooking a vital
bridging point and the widening estuary and carselands. Control of this

crossroads made Stirling a focal point in Scottish history. "The battlefield of Scotland" is no misnomer, for the area between Antonine's Wall and the hills to the north, and the battles of Stirling Bridge (1297) and Bannockburn (1314), come early in the list of conflicts that moulded Scotland's history.

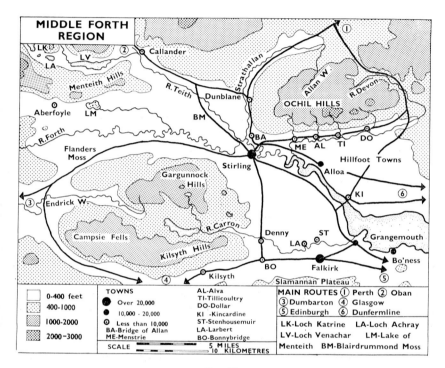

FIG. 56.

Agriculture

The higher areas with thin soils and adverse climatic conditions are devoted to sheep grazing. The lowlands, however, are intensively farmed, with generally fertile soils. The westerly position of the region gives fairly heavy rainfall (Stirling 38 in.). Together with the heavy soils, this makes arable farming often secondary to dairy farming. On the low, hilly ground in Clackmannan, heavy boulder clay soils support a high proportion of grass and fodder crops for dairy cattle.

The peat that covered most of the carse was largely removed during the eighteenth and nineteenth centuries, and a rich but tenacious soil was revealed. On these soils, specialized farming has developed, and the carse is an area of large, rectangular fields, broken only by isolated wooded

Slamannan Plateau

Stirling on the 'Tail'

Stirling Castle on the 'Crag'

Carse

Meander loop

Carse - land

To Alloa etc.

FIG. 57. Stirling, like Edinburgh, grew up on the "tail", protected by the castle on the "crag". The Forth meanders across the carse. (Photo: Valentine & Sons Ltd.)

crags and mosses. Root crops are difficult to grow, and the main crops are wheat, barley, timothy grass (for hay and seed) and beans (for fodder). While grass is extensively grown for hay or silage, it is seldom grazed. The region has celebrated dairy herds.

Farms vary in size from 80 to 250 acres, and while there is no general rotation, the sequence may be cereal, cereal, beans, fallow (for cleaning out couch grass), winter wheat undersown with timothy; the land may then be under grass for 7–20 years, depending on its continued productivity.

Once trysts at Stenhousemuir were the largest cattle fairs in Scotland, but Stirling (28,000) is the market centre for the region. Stirling is noted for trade in cattle, sheep, seeds, fertilizers, agricultural equipment, hides and skins. Among the numerous industries are some reflecting the agricultural hinterland: cooked meats, leather, and farm machinery; others include carpets, rubber goods, hosiery, cigarettes and printing.

Mining

Plentiful supplies of coal played a major role in the growth of industry in this region, and mining is still important. Coal measures extend into the region from Lanarkshire, and continue under the Forth into Clackmannanshire to join the West Fife field. Over half the output of 900,000 tons is from two collieries just east of Stirling, but a growing proportion is coming from Dollar and Solsgirth, two drift mines serving the Longannet power station.

Industrial Development

The Scottish Industrial Revolution was born in the Middle Forth region. Abundant coal, local clay-band iron ore and plentiful water led to the growth of the great **iron industry** at Carron near Falkirk. The flow of pig iron from the Carron furnaces began in 1760, and thus was set the pattern followed by many other Scottish towns. **Falkirk** (38,000) remains one of Britain's leading centres of the light castings industry; some 10,000 people are employed in metal manufacture in Falkirk, Larbert, Bonnybridge and

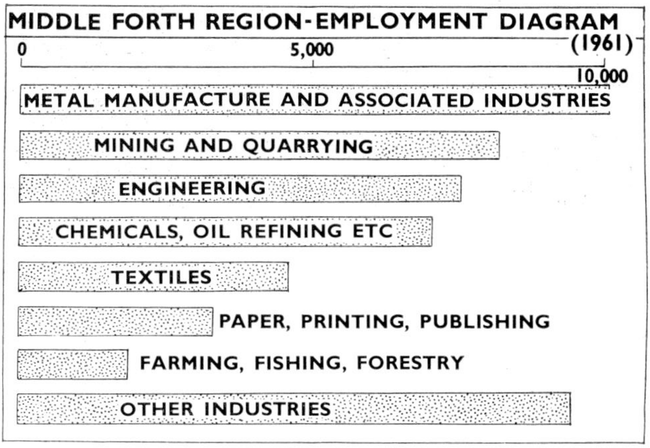

MIDDLE FORTH REGION-EMPLOYMENT DIAGRAM
(1961)

0   5,000   10,000

METAL MANUFACTURE AND ASSOCIATED INDUSTRIES
MINING AND QUARRYING
ENGINEERING
CHEMICALS, OIL REFINING ETC
TEXTILES
PAPER, PRINTING, PUBLISHING
FARMING, FISHING, FORESTRY
OTHER INDUSTRIES

FIG. 58.

Denny. The wide range of castings includes stoves, grates, boilers, baths, kiosks, police boxes, castings for ships and engineering industries. The working of brass and copper alloys and general engineering are also important. A more recent industry in Falkirk is the manufacture of aluminium sheeting: the 40-acre mills (one of the largest plants in Europe) use aluminium from the Highland refineries and from overseas, and produce sheets for many users including the aircraft and shipbuilding industries.

Other industries in Falkirk include coach building, chemicals, brewing and distilling.

Textile industries are widespread in the region with hosiery making at Falkirk and Kilsyth, and yarn spinning and carpet making at Bannockburn and Stirling. An old textile industry survives in the **"hill foot towns"**, where swift streams from the Ochils provided a source of power. The small towns of Menstrie, Tillicoultry and Alva are noted for high quality woolen goods including knitwear, blankets and tweeds. Tillicoultry also has a paper industry, though not on the same scale as at Denny and Kilsyth; in Denny several large mills use water from the river Carron.

Alloa (14,000) dwarfs the hill foot towns and, whilst it too has woollen industries, its growth has followed a different line. Originally a port aud milling centre, Alloa expanded with the local coal industry, and manufactures now include brewing, engineering, glass and printing.

As significant as the birth of the Falkirk iron industry was the rapid evolution of Grangemouth (19,000) as a port and industrial town.

The growth of **Grangemouth** was prompted by the construction of the Forth–Clyde Canal (1790), which once carried 3000 vessels a year but was

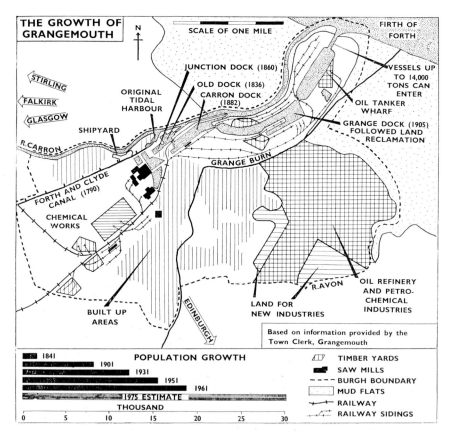

Fig. 59.

closed in 1963. Due to the foresight of Sir Lawrence Dundas, Grangemouth became a port of transhipment, controlling the flow of raw materials and manufactures to and from Falkirk and the Clyde. Built on tidal flats at the mouth of the Carron, the port expanded as railways developed and coal exports grew, and is now unrivalled as Scotland's second port. Its annual trade is almost 5 millon tons and is varied, but imports are dominated by timber from the Continent, the movement of oil for the local refinery, and iron ore and wood pulp. Exports are led by refined oil, iron and steel, coal and fireclay, but also include products from Scotland's newer industries such as cars, lorries and tractors, and a considerable container traffic. A major expansion scheme, which began in 1966, will enable the port to accommodate much larger vessels of all types, and ultimately tankers and bulk carriers up to 65,000 tons dead weight.

Early industries that remain are timber working, soap works and ship-building; the first practical steamship (the *Charlotte Dundas*) was built here in 1801—the engines, of course, were Carron-made.

On to this solid base have been superimposed the huge **petro-chemical industries.** After World War I, the manufacture of drugs and dyestuffs was established. In 1924 the suitability of the port led to the opening of an oil refinery, built to handle 350,000 tons of crude oil a year—this was still the capacity of the plant in 1938. The phenomenal growth of the industry since the last war is evident in the increase in the refining capacity, which was 1·75 million tons in 1950 and 4·5 million tons in 1964. In 1967 plans were announced to raise the capacity from $4\frac{1}{2}$ to 7 million tons; this target capacity has since been raised to 9 million tons. This will make Grangemouth not only one of the most broadly based refining complexes, but also one of the largest in Britain. As the port of Grangemouth is too small for large tankers, crude oil is piped from the Finnart Ocean Terminal (Fig. 59) where facilities for 200,000-ton tankers will shortly be available, and later modifications will enable super-tankers up to 500,000 tons to use the Terminal. Together with discharging facilities at Finnart, the capacity of the pipeline to Grangemouth is being raised to satisfy the refineries' growing demand.

Chemical industries at Grangemouth include the long-established dye-stuffs industry, but are dominated now by the concentration of petro-chemical industries, one of the largest in Europe. Using by-products from the refinery, a number of British and international firms produce in ever-increasing quantities a wide range of chemicals connected with the plastics, synthetic fibres, drug, dye, paint and detergent industries—in many aspects of this expanding field, Grangemouth leads the world. Such is the pace of development in Grangemouth that a synthetic rubber plant begun in 1963 was in production less than a year later; its initial output of 10,000 tons per annum has since increased five-fold.

FIG. 60. A Norwegian tanker discharging crude oil at the British Petroleum Company's ocean terminal, Finnart, Loch Long. From here the oil is piped to the Grangemouth refinery. (Photo: B.P. Co. Ltd.)

The Falkirk–Grangemouth area, equidistant between Edinburgh and Glasgow, at the hub of a great transport system and with the facilities of a growing international port, forms the heart of an expanding industrial region with ample room for the expansion of housing and industry. The stage seems set for continued development as is anticipated in the *Grangemouth/Falkirk Regional Survey and Plan*, published in 1968. This envisages an increase from the present population of 120,000 to 230,000 by 1985, brought about partly by improved overspill arrangements, and involving the expansion of Falkirk as the main centre of an enlarged regional city comprising Falkirk, Grangemouth, Denny, Larbert and Stenhousemuir. Further land is earmarked for the major heavy industrial growth around Grangemouth, and for lighter industries south of Bonnybridge. This expanded industrial and urban complex would have ready access by roads of motorway standard to three major ports, container services and airports, and could reach a population of 300,000 by the year 2000.

CHAPTER 9

The Middle and Lower Clyde Region

THE Central Clydeside conurbation houses over one-third of Scotland's people, over 1,800,000. If we add nearby towns, the total is over 2 million. These figures underline the paramount importance of the Glasgow region as one of Britain's (indeed, one of the world's) great manufacturing provinces. In Britain, only the London, the West Midlands and the South East Lancashire conurbations exceed Clydeside in population. The mainstay of this great population is a multitude of industries, founded upon local minerals, the development of strong trading links from the Clyde, and, above all, enterprise in exploiting these advantages, in overcoming difficulties and in adapting to frequent changes.

While certain industries, such as shipbuilding, engineering, iron and steel, and textiles are synonymous with Clydeside, there are few that do not have a place, and the range of manufactures is ever widening. Heavy industries are still dominant, but have undergone considerable concentration and modernization in recent years, and have been joined by a widening range of lighter industries often located in industrial estates and new towns. As the traditional industrial structure is changing, so population changes are also evident as the new towns grow and the overspill of population from Glasgow continues.

Physical Features

Below Lanark, the Clyde valley widens and is enclosed to the south-west by the lava Eaglesham Heights, separating the Ayrshire lowlands from the Clyde valley. This moorland rises to over 1200 ft. To the north-east of the Clyde, a low plateau, underlain by coal measures, forms the Forth–Clyde watershed. Downstream, the valley widens further and forms a lowland, 10 miles wide at the most, and floored by glacial and raised beach deposits. This is the nucleus of the region, and is linked by important valley routes to neighbouring areas: the Kelvin, the middle Clyde, the Barrhead gap and the Lochwinnoch gap. The Renfrew Heights rise to 1711 ft, and with the similar lava tableland of the Kilpatrick Hills north-east of the Clyde estuary they enclose the river in a narrow, steep-sided valley. This bottle-neck, beginning at Bowling, connects Glasgow with the sea.

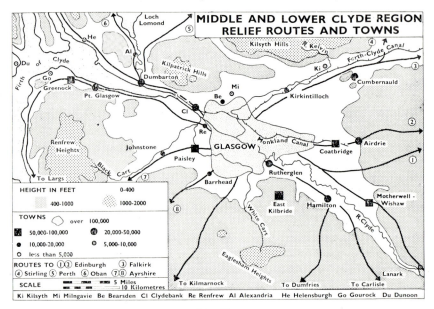

FIG. 61.

Climate and Farming

The westerly position of the region gives relatively mild winters on low ground—Paisley: 4° C (39·2° F) in January—and fairly warm summers, almost 15° C (59° F). But rainfall is heavier than in eastern areas (Paisley 44·2 in.). Comparatively heavy rainfall coupled with heavy, often ill-drained, soils mean that cash cropping is not important: oats, potatoes and turnips are the main crops, but grassland occupies the largest acreage. In the lowlands, dairying is dominant, meeting the great local demand: on a farm of 150 acres, forty milking cattle would furnish two-thirds of the income. On the higher, poorer land dairying is still foremost, though increased rough grazing makes cattle and sheep rearing more significant. Higher still, on the moorlands, only sheep grazing is possible.

In contrast to the hill sheep farms are the small, intensive horticultural units in the middle Clyde valley, from Lanark downstream to Uddingston. The alluvial valley floor and the fertile, well-drained valley sides are sheltered and comparatively frost free. This and the large urban population make possible the growth of a wide range of fruit and market garden crops. Straw-berries, raspberries, plums and tomatoes (a glasshouse crop) are the leading crops. Glasshouses also produce winter and spring flowers. Besides supplying the Clydeside and Scottish markets, exports go to northern England. Lanark (with knitwear, tanning and agricultural machinery industries) is the market centre; Carluke has jam and preserving industries.

Industrial Beginnings

The great industries of the Glasgow region date from the eighteenth and nineteenth centuries. Prior to this, Glasgow was a small fishing hamlet, the Clyde was virtually non-navigable, and pack-horses linked Glasgow to Irvine, its main port.

Trade and industry grew and flourished, particularly after free access was gained to colonies in America following the 1707 Union. Instead of trading

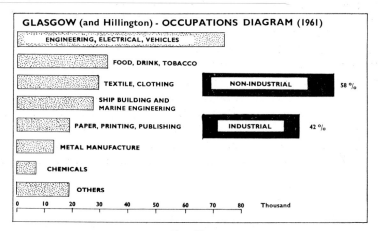

FIG. 62.

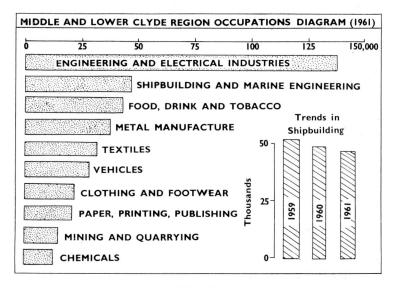

FIG. 63.

at a disadvantage with Europe, the Clyde was well positioned to exploit these new markets. The first development was the phenomenal growth of the **tobacco trade,** at its peak in the mid-eighteenth century, when over half of Britain's tobacco, as well as much rum, sugar and cotton, was imported to the Clyde. Greenock and Port Glasgow shared this trade.

A decline of the tobacco trade after the American revolt did not halt the growth of the region. Schemes to deepen and improve the Clyde for navigation, dating from the eighteenth century (and recalling such names as Golborne, Telford and Rennie), paralleled the booming trade. Continued alterations to the river have virtually made it a canal reaching up to Glasgow.

As the tobacco trade fell away, so the import of **cotton** took its place, the "cotton kings" replacing the "tobacco lords". The domestic linen and woollen industries, as well as providing exports, made available skilled labour for the growth of the cotton industry, which became paramount in the region. The use of local rivers for power and water supply (e.g. the Leven and the Cart) encouraged the industry, and the use of steam and power looms gradually ousted hand looms: here the coalfield played a vital part. Thread manufacture, fabric printing, dyeing and bleaching were firmly established in Renfrewshire and Dunbartonshire. By the mid-nineteenth century, the cotton industry employed three times as many people as mining and iron manufacture. However, brought to a standstill by the American Civil War, the industry never recovered its former greatness, though branches of the industry remain important.

Textiles Today

Paisley's great cotton thread industry grew out of early interest in silk thread and domestic weaving of Paisley shawls. Johnstone also produces thread, cotton fabric, lace and carpets. Barrhead, too, retains varied textile industries: thread, dyeing, making spools and bobbins; these augment its famous sanitary engineering industry. In Paisley, Johnstone and Barrhead, almost 12,000 people work in textile trades. Towns in the Vale of Leven still engage in calico printing, bleaching and dyeing on a reduced scale. All that remains of the flax industry is canvas and rope manufacture at Port Glasgow. The woollen industry is not important except for carpet making, for which Glasgow is a major centre: it is claimed that one-third of Britain's carpets are manufactured in the west of Scotland. In Glasgow, over 27,000 people work in clothing and specialized textile industries: shirtings, hoisery, knitwear and industrial clothing.

Coal Mining

The main part of the Central coalfield lies east of the Clyde, from Kilsyth and Kirkintilloch in the north to Motherwell in the south. The coalfield was linked to the sea when the Monkland Canal (1790) and the Forth–Clyde Canal were cut. As well as providing a valuable export, the growth of the coal industry, and the exploitation of the associated black-band iron ore, played a major role in the early growth of industry. Production grew rapidly in the nineteenth century and reached a peak in 1913, when over half of Scotland's 42½ million tons was produced in the Central field. But, with the exhaustion of reserves, the ageing of collieries and the contraction of markets, output has dropped dramatically: Lanarkshire pits produced less than 1·5 million tons in 1967–8, and over half of this came from two collieries (Cardowan and Bedlay) in northern Lanarkshire. These collieries produce good-quality coking coals essential to the nearby iron and steel industry.

The Iron and Steel Industry

Scotland's iron and steel industry is concentrated in the Glasgow region, and gives employment to almost 30,000 people. The early iron industry was naturally attracted to the coalfields where iron ore was also available, and as the demands of industry grew, the iron industry expanded rapidly during the nineteenth century. Many widely scattered areas shared in this growth, although the enterprises were often short-lived, and with the gradual closure of numerous sites in Ayrshire, a few in West Lothian and Fife and even one in East Lothian, the industry is now confined to Glasgow, Coatbridge and Motherwell. The perfection of the hot blast system by Nielson in 1828 enabled the plentiful, but low-quality, coal measure ironstones to be fully exploited—production of these reached 2·5 million tons in 1880, but dropped to 0·5 million tons by 1913 and has since stopped completely. This decline

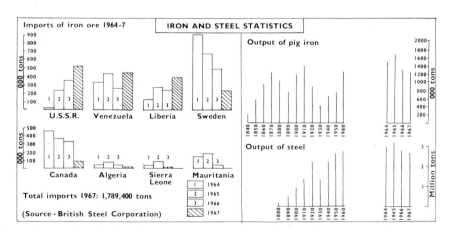

Fig. 64.

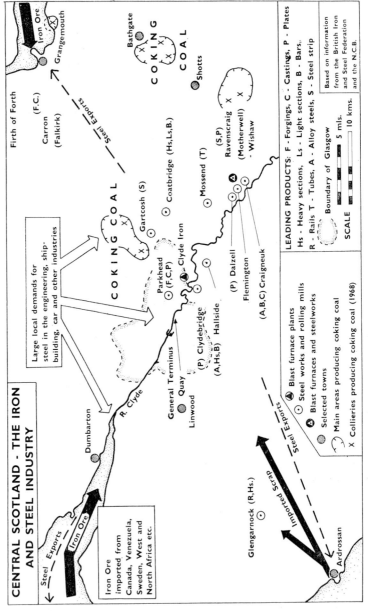

CENTRAL SCOTLAND - THE IRON
AND STEEL INDUSTRY

Iron Ore
imported from
Canada, Venezuela,
Sweden, West and
North Africa etc.

Large local demands for
steel in the engineering, shipbuilding, car and other industries

LEADING PRODUCTS: F - Forgings, C - Castings, P - Plates
Hs - Heavy sections, Ls - Light sections, B - Bars,,
R - Rails T - Tubes, A - Alloy steels, S - Steel strip

● Blast furnace plants
⊙ Steel works and rolling mills
◭ Blast furnaces and steelworks
⊙ Selected towns
⤸ Main areas producing coking coal
X Collieries producing coking coal (1968)

Boundary of Glasgow

SCALE

Based on information
from the British Iron
and Steel Federation
and the N.C.B.

FIG. 65.

has been matched by a growing dependence on foreign ores which, even by 1900, comprised 60 per cent of the total ore consumption; today, Scotland is the only steel-making district in Britain which is totally dependent on imported iron ores. Specialized port facilities in Glasgow allow the import of over 2 million tons of ore a year. Collieries in West Lothian and Lanarkshire still supply adequate quantities of coking coal to the blast furnaces at Ravenscraig and Tollcross, which produce between 1 and 1·5 million tons of pig iron a year.

The bulk of this iron is used in the steel industry which has grown remarkably this century in Mid-Lanarkshire and North Ayrshire. The major steel-making plants are at inland locations at **Motherwell, Rutherglen** and **Glasgow.** Traditionally, products of the industry are closely related to the needs of the shipbuilding and heavy engineering industries, which require heavy plates, rails, forgings, tubes and pipes, but the production of alloy steels, and, more significantly, thin sheet steel is of growing importance. Steel production now runs at between 2·5 and 3 million tons a year.

The greatest changes in recent years have taken place in the Motherwell district, which is now more clearly than ever the focus of the Scottish iron and steel industry. The new **Ravenscraig** hot strip mill with its related cold strip mill at Gartcosh (near Coatbridge) is designed to produce 1·5 million tons of steel strip a year, made possible by the construction of new blast furnaces and additional steel-making capacity; the amount of thin sheet steel produced in Scotland in 1967 was six times greater than in 1962. Hailed as the greatest single step forward by the Scottish economy, the Ravenscraig plant not only lessens the dependence of Scotland on heavy industries by providing a supply of sheet steel for new industries (such as cars and domestic appliances), but also contributes notably to exports. Much of the sheet steel is used at the car body factory at Linwood, near Paisley. The iron and steel industry also supplies exports of plates, tubes and pipes, rails and castings.

The complete dependence on foreign ore, economies in the quantity of coke consumed and the possibility of using cheap American coke may suggest that a coastal location for the new integrated iron and steel plant might have been better than the Ravenscraig site. On the other hand, Ravenscraig is in a long-established steel-making district and has easier access to the expanding markets in Lanarkshire and eastern Scotland. However, any further large expansion of steel capacity may necessitate a new location further down the Clyde (Ardmore and Hunterston have both been suggested); this would also require a new deep-water ore-handling terminal. Indeed, with the trend towards larger and larger bulk carriers, a new ore terminal may become essential as an alternative to General Terminus Quay in Glasgow.

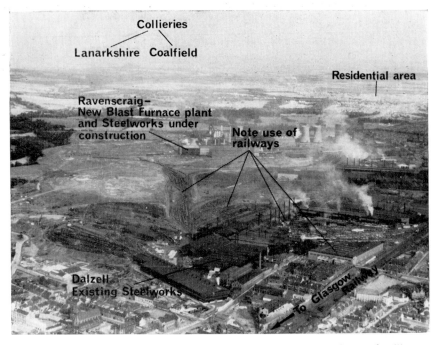

FIG. 66. The development of the new integrated iron and steel plant and rolling mills at Ravenscraig was of great significance. The bulk of Scotland's iron and steel industry is now located on this and adjacent sites. (Photo: Colville's Ltd.)

Engineering Industries

The Scottish engineering industry is concentrated in the Glasgow region, and while almost every branch of the industry has a place on Clydeside, from the very heavy to the very light products, some branches are particularly associated with the district. The early development of the iron industry and the growth of the textile industries provided the raw materials and the initial spur for engineering development; over the years the region has accumulated varied engineering skills to satisfy the diverse needs of the industry. Glasgow is thus at the heart of a great engineering province.

The coalfield towns have exploited their easy access to coal and steel. **Motherwell–Wishaw** concentrates on heavy engineering, particularly bridges, cranes, boilers and power station equipment and numerous others, ranging from railway rolling stock to nails and pins. **Coatbridge,** important for the manufacture of steel tubes, heavy castings and wire rope, is distinct from **Airdrie** where, besides steel tube production, lighter industries embrace the making of nuts and bolts and electrical equipment. To the north, Kirkintilloch houses castings industries together with engineering concerns producing cranes, colliery equipment and switchgear.

Glasgow itself has almost countless engineering industries, by no means concerned only with marine engineering: some notable specializations include boiler making and structural engineering, locomotives, cranes and commerical vehicles; the manufacture of heavy plant for the steel industry is also notable, as is the production of refrigerating equipment; another specialization is the manufacture of sugar-making machinery. With the establishment of industrial estates, the already enormous range of products has been greatly extended; over 80,000 of the city's workers are engaged in engineering, and this underlines its importance.

Towns to the west of Glasgow are also closely concerned with engineering. To its textile and foodstuffs industries, Paisley has added the manufacture of textile, mining and sugar-refining machinery; at Renfrew there is a major concentration on boiler making.

Although shipbuilding and marine engineering have for long been the main interests in **Clydeside towns,** general engineering is not neglected: complementary to Paisley's thread industry is the making of sewing machines at Clydebank, while Greenock and Dumbarton both have a wide range of heavy and light engineering industries.

Shipbuilding and Marine Engineering

The oldest shipbuilding yard in the world is on Clydeside, dating back over 250 years; indeed, vessels were built on the river Leven in Robert the

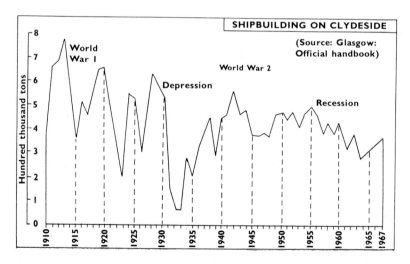

Fig. 67.

Bruce's time. However, the shipbuilding industry, with its ancillaries, has reached mammoth proportions only in relatively recent times. Along the Clyde estuary are located shipyards producing over 25 per cent of Britain's ships and 90 per cent of Scotland's. Despite reduced production and the employment of fewer people, the industry is still a leading employer on Clydeside. The 365,000 tons launched in 1967 contrasts with 750,000 in 1913.

MERCHANT SHIPPING COMPLETED IN U.K. YARDS—1967

District	Ships	Tons gross
Clyde	28	364,609
East of Scotland	13	37,582
Tyne (including Blyth)	23	202,812
Sunderland	17	339,186
Tees	8	132,368
Belfast	7	74,615
Mersey	2	7,812
Other districts	101	33,130
	199	1,192,114

The **growth of shipbuilding** was encouraged by the demand for vessels to trade with the New World, and the industry progressed rapidly as the river was improved and advances were made in the iron and steel industry. Wooden ships were gradually replaced by iron ones, and the launching in 1812 (at Port Glasgow) of Bell's *Comet*, the first ship with a steam engine, opened a new era. The industry grew quickly in those early days at Greenock, Port Glasgow and Dumbarton where, in 1879, William Denny launched the first steel ocean-going vessel.

These and other engineering achievements, such as the development of the steam turbine in 1901, gave the industry, which by now had extended upstream into the heart of Glasgow, great momentum and a world-wide reputation. "Clyde-built" is still a guarantee of the highest standards in shipbuilding and marine engineering.

The ever-increasing size of ships, particularly bulk carriers and tankers, and the decline in the total demand for ships have combined with much stronger foreign competition to effect major changes in the Clydeside ship-building industry. A number of yards in Glasgow, Dumbarton and Paisley have been closed, and the surviving larger ones have been modernized and regrouped so that the industry is now largely controlled by **two major combines:** Upper Clyde Shipbuilders, with yards at Clydebank, Scotstoun and Govan, and the Scott–Lithgow Group on the Lower Clyde with yards at Greenock, Port Glasgow and Bowling. Shipyards are thus strung out along the estuary from Greenock to the heart of Glasgow. This rationalization, together with further improvements to the estuary, should enable the Clyde to participate fully in the production of the huge tankers and carriers now envisaged.

It should be noted at this point that the shipbuilding industry of **East Scotland,** with small yards at Grangemouth, Leith, Dundee and Aberdeen, is concerned usually with the production of highly specialized vessels, and as with the Clyde there are signs of modernization and concentration.

Clyde yards produce a wide range of ships—passenger liners, tankers, ore carriers, refrigerated vessels, bulk carriers and naval craft—the construction of passenger liners is now much less important than that of specialized carriers. Perhaps the Clydebank yard of Upper Clyde Shipbuilders Ltd. (formerly John Brown's yard) is the best known as the home of the "Queens", including the recently completed *Queen Elizabeth II.*

The growth of shipbuilding was accompanied by the evolution of **marine engineering** industries in Glasgow and the Clydeside towns—boilers, diesel engines, turbines, pumps, cranes, etc., are supplied not only to Clyde-built ships, but also to many overseas areas. Many firms originally founded to equip ships have expanded their markets so that boilers, pumps, fans and other engine room auxiliaries are put to many uses quite unrelated to shipbuilding.

It is logical, too, that ships built on the Clyde, as well as many others, come to specially equipped basins for repair, overhaul and refitting. The ship-repairing capabilities of the Clyde were enhanced by the completion in 1964 of the new graving dock at Greenock—this caters particularly for large, modern tankers.

Import Industries

We have seen how the exploitation of local resources, the growth of trade and the river improvements triggered off industrial expansion. Of many industries depending upon imported materials, the iron and steel industry (using iron ore, chrome and manganese ores and scrap) and the textile industries (cotton) are amongst the most obvious. Imported wheat, maize, barley and other grains support large flour milling, animal feeding stuffs and baking concerns, particularly in the dock area of Glasgow. Similarly, Glasgow's large rubber tyre production relies on imported raw materials. Together with Rutherglen, Airdrie and Paisley, Glasgow uses imported wood pulp and esparto grass in its paper mills; the chemical industries, born to supply the cotton industry, include the making of acids, ammonia, fertilizers, paints, soap and detergents, and also draw their raw materials through the port. Tobacco industries at Glasgow and sugar refining at

Greenock rely upon imports from America and further emphasize the vital importance of Glasgow's trade.

Glasgow

With 960,000 inhabitants (1968 estimate), Glasgow is the heart of a great industrial conurbation; it is also a centre of commerce and ranks as a world port, and is the focus for many roads and railways.

The village that became Glasgow was situated at a ford 20 miles from the mouth of the Clyde, and it became a bridging point. The small township on the hill north of the ford became an ecclesiastical centre when the cathedral was dedicated in 1136, but when the university was founded in 1450 the population did not exceed 2000. Rutherglen, Renfrew and Dumbarton were relatively more important. Glasgow developed slowly during the sixteenth and seventeenth centuries, the local merchants using Irvine as a port. Development was retarded by the shallowness of the Clyde and the exports of coal, herring and coarse cloth were small. The building of the Broomielaw Pier (1662) and the opening of Port Glasgow (1668) heralded significant changes, in enabling Glasgow merchants to compete with Greenock in trade with America. This trade boomed after the 1707 Union.

So ended the first phase in Glasgow's growth. Thereafter, events moved rapidly, access to the English colonies initiating the tobacco trade, following attempts to improve the channel to Glasgow. Street names such as Jamaica Street and Virginia Street recall the tobacco era. Coal, linen, soap, shoes and saddles provided a return flow of traffic to the New World. Population grew rapidly, to exceed 23,000 by 1750.

After 1775 the tobacco trade declined and was replaced by cotton. Continued river improvements enhanced Glasgow's trading ability and the cotton industry assumed giant proportions: by 1800, 180,000 were employed in the Scottish cotton industry and by 1830, Glasgow's population reached 250,000. The coal and iron industries and shipbuilding and engineering were firmly established and were revolutionized by the invention of the steam engine. The phenomenal increases in the city's population were provided largely by an influx of people from depressed areas, such as the Highlands and Ireland.

Even the disastrous blow suffered by the cotton industry following the American Civil War could not halt the momentum of Glasgow's growth: heavy metal industries and shipbuilding, with a healthy basis on local coal and iron, furthered the process: by 1890, the population numbered 850,000, and Glasgow, at the height of its prosperity, was the sixth largest city in Europe.

Matching the growth of the population, the area of the city increased

Fig. 68. Clydebank's main industry is shipbuilding. John Brown's, birthplace of the "Queens", was perhaps Britain's most famous yard. (Photo: John Brown (Clydebank) & Co. Ltd.)

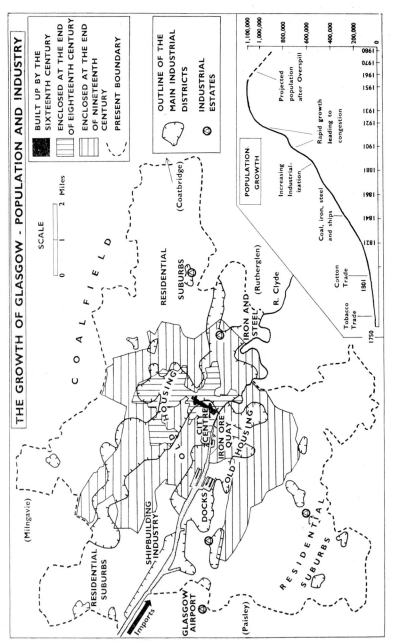

THE GROWTH OF GLASGOW - POPULATION AND INDUSTRY

BUILT UP BY THE SIXTEENTH CENTURY

ENCLOSED AT THE END OF EIGHTEENTH CENTURY

ENCLOSED AT THE END OF NINETEENTH CENTURY

PRESENT BOUNDARY

OUTLINE OF THE MAIN INDUSTRIAL DISTRICTS

INDUSTRIAL ESTATES

SCALE

0   1   2 Miles

(Milngavie)

C O A L F I E L D

RESIDENTIAL SUBURBS

(Coatbridge)

RESIDENTIAL SUBURBS

SHIPBUILDING INDUSTRY

OLD HOUSING

CITY CENTRE

IRON ORE QUAY

OLD HOUSING

DOCKS

Imports

GLASGOW AIRPORT

(Paisley)

IRON AND STEEL

(Rutherglen)

R. Clyde

RESIDENTIAL SUBURBS

POPULATION GROWTH

Tobacco Trade

Cotton Trade

Coal, iron, steel and ships

Increasing Industrialization

Rapid growth leading to congestion

Projected population after Overspill

1,100,000
1,000,000
800,000
600,000
400,000
200,000
0

1750   1801   1821   1841   1861   1881   1901   1921   1931   1951   1961   1971   1981

POPULATION

Fig. 69.

but not rapidly enough to prevent overcrowding and slum conditions, a sore that the contemporary city is gradually eradicating. Twenty-nine major areas in Central Glasgow are earmarked for clearance and redevelopment—many of these are mixed industrial and residential districts. These Central Redevelopment Areas cover over five square miles of the city, and work has already begun in eight of them.

In the twentieth century, Glasgow's rate of growth has dropped, and it still depends primarily upon heavy metal industries, shipbuilding, engineering, clothing, chemical and food and drink industries. The centre of the city is an area of industrial, commercial and administrative functions; around this nucleus, residential and industrial areas link Glasgow to neighbouring towns, thus forming the Central Clydeside Conurbation, which extends from Clydebank to Motherwell and from Paisley to Airdrie. Crossing this urban sprawl is the river Clyde.

The Port of Glasgow

The Clyde has become the major outlet for Scotland's manufactures and the mouth into which imported raw materials and foodstuffs pour. Recognition of the importance of the Clyde as a port and of the need for continued integrated development of its potential, was seen in the formation in 1966 of the Clyde Port Authority which controls all the Clyde ports and seaways down river to beyond the Cumbraes. It is a far cry from the days when Glasgow languished at a ford to the present position, when after continuous improvements to the navigable channel for over 200 years, Glasgow has eclipsed all rivals to become Scotland's leading port handling over 60 per cent of her foreign trade.

The most serious obstacle encountered in the creation of the port was the Elderslie rock bar; when this was removed by blasting (1869 and 1886), there was a continuous deep channel to Glasgow, a channel that has to be continually dredged. Since then, development has continued with the opening of new docks and dry docks, and the expansion of specialized cargo and storage facilities.

Further plans to improve the Clyde must take into account the ever-increasing size of ships, and must involve major developments downstream: one suggestion involves building a barrage (with locks) across the estuary from Greenock to Ardrinan Point, so transforming the estuary into a lake of constant depth. More recent plans involve the massive reclamation of land on the north bank from Dumbarton to Ardmore Point, and on the south bank from Erskine to Port Glasgow with a continuous deep-water channel between. This would provide not only an additional 5640 acres for industrial development, but also adequate deep-water facilities in the lower reaches for the largest tankers and bulk carriers so far envisaged. This plan implies nothing less than a Scottish Europort, with oil refining, petro-chemical and iron and steel industries. Already a large oil refining and petro-chemical development is promised for 1971 at Erskine, and proposals have been made for further oil refining capacity and an oil jetty at Bishopton and Wemyss Bay respectively. An oil-fired power station is also projected at Inverkip.

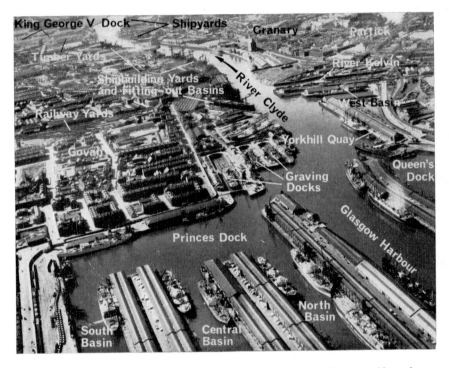

Fig. 70. Glasgow is Scotland's leading industrial and commercial centre. Along the banks of the Clyde trading and industrial activities are concentrated. (Photo: Aerofilms.)

These suggestions are an indication of the trend for growing development downstream. A concrete achievement is the new container terminal at Greenock.

These developments and plans underline the growing importance of Clydeport, and include the provision of modern facilities to service the expanding and changing industries of **Glasgow's hinterland,** which includes the whole of Scotland and part of northern England.

TRADE OF CLYDEPORT—1967

Imports	'000 Tons	Exports	'000 Tons
Petroleum and petroleum products	6045	Petroleum and petroleum products	570
Food, beverages, tobacco		Manufactured goods	
Cereals	639	Iron and steel	286
Sugar	315	Machinery and metal goods	111
Fruit and vegetables	100	Vehicles	46
Animal feeding stuffs	67	Chemicals and fertilizers	54
Live animals and meat	76	Textiles	23
Tobacco	20	Others (paper, board, etc.)	93
Others	66		
Raw materials		Raw materials and fuel (excluding	
Ores and scrap	1901	petroleum)	
Fertilizers and minerals	426	Coal, coke, briquettes	32
Timber and pulp	78	Other raw materials (scrap, etc.)	20
Others—including rubber,			
oilseed, fibres, etc.	98		
Manufactured goods		Food, beverages, tobacco	
Wood products, paper,		Beverages (mainly whisky)	163
chemicals, machinery, etc.	201	Others (sugar, cereals, etc.)	76
TOTAL IMPORTS	10,032	TOTAL EXPORTS	1474
Of which foreign	7,968	Of which foreign	949
Of which coastwise	2,064	Of which coastwise	525
IMPORTS 1966	10,178	EXPORTS 1966	1413

(SOURCE: Clyde Port Authority, *Report and Accounts 1967.*)

A Changing Scene

It has already been noted how the economy of Clydeside has frequently adapted to altering circumstances. Recently the numbers employed in traditional industries, such as shipbuilding and mining, have dropped. To take up the slack created by this contraction, many new industries of a lighter and more modern character have been introduced on **industrial estates.** Many of these industries have become very large, and though the origins of the industrial estates go back to the pre-war period and sprang from the unemployment of the 1930s, the most spectacular developments are more recent and continuing. The activities of the Industrial Estates Management Corporation cover the whole of Scotland and give employment to over 100,000 people, but most of their estates are in the Glasgow region, where they employ over 70,000.

FIG. 71. Hillington Industrial Estate is the largest in Scotland, and the oldest (1937). Situated 4 miles from the centre of Glasgow, the estate is well served by road, rail and air communications, and is within easy reach of the Clydeside dock facilities. (Photo Aero-Pictorial Ltd.)

The largest estate (at Hillington) has more than 120 factories producing a wide range of manufactures, including aircraft engines, domestic appliances, refrigeration equipment, shavers, machine tools, hosiery, etc. Such variety is typical of most estates but certain industries have become major employers: aero engines (East Kilbride, Blantyre, Larkhall and Hillington—this industry employs 14,000), electronic and instrument industries (Newhouse, Hamilton, Vale of Leven, East Kilbride, etc.), earth moving equipment (Newhouse), typewriters (Queenslie), accounting machines, clocks and watches (Vale of Leven).

In addition to estates, many individual factories have been built, including such industries as clocks at Wishaw and, of course, the Linwood factories of Rootes, producing vehicles and vehicle bodies. The range of industries on these estates has widened and secured the industrial structure of the Lower

Clyde area, and has brought a large share of the new growth industries to the region.

INDUSTRIAL ESTATES IN SCOTLAND

	Glasgow area	Ayr-shire	Middle Forth	Loth-ians	Fife	Dundee area	High-lands and islands	South-ern Up-lands
Estates at March 1968	19	3	1	0	3	3	3	3
Number of factories on estates	275	4	—	0	5	16	4	1
Number of indi-vidual sites	33	3	0	5	2	1	5	1
Total factories	308	7	0	5	7	17	9	2
Estates since 1962	4	1	1	0	2	1	2	3
Advance factories since 1962	24	7	3	3	9	2	8	9

(*Note:* This does not include industrial estates established by Local Authorities or New Town Development Corporations. SOURCE: Industrial Estates Management Corporation.)

Population and Overspill

The industrial revolution created the great concentration of industry and population in the Glasgow region. Over 2 million people live in an area of about 150 square miles, contained in a great urban mass radiating from the compact built-up area focused on Glasgow. It extends down the Clyde valley to Renfrew, Clydebank and Dumbarton; north to Bearsden and Milngavie; east to Coatbridge and Airdrie; south to Rutherglen; and west to Paisley, Johnstone and Barrhead. Within these limits the land is almost continuously built up.

To the south-east is a less continuous sprawl of industrial and residential areas, dominated by Motherwell–Wishaw and Hamilton. At the mouth of the Clyde estuary, Greenock and Port Glasgow lie slightly apart from the conurbation, as do Kirkintilloch and Kilsyth to the north-east.

In contrast to the industrial towns, the holiday resorts on the shores of the Firth of Clyde exploit splendid scenery, sheltered waters and proximity to a vast population: Helensburgh, Dunoon and Gourock are foremost.

T.F.S.—E

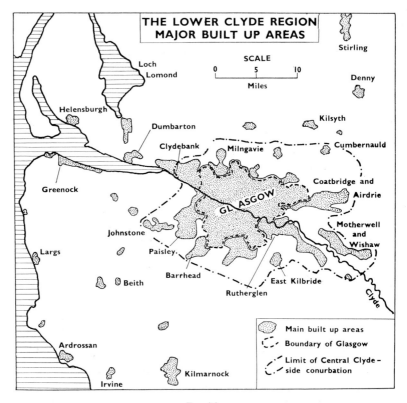

Fig. 72.

The years of unprecedented and largely unplanned growth have left Glasgow with a problem—the clearing of the old, overcrowded and unhealthy housing of the central areas. In the drive to erase slum conditions, the city has expanded in all directions, and since 1919 over 110,000 corporation houses have been built. With the city hemmed in by hills, neighbouring burghs, undermined areas and good farm land, lateral expansion is no longer the answer. The older central districts of the city are, as we have seen, being redeveloped, but in their modern form will house only 40 per cent of the original population. The remainder, at least 200,000, form the **overspill** being housed outside the city in new towns and many reception areas as far apart as Wick and Duns, and Arbroath and Stranraer. In all, by 1968, sixty-seven authorities had signed overspill agreements with Glasgow, and almost forty of these are already providing accommodation for Glasgow families; approximately half the families are being taken by the new towns. The progress of the overspill programme has gathered pace, and by late

FIG. 73.

1968, 17,440 families had been rehoused and many others were awaiting housing.

Spread over the period 1960/80, the overspill scheme is effecting many changes—the population of Glasgow will drop to approximately 850,000 and the central part of the city is being transformed; in 1968 the city's population was estimated at 960,527, a decline of 95,000 since 1961 and of over 120,000 since 1951. As a result of overspill, then, a significant redistribution of population is taking place, and is accompanied by the growth of new industries in the reception areas.

According to the 1966 Sample Census several other older industrial areas within the conurbation show a decline in population; compensating for this is a pronounced increase in the population of the less-congested peripheral areas of the conurbation.

GLASGOW OVERSPILL—DISTRIBUTION
(families rehoused by November 1968)

Total	Cumbernauld	East Kilbride	Glenrothes	Livingston	Other areas
17,440	4493	3188	330	153	9276

Contrary to the expansive picture created by the wide distribution of overspill centres, it must be observed that the greater proportion of overspill from Glasgow is being rehoused either within the conurbation or very close to it; further large overspill housing developments are suggested for Erskine (Renfrewshire) and Lennoxtown (Stirlingshire), and it is expected that Lanarkshire's large share of overspill will necessitate either the expansion of existing towns or a further new town between Larkhall and Stonehouse.

FIG. 74. Hutchesontown-Gorbals was one of the first of the central areas of Glasgow to be redeveloped. Some old housing is still visible on the photograph. Beyond the Clyde lies the city centre. (Photo: by courtesy of the Glasgow Corporation.)

The industrial towns which join with Glasgow to make the conurbation also have problems resulting from the rapid unplanned growth that took place during the Industrial Revolution, and comprehensive urban renewal programmes are solving these difficulties. For example, in Motherwell–Wishaw since 1962 when one in every three houses was classed as sub-standard, approximately a quarter of the burgh's houses have been removed and new developments completed, so that the ratio of sub-standard dwellings is now one in ten.

As one would expect, the greatest gains in population are being made by the **new towns,** of which three are developing near Glasgow. **East Kilbride,** between Glasgow and Hamilton, was designated in 1947 and is the fastest growth point in Scotland, attracting 5000 new inhabitants each year; its population exceeded 57,000 in 1968. The outstanding success of East Kilbride is to be measured not only in terms of population growth, but also in the establishment of a wide range of employment potential—over 140 new factories have been established, and these, together with the service industries, provide employment for over 22,000 people.

GROWTH OF EMPLOYMENT IN EAST KKILBRIDE

	1950	1955	1960	1965	1968
Number employed	2500	6250	9500	14,800	22,000

High-value, science-based industries dominate the scene, the largest being the manufacture of aero engines, electrical appliances, machine tools, electronics equipment and fork-lift trucks. Large research establishments have also been created.

These and other industries are located on four industrial estates on the edge of the town, which is developing five residential neighbourhoods grouped around a new town centre, grafted onto an older village.

Cumbernauld, to the north-east of Glasgow, was not designated a new town until 1956, but already its population, growing annually at the rate of 3500, has reached 25,000 (1968), and fifty new factories give employment to over 5000 people. The largest single industry is the manufacture of office machinery, but to this one could add a long list of industries including clothing, carpets, castings and a wide range of engineering.

The neighbourhood system of planning adopted in the earlier new towns, has been abandoned in Cumbernauld in favour of an integrated town located on a ridge and in which housing is grouped closely around the central area, with industry located on low-lying ground on the margins of the town.

Population and industry: summary (1961 Census)

Town	Population	Industries and functions
Glasgow	1,055,000	Industrial, commercial and communications centre—iron and steel, ships, engineering, textiles, chemicals, foodstuffs, etc. Major port
Paisley	96,000	Thread, engineering, foodstuffs
Greenock	75,000	Ships, engineering, sugar refining. Port
Motherwell and Wishaw	73,000	Iron and steel, heavy engineering of many types
Coatbridge	54,000	Iron and steel, tubes, heavy engineering
Clydebank	50,000	Ships, engineering, sewing machines
Hamilton	42,000	Metal products, electrical applicances, carpets
Airdrie	34,000	Steel tubes, nuts and bolts, electrical equipment, drugs, foodstuffs
Dumbarton	26,000	Varied engineering
Rutherglen	25,000	Chemicals, steel tubes, wire, varied engineering, paper
Port Glasgow	23,000	Ships, engineering, rope and canvas
Johnstone	18,000	Thread, lace, carpets, machine tools, general engineering
Kirkintilloch	18,000	Iron castings, engineering, electrical gear, hosiery
Renfrew	17,946	Ships, boilers, cables, varied industries on Hillington Estate
Population of the Central Clydeside Conurbation		1,801,850 (34·8% of total)
Population of Lanarkshire, Dunbartonshire and Renfrewshire		2,149,678 (41·3% of total)
Population of Scotland		5,178,490 (1961)

A feature of the town is the total separation of pedestrian and vehicular routes. The unique characteristic of Cumbernauld is the multi-level town centre being built to satisfy the shopping, commercial, cultural, civic and educational needs of the community, and which acts as a symbolic as well as a functional focus. The originality and successful implementation of the Cumbernauld plan has already won for the town an international Award for Community Architecture (the R. S. Reynolds Memorial Award, 1967).

East Kilbride and Cumbernauld are therefore playing a major role not only in the industrial life of the region, but also in the creation of new urban environments in marked contrast to the congested, sub-standard areas being replaced in the heart of Glasgow. The new town of **Irvine** (1966), although in Ayrshire, is also expected to be closely involved with Glasgow overspill.

With discussion of new towns and shifting population, of industrial estates and the contraction and streamlining of traditional industries, and of urban renewal and port growth, "change" is evidently a major contemporary element in the economic and social geography of the Lower Clyde region, and the effects of these changes are being felt far beyond the limits of this region.

CHAPTER 10

Ayrshire

AYRSHIRE owes its separate identity to the development of highly specialized agriculture and industries and important tourist attractions, although there are marked similarities to the Glasgow area in the sequence of industrial development.

Pre-eminent in milk production and the production of early potatoes, Ayrshire has developed during the last two centuries a variety of industries. First to develop were the textile industries, originally on a domestic basis but later, following the development of the coalfield, as a factory industry, and many specialized branches exist today.

The development of the coalfield stimulated not only the textile industry and a rapid growth of population, but also the iron industry using the widespread coal measure ironstones: at one time there were forty-eight blast furnaces in the county, and the iron smelting industry in turn encouraged engineering and shipbuilding. However, as in the case of the Lower Clyde region, the decline of coal and iron has provoked change, and has been accompanied by the growth of new industries.

Despite certain parallels between Ayrshire and the Glasgow region, however, distinctive agricultural practices and specialized industries combined with physical factors to give Ayrshire a separate identity.

Physical Features

A wide area of hills and moors encloses an amphitheatre of lowlands drained towards the Firth of Clyde by the rivers Garnock, Irvine, Ayr and Doon. Where the encircling hills reach the sea, north of Saltcoats and south of Heads of Ayr, a narrow coastal strip is terminated abruptly inland by steep hills. This narrow lowland forms an easy routeway and affords sites for holiday towns such as Largs. Between Saltcoats and Ayr the low, sandy coast is backed by wide raised beaches to a depth of 2–3 miles, extending up the Irvine valley to Kilmarnock. Inland stretch the undulating lowlands of Kyle, dissected by numerous streams and occasionally exceeding 500 ft.

The lowlands give way to rising ground, culminating in the fringe of hills. The rounded Renfrew Heights (over 1700 ft) extend into Ayrshire to become the Cunningham Hills, overlooking the coastal strip and stretching

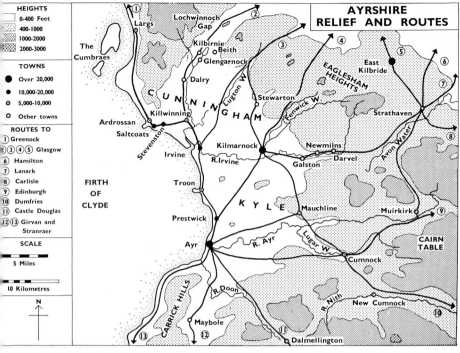

Fig. 75.

south-east as wide moorlands 1230 ft high in Corse Hill. These uplands form the watershed between the Clyde drainage and that of the Ayrshire basin, and are breached by important routes: the Lochwinnoch and Barrhead gaps have been mentioned, but notice too the Irvine–Avon valley linking Kilmarnock to Hamilton.

South of this gap, the hills are higher (almost 2000 ft in Cairntable) and merge with the still higher Southern Uplands. They swing west and reach the coast south of Ayr in the Carrick Hills. These southern hills are also broken by valleys important for communications: routes follow the Lugar valley, while the valley from Cumnock leads to the Nith valley, Sanquhar and Dumfries, and the Doon valley takes the route from Ayr to the Dee valley.

Climate

Sheltered by hills to the north and east, Ayrshire is open to the warming sea influences, and the rain-bearing winds. At low levels, winters are mild: Turnberry 5° C (41° F) in January, and the summers fairly warm; Kilmarnock 15° C (59° F) in July. Frosts after February are rare in coastal areas, where spring comes early and the growing season exceeds 240 days.

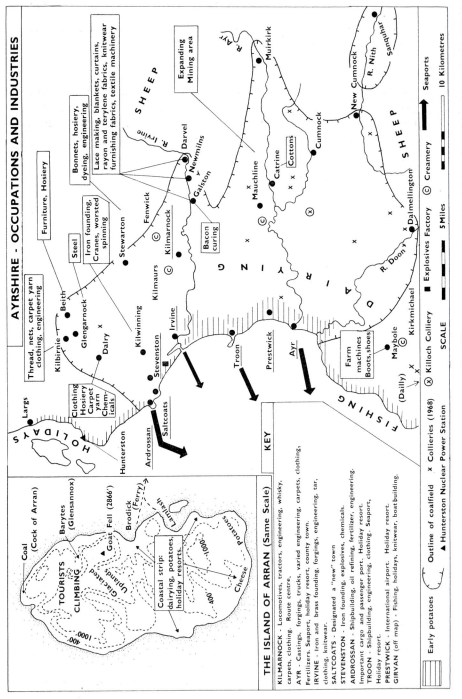

AYRSHIRE - OCCUPATIONS AND INDUSTRIES

Thread, nets, carpet yarn clothing, engineering

Furniture, Hosiery

Steel

Iron founding, Cranes, worsted spinning

Bonnets, hosiery, dyeing, engineering

Lace making, blankets, curtains, rayon and terylene fabrics, knitwear furnishing fabrics, textile machinery

Expanding Mining area

Bacon curing

Cottons

Clothing Hosiery Carpet yarn Chemicals

Farm machines Boots,shoes

S H E E P

S H E E P

A I R Y I N G

F I S H I N G

H O L I D A Y S

Largs

Hunterston

Ardrossan

Saltcoats

Stevenson

Kilbirnie

Glengarnock

Beith

Dalry ×

Kilwinning

Irvine

Troon

Prestwick

Ayr

(Dailly)

Maybole ©

Kirkmichael

Dalmellington ©

Kilmaurs ©

Kilmarnock ©

Fenwick

Stewarton

Galston

Newmilns

Darvel

Mauchline ×

Catrine × ×

Cumnock

New Cumnock

Muirkirk

R. Irvine

R. Ayr

R. Nith

Sanquhar

R. Doon ×

R. Nith

×

© ×

×

×

×

×

×

×

×

×

THE ISLAND OF ARRAN (Same Scale)

Coal
(Cock of Arran)

Barytes
(Glensannox)

Goat Fell (2866')

Brodick
(Ferry)

Lamlash

TOURISTS
CLIMBING

Glaciated
Uplands

Coastal strip: dairying, potatoes, holiday resorts.

Cheese

Potatoes

400

1000

1000

400

1000

KEY

KILMARNOCK - Locomotives, tractors, engineering, whisky, carpets, clothing. Route centre,

AYR - Castings, forgings, trucks, varied engineering, carpets, clothing, Fertilizers. Seaport, holiday resort, county town.

IRVINE - Iron and brass founding, forgings, engineering, tar, clothing, knitwear.

SALTCOATS - Designated a "new" town

STEVENSTON - Iron founding, explosives, chemicals.

ARDROSSAN - Shipbuilding, oil refining, fertilizer, engineering. Important cargo and passenger port. Holiday resort.

TROON - Shipbuilding, engineering, clothing. Seaport, Holiday resort.

PRESTWICK - International airport. Holiday resort.

GIRVAN (off map) - Fishing, holidays, knitwear, boatbuilding.

Early potatoes	Outline of coalfield	× Collieries (1968)	⊗ Killoch Colliery

× Outline of coalfield
▲ Hunterston Nuclear Power Station

■ Explosives Factory   © Creamery
▬ Seaports

SCALE

5 Miles

10 Kilometres

Rainfall is heavy and has a winter maximum—Largs has an annual average of 48·8 in. while totals on the hills exceed 60 in.

Agriculture

Ayrshire is renowned for high-quality dairy products and early potatoes. In South Ayrshire, particularly, farming is the basic industry and at the busiest seasons some 6000 people are engaged in agriculture. The damp climate does not favour intensive arable farming, and little wheat or barley

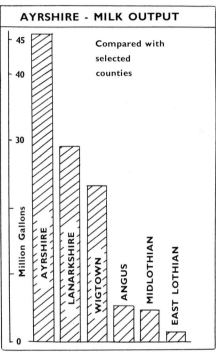

Fig. 77.

and virtually no sugar-beet are grown. Oats and fodder crops are most important, but even their acreages are dwarfed by that of grass. Grassland (for mowing and grazing) occupies over two-thirds of the good land.

Ayrshire is famed for its dairy cattle, and has led the world in many aspects of the dairy industry, notably in pioneering the attestation of cattle. Not unnaturally, dairying is the main interest of the great majority of farms on lower ground. A farm of 150 acres would carry forty milking cows, and, after a rotation of oats (or barley), roots, oats, there may be 3–4 years' grass; on poorer land the life of grassland extends to perhaps 8 years. Many dairy farms also fatten sheep, but it is on the hilly margins that sheep farming and cattle rearing are practised. On some coastal farms beef cattle are fattened, but these marginal interests cannot diminish the predominance of dairying. Over 63,000 dairy cattle in Ayrshire produce over 45 million gallons of milk annually; contrast these figures with those for East Lothian with only 20,000 dairy cattle. Much of the milk goes to the industrial towns of Ayrshire and Clydeside, but creameries consume an increasing volume of milk: Mauchline (butter, cheese and milk powder), Fenwick (cheese), Kilmaurs (butter and cheese) and Kirkmichael (condensed milk) are important centres.

It is only in coastal districts that cash cropping is important and there it is concerned with the production of early potatoes. A narrow coastal strip from near Largs south to the Wigtown border has fertile raised beach soils. These free-draining and easily warmed soils are sheltered from north and east winds by an old sea cliff, and are free from low-lying pockets where late frosts may cause damage. Conditions are ideal for early potatoes planted in mid-February. There is no definite rotation and some fields have grown potatoes continuously for two generations. Often a catch-crop of rye grass or green barley follows the potato harvest, while in some cases 2 years of potatoes are followed by a cereal, then 2 years of grass. Such continuous and intensive production of "earlies" necessitates constant feeding of the soil: sea-weed, manure and fertilizers are used.

Fishing

The fishing industry is still important and is centred on Ayr particularly, but is also important at Girvan, Dunure and Madens. Though the numbers employed full time barely reach 230, large quantities of herring, cod, haddock and whiting are landed from small vessels fishing usually in the Firth of Clyde.

Mining

The changes that have recently affected the Scottish coal industry have left their mark in Ayrshire, particularly in northern areas, and little coal is now produced north of Kilmarnock. Compared with $4\frac{1}{2}$ million tons produced in 1910 and $3\frac{1}{2}$ in 1950, output had declined by 1968 to less than 3 million tons. Despite this, however, collieries in the region still employ over 7000 men.

Coal measures in south Ayrshire afford rich reserves and production is concentrated in new or reconstructed collieries. In 1968 almost half the output came from two out of the sixteen active collieries. **Killoch Colliery** alone produced almost 1 million tons of industrial and domestic coal; this new sinking in the Mauchline basin taps reserves of 150 million tons of coal deeply buried under sandstones and lavas. Barony Colliery near Auchinleck has been reconstructed to produce 500,000 tons a year, some of it used in an adjacent power station. The output of this slurry burning station (60 MW) and the Kilmarnock power station (56 MW) has been dwarfed by the completion in 1963 of the 300 MW nuclear power station at **Hunterston**— a second nuclear power station being constructed at Hunterston will have an output capacity of 1200 MW.

In addition to the two new collieries, other pits have been reconstructed to develop deep reserves. With East Fife and Midlothian, Ayrshire will share the greater part of Scotland's future coal output.

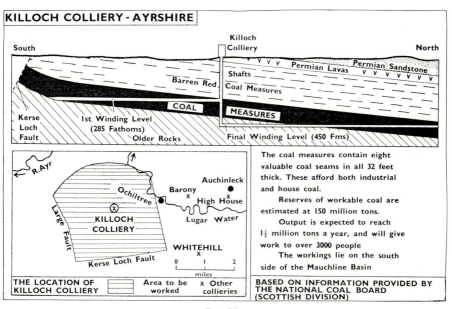

FIG. 78.

Mauchline, Cumnock, Muirkirk and Dalmellington are important mining centres in south Ayrshire, while Dailly to the south-west and Sanquhar in Dumfriesshire extend the importance of mining. As mining expanded, these villages grew very rapidly—at New Cumnock, for instance, population rose by 300 per cent in the nineteenth century and by 450 per cent in the first third of this century.

Coal played a vital role in developing Ayrshire's industries, particularly the once-great iron industry. Still of great importance for domestic and industrial uses, there remains a significant shipment of coal to Ireland and the Hebrides through Ayr, Troon and Ardrossan.

Before leaving mining, we should note the large production of road metal in Ayrshire and recall that Macadam was born near Ayr.

Industrial Development

Almost half of Ayrshire's working population is engaged in manufacturing, and the growth of industries followed a pattern somewhat similar to that seen in the Glasgow region. While some of the early industries have declined or disappeared, there remains a wide variety, being extended by the addition of the new industries.

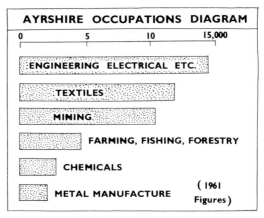

FIG. 79.

Textile Industries

These employ more than 11,000 people. The domestic handloom weaving industry, once the mainstay of life in many Ayrshire communities, has grown into a diversity of textile manufactures, involving over 100 firms. **Knitwear and hosiery industries** are widespread; Stewarton ("the bonnet town") still produces bonnets as well as knitted garments. Ayr, Irvine, Beith, Catrine, Cumnock, Dalry, Galston, Kilmarnock and Saltcoats are all closely concerned in making knitwear and hosiery. Cardigans, hosiery, carpet yarns, worsteds, flannels and blankets are local specialities.

The **cotton industry,** an old staple, is now centred on Catine, where it dates from the eighteenth century. Spinning, weaving, bleaching and finishing are carried out and sheets, pillow cases and window blinds are noted products.

The **lace industry,** concentrated in the Irvine valley, provides a famous export and is based upon generations of skill. In Darvel, Galston and Newmilns, lace weaving has been the mainstay for 200 years and was originally done on hand looms. The Ayrshire lace trade has overtaken that of Nottingham. The interests of the lace towns have widened to include blankets, curtains, bedspreads, table covers, rayon and Terylene fabrics, knitwear, furnishing fabrics and textile machinery, produced in the main by small factories.

The **linen industry** is not nearly so widespread as it once was, but is still important at Kilbirnie and Beith, where thread and fishing nets are made.

Ayrshire has a very large **carpet industry,** focused especially on Kilmarnock and Ayr, which also have numerous textile industries. Other towns concerned in the making of carpets or carpet yarn include Irvine, Dunlop, Cumnock, Kilbirnie, Kilwinning and Stewarton.

The **footwear industry** is as old as lace making, and, while a number of small firms still produce boots and shoes (notably at Maybole), the modern industry is concentrated at Kilmarnock, where a nation-wide organization has its headquarters. The production of synthetic fibres has expanded greatly in recent years with the production of nylon in a large new factory at Dundonald (east of Troon) and Cumnock. Meanwhile, at Ardeer, I.C.I. are expanding their Dyestuffs Division to become a major producer of nylon salt, an initial process in nylon manufacture.

Metal and Engineering Industries

The occurrence of coal, iron ore and often limestone led to widespread iron industries, dating in the case of Muirkirk from 1787. As in the Glasgow region, exhaustion of ore supplies led to the extinction of most ironworks and the sole relics today at Muirkirk, Kilwinning, Dalmellington and elsewhere are enormous slag bings. However, Glengarnock has large steelworks producing ingots, rails and fishplates for railways, and sections for shipbuilding and bridge building.

Upon the basis of metal working skills accumulated, the region has numerous engineering industries which, with metal manufacturing, employ almost 17,000 people. Shipbuilding, marine-engineering and ship-repairing activities are concentrated at Ardrossan, but also at Troon and Ayr. At Girvan, fishing vessels are built.

General engineering is practised mainly in the larger towns such as Kilmarnock and Ayr. The former, Ayrshire's greatest industrial centre, grew at the confluence of the Irvine and Kilmarnock, whose industries depend upon coal from the Ayrshire field and include many engineering products: hydraulic equipment (valves, water control gear), tractors and combine-harvesters, locomotives and car bearings are prominent. From Ayr come fork-lift trucks, iron and steel castings for numerous industries, agricultural machinery and electrical equipment. In both towns, these augment the clothing and textile industries. Irvine (foundries and general engineering), Ardrossan, Kilbirnie, Kilwinning, Stevenston and others have a diversity of engineering industries.

Chemical and Oil Industries

A large proportion of Ardrossan's imports consists of oil for the refinery established there—oil imports exceed 40,000 tons a month, and lead to a wide range of petroleum products. Ardrossan also has a bitumen industry. At Ayr, a large works using imported potash and phosphate ranks as one of Britain's largest fertilizer producers. A new plant at Dalry prepares vitamin products.

The most striking chemical industry is at Ardeer (between Irvine and Stevenston) where over 5000 people are employed in the I.C.I. explosives factory, the main centre in Britain for the production of industrial explosives; detonators, fuses, explosives for mining, quarrying and civil engineering are leading products which are exported through Irvine. The plant also produces acids and industrial cellulose.

Other Industries

At Beith, the furniture industry originally used local birch wood but now depends upon imported timber, moulded by traditional craftsmanship. Food industries (for instance, creameries and bacon factories) are widespread. The names Dunlop Cheese and Ayrshire Bacon are as famous as "Johnnie Walker", symbol of Kilmarnock's great whisky blending industry.

The greatest concentration of industry, therefore, is in the northern half of the county where, in addition to the established industries, new developments are most numerous. This balance in favour of the north is being accentuated with the development of **Irvine New Town**; designated in 1966, the new town area includes Irvine and Kilwinning and had a population (in 1968) of 38,400, but is expected to reach 100,000 by the late 1980s. Industry, already attracted to an industrial estate at Irvine, may also be expected to develop on a new estate being created near Kilwinning.

The southern part of Ayrshire is not so attractive to industry and remains, to a large extent, dependent on agriculture and mining. The run-down of the coal industry and declining employment in agriculture thus affect these areas particularly. The need exists to attract additional employment to mining areas such as Muirkirk, Auchinleck, New Cumnock and Dailly.

Towns

With the exception of Kilmarnock and the mining centres, most of the large towns are situated on or near the coast. **Ayr** (45,000) is the largest coastal settlement, and to its important industries (engineering, textiles, fertilizers, etc.) are added its administrative services, its port activities and its holiday industry.

From Skelmorlie and Largs in the north to Turnberry and **Girvan**

(6000) in the south, coastal towns use their positions and scenic beauty to support a large tourist industry. Together with golfing and holiday interests, **Prestwick** is an international airport (see Fig. 108), and **Irvine** (17,000), **Troon** (10,000), **Saltcoats** (14,000) and **Ardrossan** (10,000), even with their prominent industries, participate in the holiday industry. Added to the natural advantages these towns enjoy, the proximity of the vast Clydeside population has favoured the growth of the holiday industry. The islands of Cumbrae, and more especially the island of Arran, are also centres of attraction for holiday-makers and climbers.

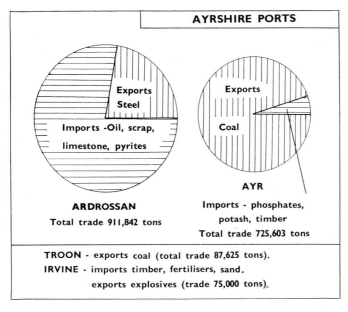

AYRSHIRE PORTS

Exports
Steel

Imports -Oil, scrap,
limestone, pyrites

ARDROSSAN
Total trade 911,842 tons

Exports

Coal

AYR

Imports - phosphates,
potash, timber
Total trade 725,603 tons

TROON - exports coal (total trade 87,625 tons).
IRVINE - imports timber, fertilisers, sand.
exports explosives (trade 75,000 tons).

FIG. 80.

While Ardrossan is now the only important port, handling 1 million tons of trade annually and more than 350,000 passengers (to Belfast, Arran and the Isle of Man), Ayr, Troon and Irvine (once the port for Glasgow) retain some trade.

The largest inland town, **Kilmarnock** (48,000), is Ayrshire's leading industrial and route centre. Her locomotive, tractor, engineering, whisky, carpet and clothing industries have been mentioned already, and attract workers from the surrounding districts. The Lugton and Fenwick valleys carry routes to Glasgow, while the Irvine valley links Kilmarnock to Galston, Newmilns and Darvel, and beyond to Lanark. Southwards, road and rail embrace the mining areas with Mauchline and Cumnock (5000) and go on to Lockerbie, Dumfries and Carlisle. Kilmarnock also has access to the Ayrshire ports. Despite her great industrial importance, Kilmarnock also functions (as it has for centuries) as a livestock market at the centre of a rich farming region.

CHAPTER 11

The Southern Uplands

SEPARATING the fragmented Central Lowlands from northern England and bounded by the discontinuous fault from Dunbar to Girvan in the north, the Solway Firth in the south-west and the great mass of Cheviot in the south-east, is the geologically complex area of the Southern Uplands (Fig. 1, p. 2), presenting a generally rounded landscape of resistant Silurian and Ordo-vician slates and shales with but occasional interruptions in the form of domed eminences like Merrick at 2764 ft and Broadlaw at 2754 ft. In contrast to the Highlands the land is neither so high nor so rugged but presents an almost monotonous appearance in the centre with long connected chains of subdued heights, almost devoid of lochs, but with numerous confluent valleys, albeit shallower troughs than in most Highland glens. The general picture is that of wide, lonely, pastoral uplands, often moor clad, with the wetter lowlands of the west (60–35 in.) concentrating upon dairying and exhibiting an entirely different agricultural pattern from that of the Eastern Lowlands or Tweed basin, where a drier and slightly more extreme climate encourages the cultivation of oats, barley, wheat, sugar-beet and turnips and hay for winter feeding of stock.

With such differences it is necessary to subdivide the Southern Uplands into its two contrasting sections:

(1) Galloway and Dumfries,
(2) the Tweed basin.

The line of division which takes the form of the upper Annan valley (Fig. 81) demarcates regions as different physically and economically as are the western and eastern counterparts of the Highlands. Galloway, much dissected and interrupted by the granitic intrusions of Cairnsmore of Carsphairn, Cairnsmore of Fleet and Criffel, rising in places over 2000 ft, presents a rugged, ice-eroded appearance, with wide glacial valleys, rock basins, peaty hollows and occasional expanses of forest reminiscent of the Western High-lands on a smaller scale. East of the Nith, the high plateau surfaces with smooth, tabular hill masses, interrupted by deep, flat-floored valleys and opening eastwards into the strath-like Merse, show a distinct affinity to the Eastern Highlands, north of the Tay.

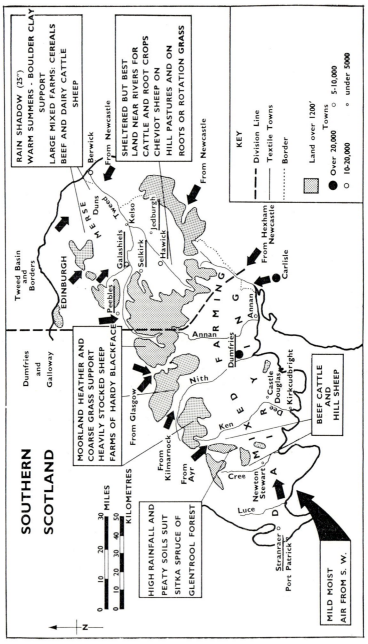

FIG. 81.

GALLOWAY AND DUMFRIESSHIRE

Physical Background

This area comprises the consequent drainage into the Solway from the Annan in the east to the Water of Luce in the west and includes the county of Wigtown in the west, the Stewartry of Kirkcudbright in the centre and Dumfriesshire in the east. Several parallel river valleys (Annan, Nith, Dee, Cree), draining into the Solway Firth, broaden out considerably in their lower stretches to afford fertile lands, humped here and there by drumlin swarms. Much of the former coastal plain has been drowned to give penetrating inlets: Wigtown Bay, Kirkcudbright Bay and Loch Ryan, which alternate with rocky headlands to give variety to the coastal scenery. Harbours, however, are small and shallow and, with large expanses of mud flats exposed at low tide, any possible use to man of these estuaries would necessitate expensive land reclamation projects.

To the north, where the counties of Peebles, Selkirk and Dumfries come together, a rounded plateau surface, incised by deep, narrow glens like the Black and White Esk, extends eastwards from the Nith valley to the border with England. Now one of the most heavily stocked hill sheep grazing areas in Scotland, the elevated surfaces of the Hartfell and Broadlaw indicate the former ice dispersal area of the Southern Uplands. Great bands of moraines in the valleys bear testimony to the waxing and waning of successive valley glaciers. Loch Doon, St. Mary's Loch and Loch Skene portray the glacial rock basin formation although the latter does appear to have been also dammed by moraine. From the outwash material, much in evidence around Selkirk, the final stages of the ice retreat can be gauged. That the Galloway ice, which fanned out from an axis extending from Merrick to Broadlaw, was of considerable significance is readily understood when one can see erratics of Criffel granite dumped at Ravenglass in Cumberland, where the Scots ice encountered another great mass radiating from the Lake District. The productive nature of the soils of the Merse and of the lower Galloway Dales must be attributed largely to the removal of material from the uplands by ice and subsequent dumping in the lowlands. A mantle of boulder clay and alluvium has thus enabled the Rhinns, Machers and Dales of Galloway to become known collectively as "Scotland's Dairy Farm" where, due to the mild winters, stock can remain out of doors all the year round nourished on the moist pasturelands which thrive in this damp corner of Scotland.

Agriculture

Where the land rises between 500 and 1500 ft, a predominance of rough grazing precludes marginal stock farming (cf. Berwick region), except for the

Glenkens and upper Cree, where hill sheep are combined with the rearing of hardy black "Belted Galloway" cattle to be fattened later on the arable farms of the lowlands. Below 500 ft the basic land use is the rearing and breeding, on large farms, of dairy cattle and the Castle Douglas–Kirkcudbright region (Lower Dee) typifies the agricultural pursuits of south-west Scotland. The largest farms are located on the fluvio-glacial deposits of the lower valley reaches rearing Ayrshire dairy herds, crossed White Shorthorn and Galloway beef stock, Cheviot sheep crossed with Border Leicesters and the latter crossed with native Blackfaces to produce Greyface sheep, and numerous pigs fed from the surplus dairy products. A feature of the crop rotation is the high proportion, between 50 and 75 per cent, under grass, either permanent or rotation in a 6- to 8-year cycle. Approximately one-sixth of the acreage is devoted to oats, barley, turnips, beans or kale for cattle and the remainder is either permanent grass, rotation grass or rough moor grazing.

Due to its relative remoteness and milder climate, south-west Scotland is ideally suited to the practice of dairy farming with daily lorry collections taken to the various creameries which, in turn, supply the dense industrial populations of central Scotland.

Writing in the seventeenth century on the Dee parishes, Andrew Symson remarked that the country "was more plentifull in bestiall than cornes". Although referring to a different kind of "bestiall", this statement could well be applied to the twentieth-century economy of the district. The emphasis has always been on stock rearing, and cropping has never played a major part in the economy of Kirkcudbright, except to provide straw and winter fodder. Time has witnessed changes from an early beef cattle droving trade to a large-scale increase of sheep farming with the enclosures, and to a subsequent swing to dairying, after the initial penetration from Ayrshire.

With the efficacy of modern transport, and with the ever-increasing demands of the industrial centres of Scotland and England, the Stewartry contributes to an integral part of the national economy. Hence the words of Jan Blaeu in 1667 that "le pays est plus propre à nourrir du bestiall qu'au labourage" hold good to this day.

Forestry

Much of the Galloway moors and rough grazing has undergone recent afforestation by the Forestry Commission to supplement the several considerable private woodlands. Forest village communities have been established in idyllic surroundings at Ae, north of Dumfries, and in the Glen Trool National Forest which, with 100,000 acres of trees planted, is the second largest forest in Scotland. Fencing and preparation of the ground for planting are the most expensive operations in the 5-year working plans. Large caterpillar diesel tractors plough deep drainage channels into the heaped soil,

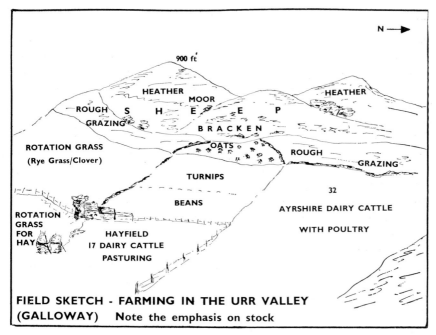

FIELD SKETCH - FARMING IN THE URR VALLEY
(GALLOWAY)   Note the emphasis on stock

FIG. 82. Land utilization in the Urr valley (Kircudbright).

FIG. 83. Drumlin, near Castle Douglas (Kirkcudbright). Note the characteristic shape and that ploughing has taken place to the very top. The boulder clay material supports grass suitable for the Ayrshire dairy cattle in the foreground.

137

forming the planting areas for the regiments of trees, and two kinds of plough must be used, one for the deep, peaty areas and one for the hard glacial gravels which occur in this area. The species planted are mainly conifers and, with many of the older trees now being over 20 years of age, a ready supply of seed for the Commission's nurseries is available. It is hoped that, in the future, a pulp mill similar to that at Corpach (Fort William) will be established to utilize the eminently suitable softwoods of the Galloway forests.

Hydro-electric Power

The 150,000-h.p. Galloway Hydro-electric Scheme, which cost initially £3 million, was one of Scotland's pioneer hydro-electric projects and has been in operation since 1935. Loch Doon (Fig. 84) normally discharged its water to the Ayrshire coast but, since being enlarged, it is now diverted by

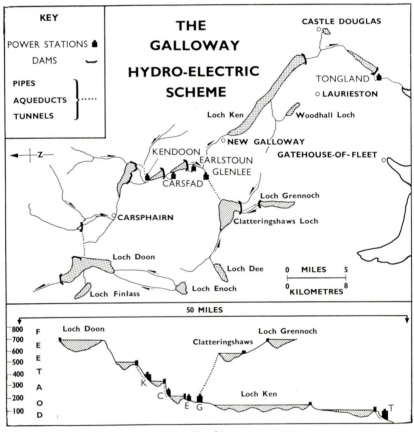

Fig. 84.

a 5700-ft tunnel to the Dee system, the water passing in turn through the power stations of Kendoon, Carsfad, Earlstoun and Tongland. A fifth station, Glenlee, is supplied by the artificial loch, Clatteringshaws, the water afterwards being discharged into Loch Ken. As with other major schemes in Scotland, fish resources are protected by means of fish ladders and resting pools for salmon on their annual movements up river.

Settlements and Industries

Towns are generally small market and service centres age-old in establishment and little changed in modern times.

Dumfries (27,000). A nodal town on the Nith, Dumfries is the largest town in the south of Scotland and consequently it functions as the administrative centre. Industries are more varied here than elsewhere in the south-west and include knitwear, hosiery, agricultural machinery, a rubber factory and several creameries. As no other town in this region comes within even half the size of pleasantly situated Dumfries, the name "Queen of the South", as borne also by the town soccer team, would appear justified.

Like Dumfries, Kirkcudbright, Wigtown, Whithorn and Stranraer were also medieval burghs but all except the latter have declined considerably. Kirkcudbright's claim to fame is as the small county town of the Stewartry with a large creamery as well as being an artist's redoubt. It is renowned as the birthplace of the founder of the U.S. Navy, the erstwhile pirate, Paul Jones.

Stranraer (9000). Regional centre for Wigtownshire, passenger–freight services are operated twice daily from Stranraer, leaving sheltered Loch Ryan on the shortest sea crossing to Ulster. Main line trains from London, Manchester, Newcastle, Edinburgh and Glasgow are scheduled to link with the *Caledonian Princess*, which accommodates 1400 passengers and 100 cars. The railway line from Dumfries to Stranraer is scheduled for closure. Motorists can drive straight on to the ship, through its stern doorways, at Stranraer and off again $2\frac{1}{4}$ hours later at Larne, a mere 20 miles from Belfast (Fig. 107). Stranraer's few industries include creameries and a recently established clothing factory for children's garments.

Portpatrick. Even nearer to Ulster than Stranraer, the little harbour of Portpatrick used also to have a link with Northern Ireland, but it now functions as a quiet, secluded holiday centre with sporadic fishing activities.

Annan (6000). Another medieval burgh, between Dumfries and Carlisle, Annan does show some resurgence due to the nearby nuclear power generating plant at Chapelcross. In operation since 1959, the four reactors of the Calder Hall type feed 1000 million units of electricity annually into the National Grid. The town itself is an important market centre with grain milling and engineering, in which cranes, machinery and boilers are made, its main activities. Annan shrimp boats fish as far away as Luce Bay for their specialized catches and it is one of the few fishing harbours on the Solway not in complete decay.

None of the newer burghs of **Castle Douglas, Newton Stewart** and **Dalbeattie** exceeds 4000 in population and all grew as market centres serving the surrounding productive farmlands.

Until comparatively recently Galloway was little known as an area suitable for holiday activities. It seemed to be detached from the rest of Scotland and, with poor transport facilities and limited hotel provision, visitors were confined to the motor tourist during the high season of July and August. With a much more mobile leisure time population nowadays, people from England are "discovering" Galloway, having been squeezed out of the crowded Lake District, during peak holiday periods. Visitors to Galloway increased from 75,000 in 1961 to more than double that figure, 161,000, in 1967, with a large proportion being fixed holidaymakers rather than tourists. The varied environmental and heritage resources await full development. Dumfries, not without its own charm and historical interest, but certainly without entertainment and large scale recreational facilities, is ideally located as a reception area. Kippford, on the Urr, already a yachting centre, Wig and Luce Bays are places suited to considerable expansion as venues for the sailing/cruising fraternity. Glen Trool Forest suggests a holiday centre of a different kind, requiring adequate accommodation, suitable parking and picnic places and properly established and supervised camping amenities. "The Galloway Project", a regional survey commissioned by the Scottish Tourist Board in 1968, has recommended the establishment of a regional tourist association for the south-west and this should give impetus and encouragement to further development of this highly individual and charming part of Scotland.

THE TWEED BASIN

Physical Background

Centred on Coldstream, a horseshoe-shaped rim of hills rising over 2000 ft in parts and tilted to the north-east encloses the drainage basin of the Tweed. Within this surrounding rim, breached in only a few places by passes, there is a definite suggestion of regional isolation which has contributed to the highly individualistic character of the Border people. The Hartfell massif is the highest point, the Moorfoot–Lammermuirs form the northern flank and southwards Ettrick forest, joined by the Cheviots, falls to the Millfield plain. On the east is the Fell sandstone escarpment and coastal plain.

Flowing in broad arable valleys the left bank tributaries of the Tweed provide routeways out of the region by the Gala, Lauder and Whiteadder, but few routes are afforded by the Yarrow, Ettrick and Teviot, which force the Tweed north-eastwards out of its general easterly trend.

Strong in local tradition, the Tweed basin must be considered a physical entity and this fact is emphasized by its restricted economic development. Lack of nodality and paucity of minerals prevented a balanced development and the principal economic resource is derived from labour on the land, with a consequent sparseness of population. The time-honoured sheep farming tradition was established by the Cistercian monks in the Border abbeys of Kelso, Melrose and Jedburgh during the eleventh and twelfth centuries. Blessed with the best of the alluvial lands, the diligent monks cultivated wheat, oats and barley and kept cows, pigs and sheep as well as enjoying the plentiful salmon from the rivers in their virtually self-supporting communities. Through the ages similar harvests have been obtained by the people of this area and the textile industry of the riverside towns owes its origins to the early stocking of the hills with sheep.

Agriculture

For farming purposes the Tweed basin is best divided into three sub-regions.

(1) *The Lowland Zone* (0–400 ft). Concentration in the Tweed lowlands and the Merse (Fig. 81) is upon arable farming and cash cropping. A triangular lowland north of the Tweed between Kelso and Berwick, the Merse has a thick mantle of glacial till and alluvium, interrupted only by long, low, east-to-west-aligned drumlins which indicate the direction of the ice turned away by the Cheviot mass. Heavy clay loams, a sheltered position, low rainfall (less than 25 in. p.a.) and summer warmth combine to render the Merse a region of intensive cultivation. Mechanized farming is well to the fore, and indeed contributory to rural depopulation, on the highly capitalized farms concentrating upon arable production half of which is grain and a third roots, potatoes, sugar-beet and turnips. The remainder is in grass on which stock are bred—not bought as in the Lothians and Angus but actually bred on the farms. Although the Tweed itself is incised into a series of bluffs, flooding is always a danger and brought considerable havoc in 1947 when several railway bridges were washed away and much farmland was inundated.

(2) *The Upland Zone* (400–800 ft). The Lammermuir slopes, Teviotdale, the Cheviot slopes and the middle Tweed are essentially stock farming areas with arable production for fodder and not for cash sale as in the Merse. Sheep here are heavier and fatter than hill sheep and the farms are generally smaller, carrying mixed stock of beef cattle, sheep and dairy cows. Heavy lambs for

meat are obtained by crossing Border Leicesters with the Cheviot breed and then the breeding ewes of this cross are in turn crossed with Oxford Down.

(3) *The Hill Zone* (above 800 ft). Farms ranging in size up to 6000 acres are stocked with breeding Blackface ewes (the native hill sheep) and are scattered along the upper slopes of the Lammermuirs, Moorfoots, Cheviot and upper Tweeddale. These ewes are the capital assets of the farms and the winter carrying capacity of the hills imposes limits on farm stock. In consequence some of the hill pastures are not being fully utilized in summer due to scant stocking and some farmers are grazing cattle on the more accessible of these.

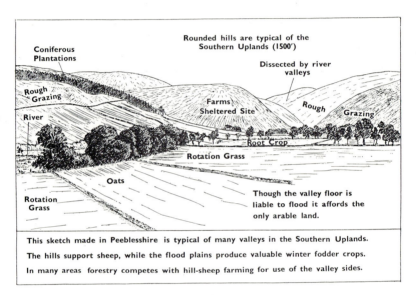

This sketch made in Peeblesshire is typical of many valleys in the Southern Uplands. The hills support sheep, while the flood plains produce valuable winter fodder crops. In many areas forestry competes with hill-sheep farming for use of the valley sides.

Fig. 85.

Roxburghshire may be considered as showing a good transect of Border farming and similar groupings to the above emerge.

Between Newtown St. Boswells and Kelso are typically large arable–stock intensive farms of over 500 acres. In addition to cattle fattening and a recent increase in barley production, stimulated by the new maltings at Tweed-mouth, Downcross lambs (see (2) above) are sold at the largest auction market in the south of Scotland at Newtown St. Boswells. On the higher slopes towards the edges of the county, hill sheep farms (of the order in (3) above) are stocked with Cheviots and, on the higher, remoter grazings, Blackfaces. These farms range between 1000 and 3000 acres, carry little else but hill sheep except for a few crossed Galloway and Shorthorn cattle and reflect the limited amount of improved land available in this part of Scotland.

The Textile Industry and Towns

Prior to the eighteenth century, spinning and weaving of wool were mainly home industries although a few mills had been established. An abundance of local wool from surrounding farms and plenty of water, not only for power, originally, but also of a quality soft enough for woolwashing, provided the necessary raw materials. Water, in particular, influenced the location of early mill sites on the narrow valley floors and, to this day, the tendency for ribbon growth in Galashiels and Hawick reflects the stringing out of mills along the riverside. Rapid expansion caused subsequent reliance upon coal, none of which was locally available, and this proved a serious handicap in face of competition from the coalfield-based Yorkshire textile industry. Manufacturers were forced to specialize in high-quality hosiery and knitwear, which now has a large overseas market, especially in the United States, and soon the local supplies of wool proved to be inadequate in both quantity and quality, necessitating large imports of Australian wool. Thus the two reasons which influenced the location of the mills in the Tweed towns no longer applied—yet another instance of geographical inertia, although the quality of the water for manufacturing and dyeing purposes together with the inherent skills remain critical factors.

Hawick (16,000). Producing £5 million worth of textile garments annually, 80 per cent of which are for overseas customers, there are nearly forty mills and factories in the hosiery, woollen and tweed industries of Hawick, the largest town in the Tweed basin. The vulnerability of the concentration on one industry, which employs over half of the town's total labour force, is underlined by the closure of nine mills during 1962 in the face of severe competition from Japan and Italy in particular.

Galashiels (12,000). In addition to the smaller towns of Peebles, Innerleithen, Jedburgh and Selkirk, Galashiels supports similar textile industries to those of Hawick. The specialization here is in high-quality tweeds, hosiery and cashmere fibres used in expensive knitwear for ladies.

Many of the workers in the Galashiels mills come from **Jedburgh,** where an encouraging step has been taken to absorb male labour with the establishing of an American-based toolmaking firm which now employs 300 workers (mostly men), and **Melrose,** which is chiefly a small residential town, and other outlying districts.

In the centre of a rich farming area **Selkirk** (6000) and **Kelso** serve mainly as market towns, the latter, in common with **Peebles, Jedburgh** and **Melrose,** having less than 5000 people.

Berwick (12,000). Although politically in England, Berwick, by virtue of its geographical position at the outlet of the Tweed, merits consideration. In the twelfth and thirteenth centuries, Berwick was Scotland's chief port but a series of setbacks culminated in its loss to England in the fifteenth century. Duns is the Berwickshire county administrative centre and Berwick's main claim to fame now rests on its position on the main road and rail routes from Newcastle to Edinburgh.

CHAPTER 12

The Central Highlands
(Grampians)

BOUNDED by two extensive fault systems, the Great Glen in the north and the Highland Boundary Fault in the south (Fig. 1), is the vast, denuded massif of the Grampians, forming the highest rampart of the British Isles with several summits over 4000 ft. Once again contrasts appear in an area which, at first sight, would seem to be little more than a broad, plateau surface, deeply trenched in parts by straths and glens. Study of a good atlas map reveals that the south-west part is much more deeply dissected and fragmentary, with the steep-sided, finger-like fiords of Loch Etive and Loch Leven contrasting sharply with the more gradual opening out of the valleys on to the Moray Firth and North Sea coast.

THE HIGHLAND ENVIRONMENT

The Cairngorms

This central mountain mass, forming the eastern part of the Grampians, is a high tableland reaching over 4000 ft in Ben Macdhui, Cairngorm, Cairntoul and Braeriach, and displays, as such, an evenness of summit levels atop the 3000-ft plateau surface, which in turn is stepped above an even more pronounced 2000-ft plateau surface. Incisions into the plateau surface appear as glacially overdeepened valleys, e.g. Glen Muick, Loch Avon and sheer-walled corries often containing tarns. The high altitude of this denuded landscape with consequent exposure to harsh climate inhibits permanent settlement. Subject to prolonged snow cover (Fig. 7), the smooth shoulders and lengthy slopes of the Cairngorms have, in recent years, seen the development of organized skiing centres as at Glenshee in the Grampians between Blairgowrie and Braemar, where a modern hotel, mountain huts, an electrically operated ski-lift system and European instructors have been provided solely for this purpose (Fig. 91).

The Monadliath Mountains

North-west of the Cairngorms, the slightly lower, but similarly stepped, plateau surfaces of the Monadliath Mountains extend from the Spey to

FIG. 86. Loch Einich (Grampians). Note the complete absence of habitation and the effects of ice action and of the elements. (Photo: Aerofilms & Aero Pictorial Ltd.)

Loch Ness. Very little settlement is possible in this extensive upland littered with peat bog and glacial debris bearing mute testimony to the meeting point of ice from the Ness valley, the Spey valley and from the north, and the predominant activity on these open moorlands is grouse shooting.

The Straths

Several large straths, or wide valleys, radiate from the mountain area on to the fringing lowlands of the north and east and, of these, Strathspey, which extends as a long tongue inland from the Moray Firth to divide the Cairngorms from the Monadliath Mountains, is the most important. Being one of the few Highland valleys to benefit from good main line railway and trunk road facilities, a string of large villages, in close proximity to the railway, extends from Newtonmore in the south to Grantown-on-Spey in the north. Several of these villages, Aviemore in particular, serve as holiday centres for the Cairngorms. In recent years there has been a rapid development of a winter sports complex and holiday centre at Aviemore. Apart from the outdoor activities on the ski-slopes of the Cairngorms (Fig. 92), there is a wide range of facilities for indoor recreation, including an indoor heated swimming-pool, games courts, an ice-rink, a cinema/theatre and excellent hotel accommodation. Vision is shown in the hope that these admirable facilities at Aviemore will be used as a conference centre when not required for winter sports. Forestry, too, is important on Speyside with the pine forests of Rothiemurchus, one of the largest natural forest areas in Britain and much depleted by war needs since Napoleonic times, undergoing progressive replanting. Farming activities vary from meagre crofting and hill sheep farming in the less hospitable parts to the selective breeding and rearing of Aberdeen-Angus beef cattle on pedigree farms, the animals being fed on rotation grasses and roots grown on the arable lands of the wide valley terraces.

On the eastern flanks of the Cairngorms the valleys of the Dee and Don are more constricted than that of the Spey. Patronized by royalty, Deeside, with Balmoral as the Highland residence of the royal family, hardly needs comment on its scenic attraction, guaranteed "By Royal Appointment". Outwith the royal estates, arable farming is practised on the alluvial flats, principally for fodder for cattle east of Ballater, and for sheep upstream of this planned nineteenth-century village. In the remoter reaches, evidence of population decline proceeding apace since the late seventeenth century may be sadly noted by the numerous abandoned and decayed crofts, often with merely the stumps of the end walls standing starkly against the empty landscape.

The Western Grampians

Physical Background. West of the Tay the jumbled, jagged landscape of sharp ridges and intermontane lochs affords a contrast to the rest of the Grampians. The cone-shaped quartzitic peak of Schiehallion (3547 ft) and the mighty Bens, Cruachan (3689 ft), Lawers (3984 ft) and Nevis (4406 ft), the highest mountain in Britain, emerge above a much more highly dissected landscape, due in part to glacial erosion and in part to the incessant gullying action of the heavier rainfall (Fig. 83) on the denuded slopes of this westerly region.

A ski-tow on the slopes of forbidding Glencoe, which is also a climber's paradise and a mere 2½-hour drive from Glasgow, and a high motor road and tarmac car and coach park on the flanks of Ben Lawers enable some enthusiasts, at least, to derive benefit from the rigorous climate of this region.

Apart from the headwaters of several notable rivers, the Tay, Earn and Forth, all of which drain eastwards out of this region, the course of most streams in the Western Grampians is a short if rapid one to the Atlantic. A feature of the drainage of this area is the profusion of lochs, varying in formation from glacially scooped rock basins and mountain tarns to moraine-dammed lochs and fault-guided troughs, one of the best examples of which is Loch Ericht in Perthshire. As well as the more obvious uses for fishing, domestic water supply (Loch Katrine in the tree-girt Trossachs supplies Glasgow) and hydro-electricity (Loch Rannoch, Loch Tummel in Perthshire), these large bodies of water tend to ameliorate the climate of their shorelands in addition to affording great scenic attractions. The recently introduced, but increasingly popular, water-skiing activities are centred on Loch Earn, the venue for the 1963 European Water-skiing Championships, and this has given a tremendous fillip to the hotel industries of St. Fillans and Loch-earnhead at either end of the 7-mile-long loch. The pronounced indentations of the deep-fiorded coastline suggest possibilities for use as natural deep water harbours but, as in the case of Norway, which has a similar coastline, remoteness from the productive hinterlands is the main drawback, although wartime exigencies demanded the use of many of these sheltered inlets as naval anchorages during 1939–45. Nowadays, enormous 80,000-ton tankers (Fig. 60) berth at Finnart (now capable of taking the giant 200,000-ton vessels) on the eastern shore of Loch Long, built as the most convenient deep-water discharge point to Grangemouth, with which it is connected by pipe-line.

Agriculture. Due to the expanse of heath and rough moorland, the inhabited parts of this area are confined to the lower slopes and alluvial valley floors and the greatest concentration of arable farming appears in wide Strathtay, with small fruit a speciality in upper Strathtay between Aberfeldy and the confluence of the Lyon and Tay where, due to the sheltered position, farmers succeed in marketing their raspberries before the main crop of the Strathmore fruit farms. However, the main agricultural activity in all of the glens is geared to livestock needs with rotation grass, oats and turnips as basic crops and the larger farms, e.g. those of the Wills's estate in Glen Lyon, carrying several thousand head of hill sheep.

Settlements. Comprising Argyllshire and Perthshire and parts of Stirling-shire and Dunbartonshire, the Western Grampians area includes several more important settlements than the Grampians north of the Tay–Garry. It is worth noting, however, that the towns listed below depend largely upon holiday-makers for their trading activities and during the holiday season places like Pitlochry, Rothesay and Dunoon more than double their population.

Dunoon (9000), on the Cowal Peninsula, and **Rothesay** (8000), on the island of Bute, are the mecca of Glasgow holiday-makers going "doon the watter" by means of the direct Glasgow steamer links with each resort.

Oban (7000). Passenger vessels leave Oban, which has a direct rail link with Glasgow, for the Hebrides and, as well as being a major holiday centre, the town has a tweed mill and a distillery, and engages in fishing activities.

Fig. 87. This sketch looking west along Glen Lyon near Slatich shows clearly the glaciated U-shaped trough flanked by 3000-ft peaks. The river Lyon meanders across the fertile floor of the glen.

Campbeltown (7000). Situated on the sheltered side of the Kintyre peninsula, Campbeltown is somewhat out on a limb and here fishing, distilling and a large creamery are really more important than the casual holiday trade.

None of the other settlements reaches 5000 in population, but **Pitlochry,** with thirty hotels and boarding houses, an open-air theatre and a convenient position on the main road and railway line from Perth to Inverness, has rapidly become the major inland Highland holiday centre. Tweed is manufactured in the town, there are two distilleries and the great dam, which has created the artificial Loch Faskally, is a source of attraction to visitors (Fig. 88).

INDUSTRIAL ACTIVITY IN THE GRAMPIANS

Isolation, scant labour force, difficult communications and paucity of economically workable minerals have all contributed to a lack of industrial development in the Central Highlands and the popular image of wonderful scenic beauty and whisky-soaked, tartan-clad pipers might well be excused! To the basic industries of whisky distilling, tourism and tweed we need only add hydro-electric power to complete the industrial picture. Recent growth of a small electronics industry and Government approval for the multi-million Alcan smelter project centred near Invergordon indicate a more balanced industrial future for this area.

Whisky

In 1966, Scotch whisky accounted for one-quarter of Scotland's £500 million export revenue. The *per capita* rate of Scottish exports is higher than anywhere else in the United Kingdom and therefore whisky, which is currently taxed in the home market at three times the value of the contents of the bottle (14/11 + tax = 58/6), figures largely in the struggle to keep Britain's trade gap as nearly closed as possible. Although most of the blending and bottling is carried out in industrial Scotland, nearly forty malt whisky distilleries are located on Speyside alone, a further ten are on the island of Islay off the Argyll coast, sixteen more are scattered throughout the Central Highlands and a new one has been established in 1963 on the island of Jura.

Whisky has been made, legally and illegally, in Scotland for over 500 years and this uniquely Highland industry provides a good example of **Geographical Inertia** as the original locating factors of

(1) proximity to barley fields, which influenced the start of distillation as a side-line to farming, and

(2) the availability of peat fuel for the malting process which, combined with peat water sources contributed, to the characteristic flavour,

are no longer so important.

Modern whiskies are blended together (malt whisky and grain whisky) to form a drink more acceptable to the palate and this blending requires specialist skills. Additionally, much of the barley now used is imported from Australia and these factors have contributed towards newer and larger distilleries, often with their own blending and bottling plants, being located in the Central Lowlands where labour, communications and import–export facilities are more favourable. One of the most significant of these developments is Dewar's large new blending and bottling plant, opened in 1962 on the outskirts of Perth and complete with its own railway sidings linked to the Perth marshalling yards. Although the manufacture and blending of whisky is a skilled process which cannot be speeded by machines, labour in this modern plant is saved by automatic handling, filling, capping, labelling and wrapping of bottles.

Hydro-electric Power

Assured heavy rainfall, steep gradients, narrow valleys, loch reservoirs and solid rock ramparts against which dams can be buttressed are some of the

Fig. 88. Pitlochry dam, looking upstream with Loch Faskally behind the dam wall. In front of the generating building is the "fish-ladder" by means of which salmon can bypass the dam. The water driving the turbines here has already been used several times by other power stations in the Tummel Valley Scheme.

advantages that have led to the Central Highlands becoming a major region for the harnessing of swift-flowing streams to generate electricity. Within the Grampians area there are no fewer than six major schemes (Fig. 17), which include the initial Highland project of the early 1930s, the Tummel–Garry scheme recently expanded to include water from Loch Ericht, and the private British Aluminium Lochaber–Kinlochleven and Foyers projects. Two major schemes, Loch Sloy and Loch Awe, merit special consideration.

Loch Sloy. Lying to the north-west of Glasgow and Loch Lomond, in an area receiving an average of 115–120 in. of rainfall annually, Loch Sloy Dam is a symbol in concrete and steel of a great national undertaking in the utilization of natural water resources to improve living standards and make the Highlands a more productive region.

Surveyed several times since 1906 as a potential power source, no development was undertaken until 1945, when work began to transform a shallow, mountain-girt loch, 788 ft above sea level, into a reservoir double its natural length and capable of producing the equivalent of a reserve of 20 million units of electricity. To accommodate water from a catchment area increased fivefold in size, by means of tunnels and aqueducts, a huge concrete buttress dam was built. This dam, as high as a six-storey building and a quarter of a mile long, was the first of its kind to be built in Britain, the great buttress on the downstream side being designed to bear the weight of water pressing against the dam. From the dam, water enters a tunnel, the main section of which is large enough to accommodate a double-decker bus, cut through the side of Ben Vorlich to the power station on the western shores of Loch Lomond, 2 miles distant (Fig. 89).

Power generated at this station is primarily for industrial Clydeside, where the demand is at its peak in winter, and, with an established annual output of 120 million units of electricity, the Sloy project renders a considerable saving of fuel at coal-burning power stations in the Glasgow district.

Loch Awe Scheme. A few miles north-west of Loch Sloy is the ambitious Awe project, designed to utilize a catchment area of 324 square miles (ten times that of Loch Sloy) and centred on one of Scotland's largest inland bodies of water, Loch Awe (Fig. 89). An average annual output of 580 million units is anticipated from the three sections of the scheme shown on the map.

Of these sections Cruachan is perhaps the most compelling by virtue of its underground power station, tunnelling for which had been completed by January 1964. Using a corrie tarn, 1300 ft up on Ben Cruachan, a massive 150-ft-high buttressed dam controls the flow of water down two steeply inclined shafts leading to the underground power station carved out of the granite core of the mountain and housing four generators driven by reversible pump-turbines. At off-peak times these generators function as electric motors, driving the turbines as pumps, which reverse the flow of water for over 1200 ft **up** the shaft from Loch Awe to the high-level reservoir in the corrie. Such a revolutionary engineering project must have repercussions on future hydro schemes as two important considerations emerge:

(1) the storage capacity of the high-level reservoir need not be as great as for conventional schemes of similar output, therefore construction costs would be less,

(2) furthermore, the catchment area can be reduced as Cruachan absorbs directly into its high-level reservoir only 2 square miles of water catchment, supplemented by a collecting aqueduct system totalling 8 square miles (cf. the Tummel Valley Scheme: 710 square miles of catchment producing 650 million units; the Awe Scheme: 324 square miles to produce 580 million units).

The Inverawe section is a self-contained conventional hydro-electric development, by which water from the river Awe, intercepted by the Awe

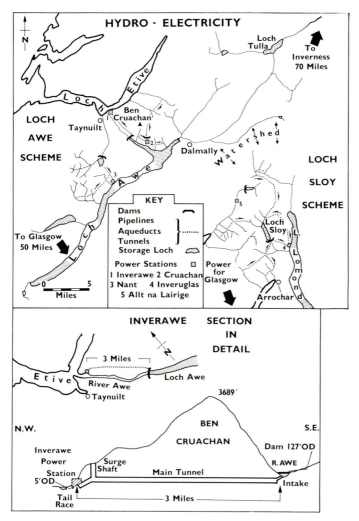

FIG. 89.

Barrage at a famous beauty spot, the Pass of Brander, is diverted through a 3-mile-long concrete-lined tunnel to generate power at Inverawe Power Station near Loch Etive. The main building of this power station is above the ground but it is harmoniously faced with locally quarried pink granite.

Complementary to the previous sections is the Nant section on which work was proceeding during the summer of 1963. This, the smallest part of the project, also includes an underground power station similar to, but with much less generating capacity than, the Cruachan Station, and in November 1963, this station began producing its estimated annual output of 28 million units.

The North of Scotland Hydro-electric Board plans a further pumped storage unit at Foyers on Loch Ness. This project would again involve the construction of an underground power station equipped with reversible pump-turbines, as at Cruachan, with a capacity of 300 MW. The intention is to use the output of the Dounreay fast reactor to pump water 600 ft up from Loch Ness to Loch Mhor at night. During daytime the Foyers station would supply electricity to Aberdeen and the north-east counties. To introduce this scheme would require a further 300 miles of transmission lines.

Aluminium in the Highlands

Most of the hydro-electric power generated in the Central Highlands is

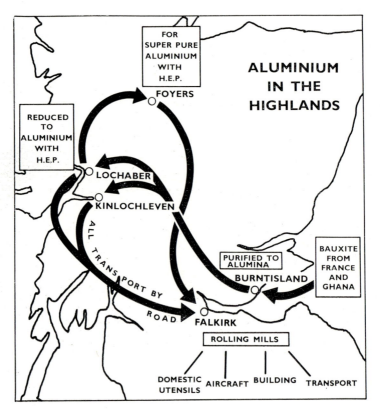

Fig. 90. Aluminium in the Highlands.

destined for the industrial centres south of the Highland line, but the British Aluminium Company, which claims to be the largest single employer of labour in the Highlands (3750), is an industrial enterprise which pioneered the use of electricity in the Highlands, long before the great national undertakings, by opening the first hydro-electric station at Foyers on the eastern side of Loch Ness in 1896. Realization that the water-power potential for electricity outweighed the absence of bauxite (as it does in Norway) prompted the company to establish its reduction plant in the Highlands as aluminium can only be reduced by electrical process.

FIG. 91. British Aluminium Lochaber Works (Fort William) which provides two-thirds of Britain's home-produced aluminium, the rest coming from the same company's works at Kinlochleven, 25 miles away. Note the five downfall pipes carrying water for electricity generation in the power house at the forefront of the plant. (Photo: British Aluminium Co. Ltd.)

There are now five aluminium plants in Scotland (Fig. 90): an aluminium factory at Burntisland, on the Forth, into which bauxite from the company's own mines in Ghana is imported and chemically purified into aluminium oxide; smelters at Kinlochleven and Fort William (Fig. 91), where the metal is electrolytically reduced; a refinery at Foyers (whose future is now in doubt) converted in 1954 to the production of super-purity aluminium using metal from other factories; and the largest location of all, the Falkirk rolling mill. Each year over 30,000 tons of aluminium are smelted in Scotland by British Aluminium, which is engaged in every aspect of the industry from the actual mining of the bauxite in Ghana to developing markets for the finished products. A great variety of industrial and domestic applications now exists for aluminium and these include uses in the chemical industry, building and construction, transport and, of course, in a wide range of scientific, engineering and domestic appliances.

Fig. 92. Electrically operated ski-lift in the Cairngorms. Note also the rounded Monadliath Mountains on the far side of the wide Spey valley. (Photo: *Daily Herald.*)

The Tourist Industry

Scenic splendour counterbalances the risk of inclement weather in attracting thousands of visitors to the Highlands each year. Increasing mobility of people in their leisure time and relatively easy access to centres such as Lomondside, the Trossachs, Glencoe, Oban and Pitlochry from the populous industrial zone of the Central Lowlands help to explain the 25 per cent increase in road traffic in the Highlands between 1961 and 1963. Not only do Highland centres cater for the tourist intent on "doing the Highlands", but hotels and other facilities are also aligned towards those seeking static holidays or specialist holidays, e.g. angling on the Tay, sailing on Loch Lomond, water-skiing on Loch Earn, pony-trekking in the Cairngorms, skiing in several centres or simply unlimited rock-climbing and fell-walking.

People on holiday are notorious spendthrifts and consequently the development of craft industries, similar in some ways to the Swiss "souvenir" industry, is reflected in the contents of "Gift Shops". In small towns and isolated villages these little shops offer "bric-à-brac" ranging from Cairngorm brooches to deer-horn-handled knives and an assortment of tartan-swathed articles, some of which the unwary buyer may subsequently find are stamped "Made in England" or "Empire Made". Specialist locally made tweed with authentic Scottish appeal can also be purchased in places like Oban, Pitlochry and Killin, as can distinctive Scottish foods.

THE POPULATION PROBLEM

Further expansion of the holiday industry with all its attendant side activities, although too often regarded as a panacea for areas lacking in industrial development, it must be admitted is helping to counteract the alarming drift of population away from the Highlands. Increasing use of the electric power generated in the Highlands with the establishment of light industries, in particular food processing in electrically operated plants, to cater for ever-increasing numbers of seasonal visitors, would provide work for young people and thereby help to arrest the drift from rural areas.

This drift is particularly pronounced in Perthshire, now suffering as acutely from rural population decline as are the more remote areas of north-west Scotland. The threat that many communities in rural Perthshire may die out with the present generation of adults is implicit in the dwindling populations of many parishes and villages. Field survey in the upper Tay region has revealed that 90 per cent of school leavers actually have to leave their home district in search of work and invariably this displacement is permanent. Increased mechanization in farming is partly responsible for the drift but the root causes go much deeper to include the "amenity pull" of city life. Fortingall, one of the most attractive little places in a county renowned for its physical beauty, has on its school roll a mere 15 pupils compared with 90 at the beginning of this century. The top-heavy age pyramid, with its lack of support from a base of young people likely to replenish the population, is further accentuated by recently increasing numbers of retired business people from central Scotland, and even parts of England, seeking peace and solitude by moving into these quiet surroundings. With little concrete inducement to retain the bulk of its young people, Perthshire's problem, reflected throughout the Central Highlands, is largely due to the fact that the county is too centrally placed and, although the physical and resources problems are similar to those of the Highlands generally, no panel or commission exists to promote its special interests. On that account it is unlikely to be accorded the same sympathy and practical aid that are the fortune of more northern counties.

CHAPTER 13

The Coastal Lowlands of the North-east

As WELL as mountain landscape, extensive lowland areas, thickly covered with glacial boulder clay and alluvial material brought down from the Highlands, appear in varied forms from the mouth of the Dee to the Pentland Firth. Most of these areas coincide with the sedimentary deposits of Old Red Sandstone (Fig. 1) and, in parts, some are wider than others, but in all cases they offer the best agricultural land of the Highlands of Scotland. With annual precipitation not exceeding 30 in. due to the rain-shadow effect of the Central Highlands, the climate is generally dry and cool but also sunny with the Moray Firth coastlands being a particularly favoured area. These conditions all contribute to a land use pattern quite distinctive from the rest of the Highlands, with much more emphasis on arable farming, especially of root crops like turnips for the feeding of livestock.

Differences in relief and structure along the east coast indicate several divisions of these lowlands (Fig. 93), each being interrupted in turn by regions less conducive to intensive farming and close settlement, and it is therefore advisable to consider each division separately.

THE BUCHAN PENINSULA

Physical Background

Deeply etched by numerous finger-like troughs extending seawards, and often termed the Buchan platform because of its stepped plateau appearance, this is a great arc between the two main rivers of the Eastern Highlands, the Spey and the Dee–Don, and it comprises the lowland parts of the counties of northern Kincardine, Aberdeen and Banff. Much of the region is composed structurally of highly folded and faulted metamorphic rocks, including relative easily eroded schists and much more resistant quartzites, which, together with exposed granitic intrusions, have helped to mould a characteristic landscape and pattern of human activities. Contrasts in coastal formation are apparent between the Aberdeenshire North Sea coast with its low, sandy beaches and the steep, cliffed, latitudinal coastline of the Moray Firth section of this peninsula. This double coastal aspect, facing north and east, and the comparative lack of protective highlands and headlands render the climate much more bleak and exposed than in Nairn, Moray and the Inverness lowlands.

Agriculture

A direct result of northerly latitude and exposed climate is the unsuitability for growth of fruit or wheat and the main cereals produced are oats and barley. Soils, derived principally from glacial drift, vary from poor material to productive loams and the main farming activity has always been the rearing of Aberdeen–Angus and Shorthorn beef cattle on rotation grass, with oats and turnips grown for winter feeding. Due to the distilleries' demands for malting barley, this cereal is widely grown, sheep are grazed on upland pastures and more than a third of Scotland's poultry are reared in this region. On the better lands stock fattening (cattle and sheep) is carried out, as opposed to rearing, and, nearer to Aberdeen, the city's demand for milk and milk products is satisfied by numerous dairy farms.

Towns and Industries

With the exception of Aberdeen, the size of which merits separate treatment below, settlements in this region are small and confined to two types:

(1) inland centres of farming regions,
(2) fishing ports and harbours.

Inland Centres. Towns in this group, some of which serve as markets, include **Huntly** in Strathbogie, **Inverurie** in the Don basin, **Alford** in the Alford basin and **Turriff,** the regional centre of the fertile Deveron valley. Of these towns only **Inverurie,** which has railway workshops and flour and paper mills in addition to the traditional woollens of this part of Scotland, has more than 5000 people.

Fishing Ports and Harbours. Proximity to the North Sea fishing grounds, a profusion of natural havens and better land communications with the south compared with the west coast, have all been instrumental in causing this area to develop as the traditional centre of the Scottish fishing industry, with the inveterate rivals **Peterhead** (12,000) and **Fraserburgh** (10,000) as the largest towns. Concentration of activity in the smaller harbours is on herring fishing, but modern dual-purpose boats and equipment enable fishermen to take white-fish as well as the pelagic herring. Aberdeen is primarily the base of deep-sea trawlers fishing in distant waters, often inside the Arctic Circle. Fluctuations in the herring industry, which employs a large number of shore-based workers as well as the fishermen, have greatly affected the fortunes of the coastal settlements and now a decided slump

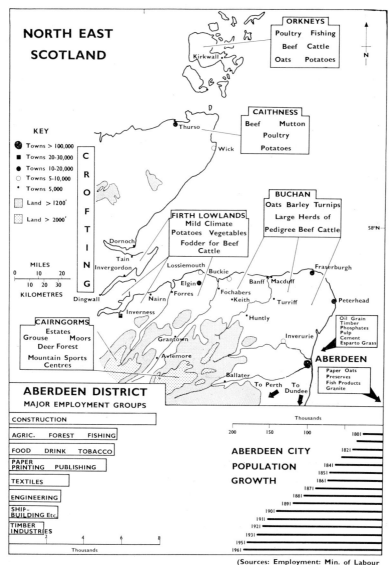

KEY

- Towns > 100,000
- Towns 20-30,000
- Towns 10-20,000
- ○ Towns 5-10,000
- Towns 5,000

Land > 1200'

Land > 2000'

NORTH EAST SCOTLAND

ORKNEYS
Poultry Fishing
Beef Cattle
Oats Potatoes

CAITHNESS
Beef Mutton
Poultry
Potatoes

BUCHAN
Oats Barley Turnips
Large Herds of
Pedigree Beef Cattle

FIRTH LOWLANDS
Mild Climate
Potatoes Vegetables
Fodder for Beef Cattle

CAIRNGORMS
Estates
Grouse Moors
Deer Forest
Mountain Sports Centres

Oil Grain
Timber
Phosphates
Pulp
Cement
Esparto Grass

ABERDEEN
Paper Oats
Preserves
Fish Products
Granite

ABERDEEN DISTRICT
MAJOR EMPLOYMENT GROUPS

- CONSTRUCTION
- AGRIC. FOREST FISHING
- FOOD DRINK TOBACCO
- PAPER PRINTING PUBLISHING
- TEXTILES
- ENGINEERING
- SHIP-BUILDING Etc.
- TIMBER INDUSTRIES

ABERDEEN CITY POPULATION GROWTH

(Sources: Employment: Min. of Labour
Popn: Registrar General)

FIG. 93.

has set in with, consequently, alarmingly high unemployment figures (Fig. 106). Considerable capital has been invested in the fleets themselves, as well as in the large canneries of Crosse & Blackwell at Peterhead, which is the biggest fish cannery in Britain, and Maconachie at Fraserburgh. Although both of these canneries process foodstuffs other than fish, the decline in quantity and quality of the herring shoals and the lessening of demand for herring at home, and in European countries now obtaining their own supplies, bode ill for the region by threatening the livelihood of several thousand people. Both Peterhead and Fraserburgh have subsidiary boat-building and repairing activities and, in addition, Peterhead is engaged in the manufacture of tweed cloth, of parts for giant Euclid earthmoving equipment, and the distilling of whisky and the making of twist-drills by a recently established American subsidiary firm.

Aberdeen (185,000)

Scotland's third largest city, Aberdeen, the commerical capital of northern Scotland, has more people than there are in the whole of the counties of Inverness-shire, Ross and Cromarty, Sutherland and Caithness combined. Situated at the mouth of the Dee, Aberdeen developed originally as two separate settlements on the Don and Dee, now fused by the construction of the modern granite-built city centred on the east–west Union Street. Because of its remoteness from industrial Scotland and the singular appearance of its granite buildings, Aberdeen shows a degree of individuality the parallel of which is difficult to find. Functioning as a port, market, holiday resort, university town, and legal, financial and industrial centre, Aberdeen fully merits its city status.

A forceful indication of the foresight of the industrial pioneers was the establishment of a first-class harbour and port which needed extensive initial dredging. More than 1 million tons of shipping now enters the port each year and special passenger services leave for Scandinavia, Iceland and the Orkneys and Shetlands, but a large part of the port facilities is devoted to handling the fish-hauls of the seine-net boats and large ocean-going trawlers. Aberdeen's position as Scotland's premier fishing port is emphasized by the city's research institutes where investigations are carried out on marine life and fish preservation methods.

Supplementing the actual fishing and wholesale marketing are fish-curing and canning, the production of fish-meal for animal foodstuffs, cod liver oil, paints, box-making, trawling gear and, most recently, the installa-tion of quick-freeze plants capable of supplying a range of quality fish products for distant markets. Although much of the boxed fish is transported by lorry to the southern industrial centres, the proximity of the extensive fish market to the main railway depot should not be overlooked as daily fish trains including *The Blue Spot Fish Train* leave Aberdeen with their perishable southbound cargoes.

Many of London's bank buildings and insurance offices are faced with polished granites hewn from the quarries at Rubislaw, as are many of the main buildings in Edinburgh and the "Granite City" itself. The streets of eighteenth-century London were not, as popularly believed, paved with gold, but had the more practical surfacing of granite "setts", or cobblestones! Almost entirely mechanized now, this distinctive pursuit lends individualism to Aberdeen's industrial character in supplying a wide market with varied forms of granite for use as monumental stone, crushed road metal and in the construction of shop and office frontages, bridges (e.g. foundations of the Forth, Tay and Tyne railway bridges), piers (e.g. Roker, Sunderland) and lighthouses (e.g. Roker and the Bell Rock).

Various other manufacturing and processing industries are located in the city and its immediate surroundings, although a considerable proportion of the working population is engaged in commerce and the professions. Such industries are shipbuilding (chiefly large ocean-going trawlers, coasters and small tankers), paper manufacture (Figs. 52, 94), the making of flax canvas hose for the nation's fire brigades and specialist engineering activities, including the manufacture of heavy quarry plant and mechanical bulk handling equipment.

Banffshire

This county of 46,000 people may be taken as typical of the development of the north-east corner of Scotland, referred to rather ruefully by farmers as "the cold shoulder of Scotland".

Agriculture. Arable land in Banff extends from sea level to about the 1000-ft contour, presenting a varied soil composition from medium loam to peat, clay and sand bases. Climatic conditions also vary from a fairly congenial coastal strip to the bleak, exposed southern flanks of the county where the higher ground is liable to severe frosts and heavy snowfalls. As a result of these diverse soil and climatic conditions, types of farming within the county show considerable differences. In coastal areas the emphasis is on crop growing and the fattening of beef cattle, whereas in upper Banff the breeding and rearing of sheep assumes importance with less intensive cropping and much use of the extensive areas of hill and rough grazing.

Although in recent years the acreage of wheat has increased slightly, oats and barley remain the principal crops with high yields being obtained in central and lower Banff, due to the use of mechanical manure spreaders and the employment of modern methods of seed treatment and chemical weed control. Important as the arable crops undoubtedly are, Banff's main claim

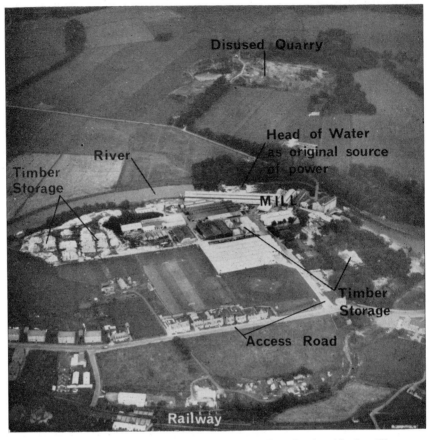

Fig. 94. Paper mill at Mugiemoss, near Aberdeen. Note the riverside site. (Photo: C. Davidson & Sons Ltd., Bucksburn.)

to fame lies in beef cattle, particularly Aberdeen–Angus, with the demand for store cattle in the feeding areas often exceeding the supply and dealers on occasion having recourse to bringing calves from England and Wales.

Industry. Banffshire industries can be grouped conveniently into two categories:

(1) those deriving their activities from the sea,
(2) those based on land resources.

The first group is naturally confined to the coastal belt and is almost entirely dependent upon the fortunes of the fishing fleets operating in varying strengths from the dozen coastal burghs and villages which house more than half the county's population. Raised beaches, especially at 25 and 50 ft, have had a direct influence on the siting of the rather austere fishing havens, each with its small bay or cove excavated by the sea, which line the coast. **Portessie** typifies this, having the lower, older part of the town clustered on the sheltered raised beach and the newer properties forming the "uptown", almost a separate community at a higher level in both "class" and elevation above the sea. **Buckie,** the largest town in Banff, reflects this dependence upon fishing with its seine-net fleet, white-fish market, modern boatbuilding yards, marine engineering, and fish curing and processing establishments. Similarly, **Macduff,** which has fifty fishing boats in its fleet, now benefits from improved harbour and handling facilities. The town of **Banff**, with its silted harbour, now functions as the county administrative centre, is largely residential and lacks the bustle and vigour of neighbouring Macduff.

The landward group of industries are distilling, textiles and limestone quarrying. With twenty active distilleries in the county no other county can boast as many within its boundaries. "Glenlivet" is now a synonym for the whisky first produced in the Banffshire glens, utilizing the plentiful supplies of peat, barley and water, where farmers and crofters engaged in illicit distilling for many years. Everybody made whisky, with over 200 illicit stills recorded in Glenlivet alone in 1824, and everybody drank it! A surplus was available, however, and, as in present times, no difficulty was encountered in disposing of it in the south. Nowadays, the bulk of the product goes south for blending, with practically all proprietary brands of "Scotch" containing a sizeable proportion of Banffshire whisky.

Keith, with abundant supplies of water suitable for the dying of delicate colours, is renowned for woollen fabrics. Two narrow bands of limestone, running in a north-east to south-west direction, have been used for over 200 years for the production of agricultural lime. Five main quarrying–grinding plants at Keith, Boyndie, Grange, Drummuir and Dufftown produce over 250,000 tons each year, much of which is in evidence on the fields of northern Scotland.

Banffshire, with a decline in population of 8 per cent between 1951 and 1961, reflects the acute problem of depletion of population resources in the Highland counties, a problem shared by all the counties of the north-east with the exception of Moray, which shows an increase of 2 per cent between 1951 and 1961, due to the influx of families of servicemen stationed at Kinloss and Lossiemouth.

THE FIRTH LOWLANDS

Extending from the mouth of the Spey to Dornoch and interrupted by three narrow arms of the sea in the form of the Beauly, Cromarty and Dornoch Firths, the character of this lowland is markedly different from the shorelands east of Buckie, due to structural and climatic causes. To preserve continuity it is better to consider firstly the Moray–Nairn and Inverness region separately from the lowlands of Easter Ross.

Moray–Nairn and the Inverness Lowlands

Here, in place of the resistant metamorphic rocks of Banffshire, are softer sedimentaries of Old and New Red Sandstone age, thickly masked by boulder clay. Between the basins of the Findhorn and Nairn rivers, large morainic dumps enclose patches of ill-drained, peaty land and, etched into the coast, the pronounced 25-ft raised beach forms a butt of flat land varying in width from 200 yd to $3\frac{1}{2}$ miles and succeeded inland by 50- and 100-ft levels. West of the mouth of the Findhorn, the sand dune wasteland of the Culbin Sands has been successfully afforested with Corsican Pine and the late-seventeenth-century encroachments onto arable land have been completely arrested, although on windy days a film of fine sand can often be seen on exposed coastal roads.

Climate. Warmer, drier and generally more pleasant conditions which obtain in Moray–Nairn, as opposed to the bleak and boisterous "cold shoulder" of Buchan, might conceivably be explained by the idea of a föhn effect in this region, which enjoys an average rainfall of 25–27 in. A large element of the wind force must cross appreciable highland barriers, including the most extensive area over 3500 ft in Britain, before reaching this district. Some considerable warming effect takes place as winds from the south-west have to descend from the 4000-ft Cairngorms to sea level in the space of 30 miles. Such an abrupt descent does not take place over the more continuous Buchan platform which, being exposed to the North Sea on two sides, is likely to have any heating effect neutralized.

Farming. Farming is typically of the east coast pattern with arable production largely destined for stock feeding. Small quantities of wheat, potatoes and vegetables are grown but the piegram of Elgin Parish (Fig. 96) taken as typical of this region clearly indicates that the bulk of farm production is

AVERAGE YIELDS PER ACRE OVER A 10-YEAR PERIOD

	Oats	Barley	Wheat	Potatoes	Turnips/swedes
		(cwt/acre)			(tons/acre)
Scotland	16·5	20·2	22·1	7·2	17·1
Moray	17·2	19·9	25·0	6·3	20·3
Angus	20·6	20·4	21·2	7·4	19·5
East Lothian	22·1	22·6	23·8	9·1	20·1

Fig. 95. Twin fishing ports on the Banffshire coast. (Photo: Air Ministry. Crown Copyright Reserved.)

FIRTH LOWLANDS

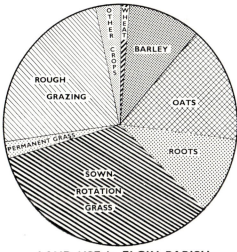

LAND USE in ELGIN PARISH

Fig. 96.

167

geared towards the feeding of livestock. It is not commonly realized that the Moray Firth lowlands are a highly productive agricultural region. Regional comparisons from the table on p. 166 indicate that this region obtains above-average yields per acre in oats, wheat and turnips, although it must be borne in mind that total production will not approach that of either Angus or East Lothian, both of which are intensively farmed counties.

Forestry. A striking feature of the landscape of Moray–Nairn is the high proportion of woodland and it does not come as a surprise to note that, with 22 per cent of its area under forest, Moray has the highest percentage in Britain, with Nairn a close second at 19 per cent. This is of special significance when one considers 6 per cent as the national average for Scotland. Conifers predominate with Scots Pine, Sitka Spruce and Norway Spruce being supplemented by European Larch and, of course, the Corscian Pines of Culbin.

Industries and Settlements. As well as farming, forestry and fishing, which is centred largely on Lossiemouth, distilling is important, with Speyside showing the main concentration of this activity. Specialized woollens are produced in Elgin and a preserve works at Fochabers produces high-quality canned food-stuffs ranging from Scotch broth to canned whole grouse with sales in over seventy countries.

East of Inverness the largest towns are **Lossiemouth** (6000) and **Elgin** (12,000). Whilst Lossiemouth is a major fishing port and the home of a large naval air base, Elgin with its cathedral city status, ornate flower gardens and respectable, "solid" architecture has a distinctly non-Highland appearance and serves as a desirable residential area for retired people. Industries of the town take the form of small concerns discreetly tucked away from the central thoroughfare and comprise two woollen mills, three grain mills, an aerated water works, a cod liver oil factory and an egg packing station. The specialized woollen industry is noteworthy and includes the production of luxury clothing from cashmere and vicuna wools. A rare fibre from Peru, vicuna, is often termed the mink of the woollen industry and a vicuna coat for a lady could cost £300. **Nairn** is primarily a small holiday resort and **Forres** a small residential town.

Inverness (30,000). Approaching Inverness from the south there is a sudden drop from relatively high land to the open expanses of the Moray Firth and the bottleneck situation of the Highland capital lying athwart four routes becomes apparent. Of the routes, the major one to the south, via Aviemore and upper Strathspey, presented initial difficulties in the breaching of the watershed between the Ness and the Spey.

Sited at an early fording point on the Ness river (now bridged by road and rail) on morainic ridges and fragments of the raised beaches common to these lowlands, historical records reveal port activities at Inverness trading with the Baltic and Mediterranean countries in skins, hides and wool. The limited productivity of the hinterland, little use of the Caledonian Canal and increasing size of vessels have, however, restricted its modern functions to those of market and tourist centre. Industrial activities in Inverness are confined to the production of specialized woollens, whisky and automatic electric-welding machines for use in the automobile, shipbuilding and steel industries. To the north of the town, on the delta flats known as the Longman, some progress has been made in developing a light industrial estate accessible to the harbour but inducements hardly seem sufficient to establish industry on a large scale. Although well linked by road, rail and air, Inverness is 115 miles from Perth and 170 miles from Glasgow and therefore it suffers by being remote from the main markets.

Easter Ross and the Dornoch Firth Region

Although less extensive than in Moray–Nairn these drift-covered lowlands have similar geological and climatic characteristics: foundations of Old Red Sandstones, low rainfall and appreciable warmth for such a northerly latitude. Consequently, the agricultural response is similar to that of the lowlands south of the Moray Firth.

Farming. Farming in Easter Ross may be summarized in the following way:

(1) Large 200–300-acre arable farms producing rotation grass, oats and turnips all for cattle feeding, in addition to barley for distilleries (e.g. Tain), wheat in selected, favourable, sheltered areas below 100 ft and, occasionally, seed potatoes on sandier soils. These farms are mainly located on the productive soils of the Black Isle and carry large herds of Aberdeen–Angus–Shorthorn cross beef cattle, which are often marketed at Tain or Dingwall when about 2 years old.

(2) Dairy farms occur in small numbers, generally in proximity to the small burghs Tain, Invergordon and Dingwall.

(3) Small farms on the poorer marginal lands working arable with mixed cattle and sheep, with the latter increasing in proportion with altitude.

(4) Crofting (see Chapter 14).

(5) Hill sheep farming in the higher, central parts towards Wester Ross and Sutherland.

Two interesting recent developments have emerged in the farming of the Dornoch Firth region:

(1) An expanding market in Caithness, caused by the Atomic Energy Authority scheme at Dounreay, has stimulated an increase in beef and mutton production as well as in potatoes.

Fig. 97. Dounreay Experimental Reactor Establishment. (Photo: U.K. Atomic Energy
Authority.)

(2) Coastal farms are now so heavily stocked with fattening cattle and
    sheep that hill sheep farmers seeking good-quality winter grazings
    now have to winter their flocks in Morayshire.

Settlements. **Dingwall,** with just under 4000 people, is the largest settlement of this region, functioning as the county administrative centre for
sparsely populated Ross-shire. A large creamery, agricultural engineering
and livestock auction markets comprise its main activities and a site on
the west side has been made available for industrial development.

Tain, on the shallow Dornoch Firth, is a decayed port long since blocked
by progressive silting.

Invergordon, on the Cromarty Firth, now developing as a holiday resort,
has a naval base establishment with a deep-water harbour and more than
forty large oil storage tanks for refuelling. The presence of this deep-water
anchorage was one of the critical factors in selecting the Invergordon–
Alness area as the most suitable site for the projected Alcan aluminium
smelter with its attendant power station.

Strathpeffer, 5 miles to the west of Dingwall and situated in the deep, sheltered trough of a thickly wooded glaciated valley, has mineral springs and has long been a favoured holiday resort for elderly people.

Dornoch, at the seaward extremity of the firth of that name, is the county town and only burgh of Sutherland and it relies largely on summer visitors who double the population of 933!

In an area which has suffered considerably from a decline in population the only present industries of note are oatmeal milling, chiefly at Dingwall, traditional Highland weaving in several centres and whisky distilling at Alness and in the Black Isle. All of these industries reflect a total dependence on agricultural products but the Alcan project on the shores of the Cromarty Firth is indicative of, at long last, a move towards a balanced industrial development, which would halt the decline in population and arrest the drift away from this area. The Alcan development should herald a rapid rise in population as, apart from the construction workers, over 1000 workers, mostly men, will be needed in the plant when it becomes operational. Scenically most attractive and climatically mild for the latitude, the Cromarty–Moray Firth region would be a pleasant area in which to live, provided there was also some provision of ancillary industries to absorb the female labour which would become available on the Alcan development.

THE CAITHNESS LOWLANDS

Northern Caithness, largely a low plateau of sandstones (Caithness flagstones) and conglomerates, masked by deposits of boulder clay, presents the most suitable expanse of land for farming and settlement in the northernmost extend of the mainland of Britain. Much of the landscape is flat and treeless and the settlement pattern is one of small farms and dispersed crofts on the poorer soils and coastal edges. A short growing season is inimical to intensive arable farming and cultivation is mainly confined to oats, barley and potatoes. More emphasis is laid on the fattening of Cheviot sheep than on cattle as in the south. Poultry and dairy farming show an increase in recent years, stimulated by the demands of the families of atomic workers recently settled in the Thurso district.

Settlements. Over half of the population of Caithness (30,000) is contained within the two burghs of Wick and Thurso.

Wick (7000). The county town Wick owes its importance largely to fishing and fish processing, although it has now been surpassed in size by neighbouring Thurso. Amongst its industries are the making of components for a small tractor suited to croft work, an ice factory which often supplies Polish and Russian trawler fleets, textiles including hosiery and blankets, and a relatively new enterprise, the production of high-quality blown glassware. Possessing a harbour capable of accommodating vessels of up to 3000 tons, Wick is, at present, linked to the south by road, rail and air. The airport, however, is not greatly used and the railway is scheduled for closure under the Beeching Plan.

Thurso (9000). At the mouth of the river of the same name, Thurso suffered from competition from Wick until the establishment of the Dounreay experimental atomic centre (Fig. 97), 10 miles to the west of the town. Containing the first fast reactor in the world to generate electricity, this £25 million plant gives employment to 4500 workers, large numbers of whom are engaged upon the scientific research activities of the establishment. In 1951 the population of Thurso was 3200 and by 1963 it had virtually trebled to become the largest town north of Inverness—a healthy reversal of the usual downwards trend of population in the Highlands. New life has been injected into this formerly remote backwater of Britain with a happy fusion of the Thursonians and the incomers, known locally as "The Atomics", to the extent of a large representation of Dounreay people on the town council and a galvanizing of social and community life. Much more of this is needed in the ailing, ageing Highlands.

THE ORKNEYS

Linked by a daily ferry service from Scrabster on Thurso Bay, only 6 miles of the rough Pentland Firth at its narrowest extent separate the Orkneys from the mainland of Scotland. Composed largely of Old Red Sandstone (cf. Caithness) and engaging mainly in beef, sheep and poultry production, the Orkneys have closer affinities to the eastern lowlands of northern Scotland rather than to the Hebrides and Shetlands with which they are all too often treated.

Lying in the track of deep depressions and therefore much battered by gales and heavy seas, treeless Orkney exemplifies some of the finest marine erosional features in Britain, e.g. the Old Man of Hoy, a stack of Old Red Sandstone rising 450 ft above a lava platform base. Although having generally milder winters than the eastern parts of northern Scotland, the July isotherm of 12° C (54° F) is hardly conducive to attracting large numbers of summer visitors.

Economy

The economic basis of the county rests on arable farming, principally for stock rearing and fattening, with fifteen times as many beef cattle and twice as many dairy cattle as are carried on the Shetlands. An independently progressive and hardworking community, the Orcadians shatter the popular misconception of scattered hamlets along windswept shores gleaning a

Fig. 98. The erosive power of the sea on the northernmost coast of the mainland of Britain. These sandstone cliffs facing the rough Pentland Firth receive an incessant battering. (Photo: H.M. Geol. Survey. Crown Copyright Reserved.)

meagre existence from the barren soil or harsh sea. With the emphasis on beef cattle, the most important crops are oats and turnips for fodder and the enterprising farmers, who operate small, family holdings (80 per cent of the farms are less than 50 acres) often highly mechanized, are constantly working to reclaim heath and "machair" land.

Consideration of climatic and economic handicaps, especially remoteness from markets and high freight charges, evokes nothing but admiration for results achieved by Orcadian farmers.

Kirkwall, the county capital and largest town, does not itself exceed 5000, and with its large creamery for milk, milk powder, Orkney farm cheese, butter and frozen cream, small tweed mill, distillery, kipper factory and egg-packing stations, reflects the complete dependence of Orcadian industry upon sea and farm produce.

Population

Although declining at an alarming rate, the Orkneys are actually still more densely peopled than Nairn County. Of the twenty-one inhabited islands occupying 350 square miles, two-thirds of the population is on Mainland. The island of Hoy could be taken as an alarm note. Scapa Flow, the area around Lyness, was an operational centre for 20,000 servicemen during two world wars with obvious stimulus to the island's economy and, since the Royal Navy closed the base in 1951, the "native" population has plummeted from 1275 to 570 in 1962 and is still falling. So aged is the population now that Hoy school has been converted into a youth hostel to encourage young people to at least visit the island! The progressive nature of farming, too, with introduction of much mechanization and a consequent reduction in hired labour, only serves to aggravate the problem in an area completely devoid of light industry.

CHAPTER 14

The Crofting Counties

COLLECTIVELY known as the Crofting Counties for the purposes of the Crofters' Commission Advisory Panel, the crofters themselves constitute approximately half of the population of the counties of Argyll, Inverness, Ross and Cromarty, Sutherland, Caithness, the Orkneys and Zetland (Shetland Islands). The more productive parts of these counties, almost wholly on the sheltered eastern side, have already been considered and consequently the main treatment in this chapter must be related largely to the activities of the crofting communities of favoured coastal and valley areas on the mainland and on the Hebridean and Shetland Islands.

PHYSICAL BACKGROUND

North-west of the Great Glen, which separates the bulk of the crofting counties from the higher plateau surfaces of the central Highlands, the landscape is one of continual variation due to changes in rock structure. The upstanding quartzite caps of the Paps of Jura and the butte-like formations in Wester Ross offer sharp contrast to the smooth, mammillated Lewisian gneiss surfaces of the Outer Hebrides. Still further differences can be attributed to the far-reaching effects of mountain glaciation, with perhaps the most striking being the number and form of the fiords which disrupt the whole of the western coast. Moraine-dammed lochans, huge ice-smoothed bosses of rock, peat-filled hollows and a pathetically thin soil covering on the few patches of flat land provide scant basis for economic agriculture. As can be seen from Fig. 4, the watershed lies very close to the west coast and any westwards-moving glacier must have exercised maximum effect on its relatively short passage to the sea, gouging out great, deep valleys to be subsequently filled with water as inland ribbon lakes like Loch Shiel, or drowned by marine incursions to form long, narrow and often steep-sided sea lochs, or fiords, like Loch Etive.

CROFTING

The Crofters' Act of 1886 defined a crofter as "a small tenant who finds in the cultivation and produce of his croft a material portion of his earnings and sustenance". This stark definition, together with the remoteness and isolation of this area from the rest of Britain, are contributory factors to the popular misconception that the crofter is little more than a backward peasant living in a crude, low hut with a hole in the sod roof to let the peat smoke escape. Although self-sufficiency is higher here than in other farming communities, the subsistence element associated with peasant life has all but disappeared. Derived from the division of farmland in the eighteenth and nineteenth centuries, crofts are small-holdings 5–10 acres in size on which the tenant has complete security of tenure, a social necessity brought about by the wholesale evictions prevalent before. Crofts may be entirely separate and isolated, but more often are grouped together in "crofting townships" (hamlets) wherein the crofters share "souming" (grazing rights) on common pastures. Joint land ownership used to prevail and this was a fundamental reason for the grouping together, but combined efforts are still made in the cutting and carrying of peat, harvesting, boatbuilding and fishing.

Cultivable land in the crofting region is restricted to alluvial deltas on loch shores (Fig. 99), raised beaches or "machair" (sandy stretches) and peat-skimmed tracts. Poverty of soil and, in many areas, a raw climate inhibit crop growing and influence a basically pastoral economy with arable patches near to the croft cottage (Fig. 100). Where possible, oats, potatoes and turnips are grown, normally on a 2–4-year rotation basis, with the additional odd hay patch for winter feed. The low standard of animal husbandry is clear from the small amount of rotation grass and turnips, reflecting a low standard of living for the crofters themselves and rendering necessary a supplementary income through fishing, weaving, working on road maintenance or, more latterly in the more accessible areas, letting part of the croft to holiday visitors. Regional differences do occur and it is advisable to consider the crofting counties under separate headings.

ACTIVITIES ON THE MAINLAND
(WESTER ROSS, SUTHERLAND, PARTS OF
CAITHNESS AND INVERNESS)

A deeply indented western coastline, which makes journeys from peninsula to peninsula tedious detours, together with adverse soil conditions, helps to account for the north-western seaboard being one of the least populous parts of Britain and the degree of isolation and remoteness is clearly reflected in the widely dispersed settlement pattern.

In the extreme north-west, the Cape Wrath area, desolation is the picture with scarcely any habitation at all, and over much of Sutherland can be seen numerous abandoned crofts supporting only the census returns which clearly show that there must have been more people in the Highlands and Islands

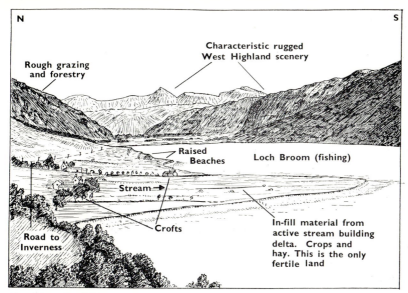

Characteristic rugged
West Highland scenery

Rough grazing
and forestry

Raised
Beaches

Loch Broom (fishing)

Stream →

Crofts

In-fill material from
active stream building
delta. Crops and
hay. This is the only
fertile land

Road to
Inverness

FIG. 99. Lake delta formation on the north shore of Loch Broom, near Ullapool
(Wester Ross).

Hummocky Lewisian Gneiss (Ice-Smoothed)

Rough
Grazings

Cultivation

Hay for animal
winter feed

Arable Patch

Peat Stack

Access
to Sea
(fishing)

Potato Clamp
(storage)

Thatch
weighted w/rocks
(high winds)

Peat
Stack

FIG. 100. Small crofting township of Garinin on the west coast of Lewis. Note weighted
thatches of the cottages, use of local stone for building, and tiny arable patches. (Photo:
J. L. Rodger, Stornoway.)

177

when Dr. Johnson journeyed there in the late eighteenth century than there are now. Beauty of landscape here cannot be surpassed anywhere in Britain, but this is small compensation for a dying population, as the only young children one sees belong largely to the holiday-making fraternity. Deaths exceed births in most parishes and in fact in some crofting townships no child has been born for 40 years. Many of the old people remaining are unable to cope with the upkeep of the croft in attending to drainage, wall repairs and the husbanding of stock and, consequently, the pattern emergent is one of senile decay in both man and holding. The ageing population, low density and absence of young people really means that there are insufficient people

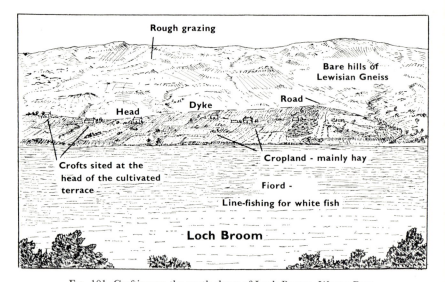

Fig. 101. Crofting on the south shore of Loch Broom, Wester Ross.

to fulfil even a rural economy, and in many areas this generation is the last one.

Ullapool, on the north shore of Loch Broom, with direct road links to Inverness and Kyle of Lochalsh, is less remote and in the past few years it has seen the development of a considerable tourist trade to supplement the traditional crofting and fishing activities. Indeed, in the summer of 1962, it was noticeable that, as well as two large caravan sites, a rash of bed and breakfast establishments had appeared, catering largely for transitory people from central Scotland and England. Ullapool itself is sited on a very fine raised beach, with a southerly aspect, and during the herring season the little harbour is a hive of activity (Fig. 16). Farming on Broomside is restricted by slope, humidity and general sterility of the soil to strips at right angles to the shore of the loch (Fig. 101), extending from upper terraces, on which the crofts are built, upwards on to rough grazing land and seawards on to arable patches, through which the crofter has access to his boat. This is used to supplement his income by line fishing for whiting and haddock, caught near the sea floor, 100 ft below the surface of the loch. The few children of secondary school age have to board out at Dingwall, 40 miles away, for five nights a week and during severe winters, when roads are impassable inland and eastwards, they may not be home for several weeks. Winters on the west coast, open to the mild air stream of the Atlantic, but at the same time well protected by the headland of the highly indented coastline, are never severe and summers tend to be muggy and warm for the latitude.

South of Loch Torridon, the Applecross peninsula, being near to the main arteries of communication from Kyle to Inverness, shows a more favourable degree of development on better soils, but here, as in the north and in Sutherland, a county which has no more people than there are in the small border town of Galashiels, derelict and abandoned crofts dot the landscape. The highly indented coast, a preponderance of mountain and moorland and a heavy rainfall, often over 60 in., with consequent leaching of the soils, present insuperable difficulties for progressive farming and it is only in the eastwards-opening glens (e.g. Glen Moriston and Strath Glass) that broad stretches of alluvium permit arable farming and make ploughing possible up to 800 ft.

Kyle of Lochalsh, the steamer port for the Outer and Inner Hebrides, has, together with Mallaig 20 miles to the south, channelled all the former fishing activities of Kishorn, Toscaig and Plockton, due to better handling facilities and a direct rail link with Inverness (Mallaig is linked by rail to Glasgow). During the summer season the Kyle ferry service is overworked with motorists bent on enjoying the scenic splendour of the Cuillins of Skye.

Wester Ross, although not yet as popular as Skye with summer tourists, is a region of commanding beauty with enchanting glens, long beaches of silver sand, often practically deserted, and excellent fishing in the numerous lochs and rivers. Careful negotiation of steep, but normally well-surfaced mountain roads, so narrow that even small cars have to pull into a lay-by to permit passing (Fig. 102), may often be rewarded by a sunset of riotous colour shedding a reflected glow on the plum-coloured Torridonian Sandstone.

Apart from further expansion of the holiday industry in Wester Ross, and, for that matter, over much of the rest of the crofting counties, afforestation and hydro-electricity appear to offer the only other avenues of development. The Forestry Commission already has extensive properties east of Loch Broom and in Strath Oykell and further expansion is anticipated. Utilizing the heavy rainfall on the hills of north-west Scotland, the North of Scotland Hydro-electric Board has already seven major schemes in operation and,

T.F.S.—G

Fig. 102. The main and only road from Ullapool to Inverness. The small lay-by is really a loop to enable vehicles to pass.

in fact, almost the whole of the west side of the Great Glen has been developed for hydro-electric generation (Fig. 17).

THE INNER HEBRIDES

Generally thinly masked with glacial deposits from the mainland, this group of scantily populated islands extends from Islay in the south of Skye and includes Tiree, Coll, Jura, Colonsay and Mull. Here again the landscape reflects structural differences from the well-worn gneisses of Tiree and Coll to the resistant quartzites of Jura, massive Torridonian Sandstone of Islay and unique dyke formations radiating from the former volcanic centres on Mull.

Of the largest islands in the group only Islay and Skye have a population in excess of 5000 and, in fact, Lewis in the Outer Hebrides, despite its greater isolation, has more people than all of the Inner Hebrides put together. Apart from Skye marble and diatomite, Mull granites and the occasionally worked Jurassic ironstones of Raasay, the Inner Hebrides depend almost wholly upon agriculture. About 5 per cent of the total area is under crops and grass with the remaining usable land as rough grazing or, as on Skye, Mull and Jura, in deer forest. The lime-rich, sandy deposits of Tiree have resulted in its becoming the most progressively farmed island in the group, with a specialized cultivation of tomatoes and bulbs. Whisky distilling is the only industry of real note and is concentrated upon Islay, but even this depends on barley grown outside the area. In the summer of 1964, the introduction of the new car ferry services from Oban to Craignure on Mull, and Mallaig to Armadale on Skye, has given an added stimulus to the tourist industry which has basic attractions in the unrivalled scenery of Skye and in pilgrimages to Iona, the little islet off the coast of Mull, where St. Columba landed from Ireland in A.D. 563.

THE OUTER HEBRIDES

This archipelago forms a 130-mile-long barrier of islands between the north-west coast of Scotland and the Atlantic Ocean. Predominantly subdued in relief, due largely to extensive ice erosion, the land rises above 2000 ft only in the northern part of Harris and the general appearance is one of interrupted ridges on the east of the chain of islets, overlooking a hummocky plateau surface in the west. Huge slabs of bare rock, worn smooth by glaciation and the elements, alternate with boggy peat hollows and innumerable lochans in a virtually treeless landscape and, only where there is a thickening of glacial drift, as in the north of Lewis, or an expanse of "machair", as in South Uist, is there continuous cultivation. The climate is rigorous rather than harsh, with gale incidence a feature and rain expected on two days out of three. Although the latitude compares with Port Churchill on Hudson Bay and northern Labrador, the ameliorating influences of the Atlantic and the south-westerly winds are most pronounced, with a long frost-free period, remarkably little snowfall compared with the mainland, and relatively high winter temperatures. Stornoway enjoys a mean January temperature of 6° C (43° F) compared with 3° C (38° F) at Cambridge, several hundred miles further south.

Crofting is at its peak in the Outer Hebrides, with over 6000 crofts and a mere dozen farms. Due to the inhospitable peat-ridden interior, settlements are all close to the sea, where at least some supplementation of income is possible by fishing. North Uist, which may be taken as typical, has 35 crofting townships varying in size from 3 to 34 crofts, with an average acreage of 12 per croft. As well as access to the coast and a range of best land deteriorating to poor peaty soils, each croft has grazing rights on the township's common pastures.

Crossed Highland and Shorthorn cattle and the hardy Blackface sheep are reared on pastures which are inadequate to support winter grazing and, therefore, the bulk of the arable land is under fodder crops, chiefly oats. Potatoes and vegetables for own consumption are grown on a patch near to the croft and fuel is obtained from peat cuttings, due to the high freight charges for coal. Most crofters sell two or three animals each year but the buyers, in the knowledge that they must meet the transport costs to the mainland and that the crofters have to sell, keep prices low. Consequently, with an average income of £82 on these transactions, the crofter seeks income supplementation by lobster fishing and weaving. Cattle, sheep and wool are the chief products of the Hebrides and although some cattle are kept for milk supply, import of milk from the mainland is still necessary. Sheep are reared in large numbers, but with a high lambing mortality rate, due largely to overgrazing and disease, few sheep are sold, emphasizing the uneconomic working of the crofts, which return a very low average income figure.

Two fairly recent developments of interest have been the progressive introduction of re-seeding of grasslands, which has increased the cattle units per acre, and the use of artificial insemination. Four miles from Renfrew Airport, near Glasgow, is the Southbar Artificial Insemination Centre where samples from Shorthorn, Aberdeen–Angus and Ayrshire animals are sealed in containers to be flown in less than 2 hours to Stornoway. Delivery to the scattered crofting townships may then entail a journey of 100 miles by road but with resultant improvement in stocks it is considered more than worth while.

Remoteness, isolation and poverty of natural resources inhibit industrial development and consequently there is only one town in the Outer Hebrides with over 5000 people, **Stornoway.** Outwith this, the only burgh, the industries are confined to weaving of Harris tweed and seaweed collection for processing into gelatine and tomato fertilizer at Lochmaddy in North Uist.

Harris tweed, surprisingly, is produced in greater quantities in Lewis than in Harris and this is largely due to Stornoway's influence, for here the wool is spun in the mills and supplied to the crofters who undertake the weaving process. The world-famous orb stamp on genuine Harris tweed garments is a guarantee of high quality, but at the same time it must be noted that the product suffers from a $66\frac{2}{3}$ per cent purchase tax imposition which does little to encourage further development.

As the kelp-making (burning of seaweed for the soap and chemical industries) has now died out, the only other industry of note is fishing, with a concentration of activity in Stornoway and on Barra, and it is a sad reflection that in Stornoway harbour Norwegian and Dutch vessels often outnumber Scottish fishing boats.

Linked by air to Glasgow and $4\frac{1}{4}$ hours by sea on the daily steamer service to Kyle of Lochalsh, **Stornoway,** with 5221 people, contains 25 per cent of the population of Lewis and is tending to increase at the expense of the rural areas. Plummeting of the fortunes of the fishing industry is reflected in the

27 per cent unemployment rate, despite the fact that many Lewis men serve in the Merchant Navy and many girls have left to work on the mainland. With this in mind, the significance of the tweed industry, employing nearly 1000 in the Stornoway mills and even more weavers in the crofts, becomes apparent. Should this industry suffer a recession, the repercussion would be destitution and mass emigration. High hopes are held of a boost to the little-developed holiday/tourist activities with the introduction of the car ferry services from Mallaig to Tarbert, only 30 miles by road to Stornoway.

THE SHETLAND ISLANDS (ZETLAND)

Lying north of 60° N and actually nearer to Bergen in Norway than to Aberdeen, their main sea link with the mainland, the Shetlands, with an area similar to Fife, comprise over 100 islands and islets, 18 of which are inhabited and support a population of under 18,000. Isolation from the mainland and relative proximity to Norway has produced a long history of Norse colonization and culture, some of which is still preserved in traditional Shetland activities, and some shown by the recent Sumburgh excavations where, on the edge of the present-day airfield, an archaeological maze of low turfed walls and paving slabs indicates a former Viking stronghold. This northerly isolation has restricted human activities by heavy freight costs and exposure to the full fury of the inclement North Atlantic with its high incidence of gales. Physically, the islands are composed largely of ice-moulded igneous and metamorphic rocks similar to those of the Highlands and Hebrides and quite different from the sandstone of the Orkneys, and for this reason and consequent differences in the economy the Shetland Islands should never really be considered as an adjunct to the Orkneys.

Fishing, farming, woollens and tourism are Zetland's assets awaiting exploitation to the full. Unable to face competition from heavily capitalized ports and fleets in the south and from foreign vessels, the Zetland fishing industry is living in precarious times. At the same time it should be noted that fishermen operating from Scalloway, Lerwick, Whalsay and Burra are only exceeded by crofters as a work force. The basic problem concerns the cost of transport to distant markets and much of the catch goes into the quick-freeze plant, or is converted into fish-oil and meal at Bressay. Distant water vessels have to pass Shetland, therefore a fish processing factory there would save time, provided the transport problem to urban markets could be overcome, as within 100 miles radius of Shetland are some of the most productive North Sea fishing grounds.

Acid soils, a low July average temperature, 11° C (52° F), and frequent, strong, salt-laden gales restrict farming capabilities, confining the arable land to 4 per cent of the total area, with oats, hay and potatoes as the chief crops, although farming using modern electrical equipment has expanded on Mainland since the installation of the diesel power station at Lerwick. The outlying islands suffer most from transport difficulties and Fetlar, which has reasonable soil, worked long ago under less exacting economic conditions, could be taken as typical as it does not even possess a pier suitable for the island steamer to use. In 1881, 431 people were living on Fetlar, growing enough food for themselves with a surplus to market in Yell. Now, with most of the land given over to sheep, less than 200 people have to import basic farm produce in order to live—the price of modern economic progress! Uneconomic crofting is the primary reason for the slump in Shetland farming, with two-thirds of the 3000 crofts less than 5 acres in size and too much land allocated to sheep. At one time there were three sheep to every cow; now the ratio is nearer 30 : 1 and costly imports of beef and dairy produce must be made. There is little room for the crofter–fisherman, or the crofter–road-man, if agriculture is to be put on a sound basis in Zetland, with the merging of crofts, improvement of pastures and absorption of some of the better hill grazings, by progressive reclamation and re-seeding.

Members of the successful Everest expedition could testify towards the warmth and quality of Shetland Isle woollens, and although machines, sent out from centralized premises, are widely used for knitwear throughout the islands, as a direct inheritance of traditional hand-knitting in the crofts, the industry has not yet been centralized as a hosiery–knitwear mill industry. All the wool is spun in mills outwith Zetland, to be subsequently returned, and the case for a Government-sponsored woollen mill in Lerwick costing about £100,000 would appear to have strong economic and social grounds.

In addition to improving the overall economic functions of the islands a radical improvement in transport facilities, using up-to-date car ferries, large helicopters or even hovercraft, woulds timulate the tourist industry, very much in its infancy at present. For jaded city-dwellers, the prospects of a quiet holiday amongst hospitable people in clean, invigorating air not polluted with diesel fumes and affected by traffic din should be sufficiently attractive to bring them to this, our most northerly outpost, and tempt them to take a chance on reasonable weather which, for that matter, one does in any part of Britain during the holiday season. On this basis the holiday industry would have more to contribute to island revenue than a dwindling fishing industry is likely to do.

SUMMARY ON THE AILING ECONOMY OF
THE CROFTING COUNTIES

Two critical interacting factors emerge as basic causes of the present malaise in the Highlands and Islands of Scotland:

(1) the decay of the crofter's way of life,
(2) the alarming decline in population and top-heavy pyramids of population (Fig. 21)—the legacy of the unrelenting drift of young people in search of work.

To these must be added the "bursting of the herring bubble" and the slump in the white-fish industry in face of severe competition from highly organized and capitalized concerns, often foreign based, with consequent repercussions on (1) and (2) above.

Nowhere is the fact clearer than in Zetland, that the crofter was once virtually self-sufficient, relying upon his own resource to produce oats for oatmeal, eggs, meat, dairy produce and fish. Saleable items, like cattle and spun and woven wool, provided the wherewithal for extra purchases although the crofter's needs were simple and few. With a deal of sweat and toil, peat was, and still is, obtainable as a fuel, and life's work followed a distinct cycle, making the fullest use of traditional skills, with the harvest, peat-cutting and stacking and herring fishing as seasonal highlights.

Nowadays, the clearances could hardly be blamed for the continued decline in population which in the crofting counties is predominantly an ageing one. Those who have savoured city life, either in war service or on voyages as Merchant Seamen, are reluctant to gamble all on their inheritance, the croft, especially when they cannot be assured of sufficient arable land to support a family in the way they would wish. Similarly, opportunities for professional people, who may be islanders by birth and upbringing, in a decaying society are distinctly limited. Modern planning, in the Atomic Age, with the establishment of Dounreay (see Chapter 13) has shown some of the benefits of the introduction of "new" industries to these declining areas. During 1951–61, whilst the six other crofting counties lost 5 per cent of their population, Caithness returned an increase of 20 per cent and Thurso (Dounreay district) had, by 1963, trebled its 1951 population.

Recent investigations by Glasgow University Crofting Survey over a period of 4 years give valuable pointers to the alarmingly unhealthy state of the crofting society. In the four island districts of Barra, South Uist, Lewis and Skye the following figures emerge:

(1) Only 15 per cent of males of insurable age were **full-time** crofters.
(2) A further 14 per cent of males of insurable age were crofters with other regular employment, mostly in servic eoccupations (transport, etc.).
(3) A further 7 per cent were seasonally employed on roads, water schemes, etc., in addition to their croft work.
(4) 17 per cent had non-crofting occupations.

(5) 30 per cent were either seasonally or permanently employed outwith their own region. Significantly this permanent migration for work is least in South Uist where the crofts are more viable and greatest in Barra with poor crofting returns. Over 60 per cent of Barra men were employed outside the island, mostly as merchant seamen.

(6) Additionally large numbers of women seek employment outside the islands in domestic, hotel or nursing service.

This lack of employment and the difficulties of rendering the crofts into economic holdings are the main contributory factors in the twentieth-century depopulation of the crofting counties, accelerated by changing senses of values and the demands of modern living. It is interesting to note that in November 1968, the Crofters' Commission advocated changing the age-old crofting tenure into owner occupancy to enable crofters to develop their land for both agricultural and non-agricultural uses.

COUNTY POPULATIONS BY THOUSANDS

County	Census 1851	Census 1951	Census 1961	Change± 1951–61
Argyll	89	63	59	−4
Banff	54	50	46	−4
Caithness	39	23	27	+4
Inverness	96	85	83	−2
Moray	39	48	49	+1
Orkney	31	21	19	−2
Ross and Cromarty	83	61	58	−3
Sutherland	26	13·6	13·4	−0·2
Zetland	31	19	18	−1
(Perthshire)	139	128	127	−1

CHAPTER 15

Trends in Scottish Industrial Development

AGRICULTURAL problems, the expansion of hydro-electric power, foreign-based industry, forestry and tourism have all been dealt with in relevant foregoing chapters and it now remains to summarize trends in the development of Scottish industry, upon which the prosperity of the country really depends.

Although at present facing temporary problems, as traditional industries decline at a faster rate than the establishment of new growth, Scotland has undergone, since the last war, a fascinating industrial transformation. With a wide variety of modern industry and, as one of the few remaining areas of industrial Britain free from congestion and labour shortage, Scotland should play a key role in the future development of British industry.

In order to appreciate this change one must also know something of the past. The cornerstones of Scottish industry have been coal, iron and steel, shipbuilding and marine engineering, all of which industries are showing a decline nowadays. From the Scottish shipyards came half the British Navy and, of course, the Transatlantic "Cunarders". Industrial equipment produced by skilled Scottish craftsmen can be found all over the world. Founded on the demands of the nineteenth century, Scotland had a well-established range of industries. However, some of these industries were excessively expanded to meet the inflationary needs of two world wars, particularly heavy industries, and it was ruefully discovered, after World War II, that many shortcomings existed in the Scottish industrial structure. Three distinct gaps emerged:

(1) shortage of consumer goods production,
(2) shortage of science-based industries,
(3) too few industries using sheet steel or engaged in light engineering.

Engineering industries witnessed the greatest progressive changes in the immediate post-war years with firms producing aero-engines, typewriters, cash registers, clocks, watches, precision tools, refrigerators and earth-moving equipment. These new industries have not only created a large number of new jobs, with incoming American firms employing over 40,000 people alone, but they have also introduced a whole range of new techniques and skills. Research by the Scottish Council has revealed that, in 1966, recently established incoming firms engaged in manufacturing instruments, electronic equipment and business machines were producing £473 million worth of goods of which more than one-third was destined for export. American-based firms showed the greatest rate of progress and, in particular, 82 per cent of the business machine items were for the export market. From the table below it is clear that growth industries, once established, can progress rapidly in Scotland.

PERCENTAGE INCREASES IN EMPLOYMENT 1959–61

	Scotland	United Kingdom
Office machinery	32	21
Radio/electronics	47	11
Watches/clocks	30	10
Electrical machinery	13	7

The above figures do not represent merely initial growth from a small base but include the employment of over 40,000 workers in the four named sectors of industry.

With Government help a vital opportunity was created by the establishment of the steel strip mill at Ravenscraig, making it possible for the users of sheet steel to buy their material in Scotland. This facility attracted the two

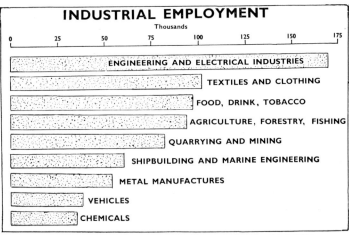

(Source: Scottish Digest of Statistics April 1963)

FIG. 103.

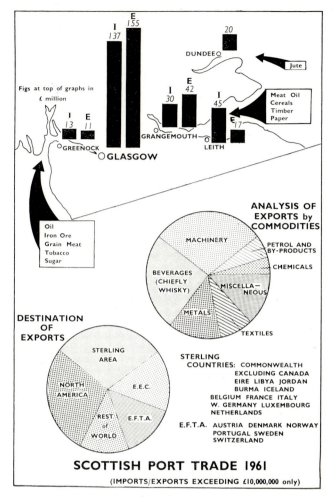

Figs at top of graphs in £ million

SCOTTISH PORT TRADE 1961

(IMPORTS/EXPORTS EXCEEDING £10,000,000 only)

FIG. 104.

large motor companies British Leyland and Chrysler/Rootes to establish factories at Bathgate for British Leyland lorries and at Linwood, 12 miles from Glasgow, where the whole production of the popular "Hillman Imp" takes place. It has been estimated that the combined output of these two plants, which now employ over 20,000 workers, will soon equal in value that of the shipbuilding and marine engineering industries, traditional bulwarks of Scottish industry.

Thus, significant industrial developments have taken place in Scotland in recent years. In particular, the recently established electronics and motor

Fig. 105. Rootes (Scotland) Ltd.—Linwood plant. Operators at their work stations on the main assembly line of "Hillman Imps"—note the special containers with component parts easily accessible. (Photo: Rootes Ltd.)

vehicle industries and the Alcan project at Invergordon, which will give rise to a nucleus of industrial population in an area well suited to such a development, indicate a refreshing note of optimism for the future. Within the Central Lowlands the rate of growth of the electronics industry is among the highest achieved by any industry in Britain. Already this new industrial activity employs half as much labour as does the traditional coal-mining pursuit of that region. Factors which have influenced the location of these investments have been: low land values, local authority co-operation, availability and adaptability of the labour force and further expansion possibilities.

With the above facts in mind it is not unreasonable to ask why more industry has not been attracted to Scotland without constant appeals for Government support. The answer lies largely in the magnet of the Midlands and the South-east, with mass markets, easy communications, head offices and a general focus of industrial and commercial activity, allied to a crass ignorance in the South of opportunities and amenities which can be provided in Scotland.

Against this growth, which is effecting changes not only in the character but also in the distribution of industries, with less concentration on Clydeside

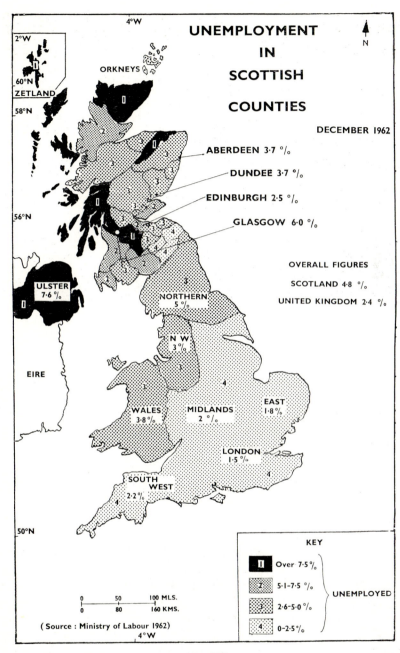

FIG. 106.

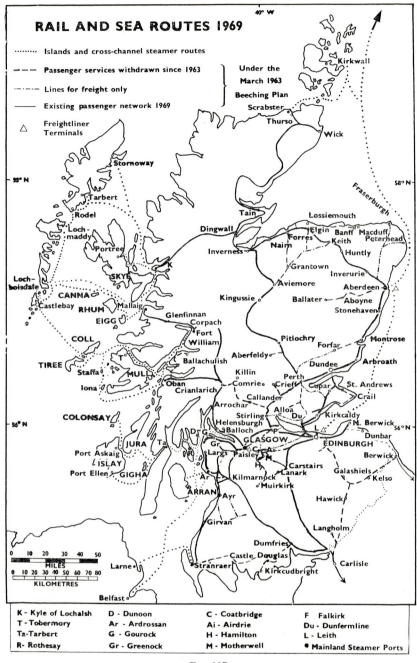

RAIL AND SEA ROUTES 1969

········· Islands and cross-channel steamer routes

– – – Passenger services withdrawn since 1963

–·–·– Lines for freight only

——— Existing passenger network 1969

△ Freightliner Terminals

Under the March 1963 Beeching Plan

K – Kyle of Lochalsh   D – Dunoon   C – Coatbridge   F   Falkirk
T – Tobermory   Ar – Ardrossan   Ai – Airdrie   Du – Dunfermline
Ta – Tarbert   G – Gourock   H – Hamilton   L – Leith
R – Rothesay   Gr – Greenock   M – Motherwell   ● Mainland Steamer Ports

Fig. 107.

being succeeded by developments in overspill and new town locations, must be set the inevitable decline of older industries. The production of shale oil has ceased; coal output is declining, although efficiency is being improved; shipyards, although regrouping and modernizing, find it increasingly difficult to compete with foreign tenders and employ fewer men; and the same pattern can be seen in other sections of heavy industry. The draught being felt from pit closures, mill closures (in the Border towns), empty shipyards and abandoned railways, all with obvious repercussions on the employment rate, suggests, at first sight, a gloomy economic future. From the unemployment map (see Fig. 106) and population movement analysis (see Fig. 19) it would appear that the economic health of Scotland is deteriorating.

Emphasis to this impression cannot help but be drawn from the Beeching proposals of 1963, by which the railway route mileage in Scotland was to be reduced by 40 per cent and two-thirds of the passenger stations were to be closed. Thankfully, not all of the proposals have been implemented and it seems that some consideration is, at last, being given towards future economic and social development instead of empirical decisions being taken based on short-term economic planning. Government aid, announced in December 1968, to certain socially desirable railway services which are not actually paying their way will help to keep the needs of regional development in Scotland to the fore.

With the resurgence in industrial development, especially in the Central Lowlands, air services must be expected to play an integral part. American or European businessmen are accustomed to rapid and frequent air travel as to them time is money and, naturally, they expect this provision. The distinct possibility of stronger links with the Continent on a Common Market basis indicate that a close watch should be kept on the feasibility of developing links from Scottish industrial centres direct with major European regions. Distances between the main centres of industrial activity in Scotland are not great by foreign standards and, therefore, existing airfield locations (see Fig. 108) ought to suffice. A greater emphasis would be needed, however, on "air taxi" feeder flights linking with normal service flights from Inverness, Aberdeen, Edinburgh and Glasgow to England and the Continent.

Distance from scientific sources and major markets has, for long, often deterred companies from seeking location in Scotland and the provision of better transport facilities would help to redress the balance at present overweighted in favour of the Midlands and South. The newly established "Freightliner" terminals at Aberdeen, Glasgow and Leith (Edinburgh) and the nightly chartered freight train from the Chrysler/Rootes plant at Linwood to England serve to indicate the vital importance of such specific transport links. Thus industrialists can then reap the benefits of lower land costs and overheads and of the large, competent labour pool in Scotland,

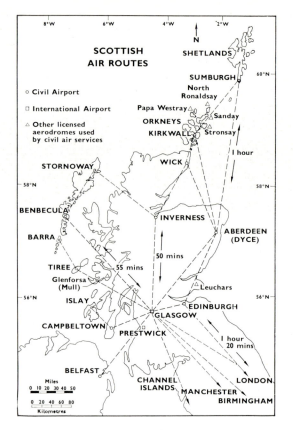

FIG. 108.

Unemployment is still a critical problem in Scotland. Up to 1966, the level of unemployment in Scotland had been rising steadily for 15 years at a greater rate than in Britain as a whole (Fig. 106). In 1958–9, Scotland had 18·3 per cent of the nation's unemployed. In 1962–3, the figure was 17·2 per cent. In other words, 10 per cent of the population of Britain was suffering nearer 20 per cent of the national unemployment—hardly fair treatment! Progress in this relative position has been made, particularly considering the industrial developments in Central Scotland, to the extent that the Scottish unemployment figure for 1967 was just under 15 per cent.

Nothing can resolve the chronic unemployment problem in Scotland which, even since 1945, has been consistently twice the U.K. national average, other than a *sustained* policy of growth. Short-term "crash" programmes are of mere stopgap value in not reaching the root causes. This policy of growth must be supported by long-term planning in which a sound development of power expansion, utilizing all sources—coal, hydro, oil and nuclear—is geared to improved transport facilities. Only then will balanced economic expansion be feasible and thereby will Scotland be enabled to play a vital role in the industrial development of Britain as a whole.

Bibliography

THE following sources were consulted and appear approximately in the order of contents of this book. This list is by no means intended to be exhaustive and readers may well consult the select bibliography published in the *Scottish Geographical Magazine*, **80** (11), September 1964. This is much more complete, although much literature of interest has been added since 1964.

1. A. GEIKIE, *The Scenery of Scotland*, Edinburgh, 1887.
2. J. PRINGLE, The South of Scotland, *British Regional Geology*, H.M.S.O., 1948.
3. M. MACGREGOR and A. G. MACGREGOR, The Midland Valley, *British Regional Geology*, H.M.S.O., 1948.
4. H. H. READ, The Grampian Highlands, *British Regional Geology*, H.M.S.O., 1948.
5. J. PHEMISTER, Scotland, the Northern Highlands, *British Regional Geology*, H.M.S.O., 1948.
6. *Natural Resources in Scotland*, Royal Edinburgh Symposium 1960. Published by the Scottish Council (Development and Industry).
7. *Types of Farming in Scotland*, Department of Agriculture for Scotland, Edinburgh H.M.S.O., 1952.
8. *Census of Woodlands, 1947–49*, Summary Report, H.M.S.O., 1951.
9. *Preliminary Report on the Sixteenth Census of Scotland*, H.M.S.O., 1961.
10. *Scottish Digest of Statistics*, H.M.S.O., various.
11. *Scottish Sea Fisheries Statistical Tables*, H.M.S.O., 1961.
12. *The Tay Valley Plan*, published by the East Central Scotland Regional Planning Advisory Committee, 1950.
13. J. C. DEWDNEY, Changes in population distribution in the county of Fife, *Scottish Geographical Magazine*, **71** (1), April 1955.
14. D. SEMPLE, The Growth of Grangemouth: a note, *Scottish Geographical Magazine*, **74** (2), 1958.
15. C. J. ROBERTSON, Locational and structural aspects of industry in Edinburgh, *Scottish Geographical Magazine*, **74** (2), 1958.
16. A. G. OGILVIE *et al.* (Ed.), *A Scientific Survey of South Eastern Scotland*, British Association for the Advancement of Science, 1951.
17. R. MILLER and J. TIVY (Ed.), *The Glasgow Region*, British Association, 1958.
18. *The Survey Report of the City of Glasgow Development Plan: Quinquennial Review*, 1960.
19. *Industry on the Move*, Glasgow Corporation, 1959.
20. *British Shipbuilding Facilities and Services in 1942*, published by the Shipbuilding Conference.
21. *National Coal Board (Scottish Division) Five-year Review, 1962–6*.
22. *Iron and Steel: Annual Statistics—1962*, published by the Iron and Steel Board and British Iron and Steel Federation.

23. J. Mitchell (Ed.), *Great Britain, Geographical Essays*, Cambridge University Press, 1962:

    J. B. Caird, The North Western Highlands and the Hebrides;
    W. Kirk, North East Scotland;
    A. C. O'Dell, The Orkney and Shetland Islands;
    J. Tivy, The South of Scotland.

24. *The Crofters' Commission Annual Report for 1962*, Edinburgh, H.M.S.O., 1963.

25. J. N. Toothill, *Report on the Scottish Economy 1960–61*, published by the Scottish Council (Development and Industry).

Also numerous towns and county planning reports and surveys.

Glossary of the More Unusual Terms

Alluvium. Sediments derived from the work of rivers.

Black band iron ore. These are clay band ironstones that have a high carbon content. Their widespread use dates from the mid-nineteenth century.

Boulder clay. An uneven layer of boulders and clay deposited by a melting ice sheet. This often develops into fertile soils but may be waterlogged (syn. "till").

Clay band iron ore. Deposits of iron-rich clays that occur widely in nodules in the Carboniferous rocks. Used in the early iron industry for example, at Carron.

Coal measures. The youngest division of the Carboniferous period. These rocks include numerous coal seams, interspersed with other rocks.

Corrie. A circular hollow, or depression, on a mountain side, surrounded by steep slopes on three sides to give an "armchair" effect. Many corries have a small, round lake (tarn) occupying the hollow, from which a stream may issue.

Diatomite. A deposit of siliceous remains used as a polishing powder or insulator in glazes and cements.

Drumlin (see Fig. 83). Smooth, oval-shaped hills, generally composed of boulder clay (see above) with the long axis indicating the direction of the ice.

Dyke. An igneous rock (see below) formed by magma ascending in a molten state through vertical fissures and cooling to present a wall-like vertical sheet of rock, usually only a few feet in thickness, which may protrude on the landscape.

Fault scarp. Formed as a result of faulting, the downthrow side being overlooked by a steep scarp slope.

Fireclay. Fireclays occur widely throughout Carboniferous rocks in Scotland and often represent the soil in which the coal forests and swamps had their roots.

Fluvio-glacial. Deposits formed by glacial meltwater streams.

Föhn. A warm, dry wind which blows down the leeward slopes of mountains.

Glacial deposits. Varied deposits of boulder clay, sand and gravel left by the melting ice sheets.

Gneiss. A coarse, crystalline rock formed by metamorphic activity (see metamorphic, below) and often showing a banded appearance (Lewisian gneiss).

Haars. Cold sea mists, common on the east coast in spring.

Highland front. The steep fault scarp edge of the Grampians.

Igneous rocks. Rocks formed by the cooling of molten magma, whether inside the earth (plutonic—coarse-grained) or on the surface (volcanic—fine-grained).

Ley grass. Sown grass which remains, on average, for seven years.

Machair. Stretches of calcareous sand.

Massif. A large, compact mountain mass.

Metamorphic. Rocks derived from pre-existing rocks by means of chemical, mineralogica and structural changes brought about by heat or pressure.

199

Moraine. Glacial debris which may take several forms, e.g. ridge-like terminal moraines athwart glaciated valleys.

N.R.R. (net reproduction rate). Where deaths balance equally with births the population, which is merely replacing itself, is expressed as the unit (1).

Quartzite. Metamorphosed sandstone.

Raised beaches. Terraces backed by old cliff lines which mark a former level of the sea They normally provide light, productive soil.

Schist. A metamorphic rock which splits easily into thin flakes, e.g. mica schist.

Till. A mixture of unsorted glacially deposited sand, gravel and boulders (syn. "boulder clay").

Volcanic plug. The resistant remains of an old volcano consisting of lava which occupied the former throat of the volcano.

Volcanic rocks. Fine-grained rocks formed by the cooling of molten magma poured out on the surface of the earth.

Index

References in **bold type** are to figure numbers

Aberdeen   **93;** 27, 162–163
Aberdour   65
Aberlady   87
Ae   **15;** 25, 136
Agricultural resources   19 *et seq.*
Agricultural unit   **11, 12**
Air transport   **69, 71, 108;** 193
Aircraft industries   114, 119
Alford   160
Alloa   92, 94
Alloys   92
Almond   73, 77
Alpine   3
Aluminium   **90, 91;** 69, 93, 155–156, 170–
    171, 189
Alva   94
Alyth   52, 57
Annan   139
    River   **81;** 133, 135
Anstruther   64, 65
Applecross   179
Arable farming   **30, 38, 39, 40, 46, 47, 82, 109;**
    19, 42, 49, 52, 63, 64, 75, 77, 91, 92, 98,
    125, 126, 136, 141, 163, 166, 168, 172,
    173, 176, 183–185
Arbroath   **35;** 53, 56
Ardeer   129
Ardrinan Point   111
Ardrossan   **65, 80;** 127, 128, 129, 130, 131
Area, Scotland   1
Argyll   145–147
Armadale   78, 83
Arran   **76;** 3, 131
Aspect   45
Auchinleck   126
Auchterarder   57
Auchtermuchty   **40;** 69, 72
Aviemore   146
Ayr   **80;** 126, 127, 128, 129, 130, 131
    River   122
Ayrshire   **75, 76, 77, 79, 80;** 43, 122–132
    agriculture   125–126

climate   123, **125**
fishing   126
industries   128–132
mining   126–127

Bacon factories   130
Balmoral   147
Banff   **95;** 165
Banffshire   163–165
Bannockburn   90, 92
Barley   **12, 96;** 49, 63, 75, 77, 82, 125, 126,
    136, 160, 163, 166, 169, 171, 181
Barony Colliery   **78;** 126
Barra   **21;** 182
Barrhead   **116;** 100, 115
Basalt   3, 4
Bathgate   **45, 47;** 80, 85, 89
Bauxite   **90;** 69, 155–156
Beans   52, 92, 136
Bearsden   115
Beeching Plan   **107;** 1, 25, 193
Beef cattle   **13;** 21, 49, 52, 58, 63, 75, 77
    126, 136, 147, 160, 164, 169, 172, 182
Beith   128, 130
Ben Cruachan   **89;** 152
Ben Nevis   11, 147
Benarty Hill   59
Berwick   144
Bilston Glen Colliery   **48;** 78
Bitumen   54
Black Isle   169, 171
Blackband Ironstone   16, 42, 100
Blairgowrie   52, 57
Blairhall   65
Blankets   72, 128, 171
Blantyre   114
Bo'ness   80, 85
Bonnybridge   93
Bonnyrigg   88
Boulder Clay   **83;** 63, 91, 135, 166, 171
Bowling   97

Brechin   53, 57
Brewing   75, 83, 87, 93, 94
Broadlaw   9, 135
Broomielaw   108
Brown coal, Brora   16
Broxburn   80, 85, 86
Buchan   **93;** 159–165
  platform   159
Buckie   165
Buddon Ness   52
Burntisland   **90;** 69, 156

Cairngorms   **92;** 6, 145–147
Caithness   **93;** 171–172
Calders   80
Caledonian Canal   **2;** 169
Caledonian system   3
Calico   100
Callander   90
Camp Ridge   **48;** 73, 78
Campbeltown   149
Campsie Fells   **56, 68;** 8, 90
Canning industry   **30;** 52, 54, 57, 162, 168
Car
  bodies   **105;** 103
  industry   **27**
Carluke   98
Carnoustie   52, 56
Carpets   53, 58, 69, 88, 92, 93, 129, 131
Carrick Hills   123
Carron   **65;** 93, 95
Carse
  of Earn   52
  of Forth   **57;** 90, 91
  of Gowrie   **28, 31;** 8, 42, 52
Cash registers   54
Castings   85
Castle Douglas   **81;** 140
Catrine   128
Cellardykes   69
Central Highlands   145 *et seq.*
Central Lowlands   **1, 24;** 8, 41 *et seq.*
Chapelcross   **17;** 32
Cheese   130
Chemicals   **58, 63;** 84, 87, 92, 95, 107, 130
Cheviots   9, 133
Chocolate   83
Chromite   17
Clackmannan   91
Clayband Ironstone   16, 42, 93
Cleish Hills   8, 59, 60
Climate   **6;** 9 *et seq.*
  see also regional chapters
Clyde valley   42, 97 *et seq.*
Clydebank   **68;** 68, 105, 106, 107

Clydeport   **70;** 111–113
  Authority   111
Coach building   93
Coal
  exports   66, 127
  in Ayrshire   **76, 78;** 126–127
  in Central Coalfield   **65;** 100–101
  in Fife   **41, 42;** 65–72
  in Lothians   **47, 48, 49;** 78–80
  in Middle Forth Region   92–93
Coalfields, general   **25, 26;** 45
Coatbridge   101, 104, 115
Cockenzie   45, 78
Coking coal   **65;** 80, 101
Colonies, trade   99, 100, 108
Colvilles   66
"Comet", Bell's   106
Commercial fishing   27
Commercial vehicles   85, 189
Container terminal   112
Copper pyrites   17
Corby   34
Corpach   25, 138
Corse Hill   123
Corsican Pine   166, 168
Coupar Angus   46, 52, 56, 57
Cowdenbeath   65, 70
"Crag" and "Tail"   **50, 51**
Crail   **38;** 64
Creameries   126, 130, 136, 139, 160, 170, 174
Cree River   **81;** 135
Crofters' Commission   28
Crofting   **99, 100, 101;** 19–20, 175 *et seq.*
Crop comparisons   **14**
Crude oil   **60;** 79, 95, 130
Cuillins   1, 179
Culbin Sands   166
Cumbernauld   **72;** 37, 43, 118, 119, 120
Cumbraes   131
Cumnock   **75;** 123, 127, 128, 129
Cunningham   122
Cupar   **36, 37;** 63, 68, 72

Dailly   127, 130
Dairying   **13, 77, 81;** 63, 77, 91, 98, 125, 126, 135 *et seq.*, 169, 172, 174
Dalbeattie   140
Dalkeith   **47, 48;** 87
Dalmellington   **76;** 127, 129
Dalry   **76;** 111, 116, 128, 130
Damask   68
Darvel   128, 131
Dee, River   **48, 81;** 123, 135, 136, 147, 159, 162

Deeside 147
Denny 94, 96
Development areas **27;** 70, 83
Devon valley **56;** 59, 90
Diesel power stations **17;** 29, 184
Dingwall **93;** 169, 170
Don, River **48;** 147, 162
Donibristle 70
Dormitory towns 56, 88
Dornoch **83;** 165, 171
 Firth 165 *et seq.*
Dounreay **17, 97;** 32, 165
Drainage **4;** 6, 9
Drumlins **83;** 199
Dumbarton **61, 72;** 105, 106, 111, 115, 120
Dumfries **81;** 139
Dumfriesshire 135–140
Dunbar **47;** 88, 89
Dundee **27, 28, 30, 33, 101, 104;** 45, 52, 53,
 54, 55, 56, 57, 107
Dunfermline **36, 37;** 68, 69, 70, 72
Dunkeld 57
Dunlop 129, 130
Dunoon 115
Duns 144
Dunure 126
Dyeing 58, 69, 110
Dyestuffs 95
Dykes 3, 180, 199

Eaglesham Heights 97
Earlsferry 65
Early potatoes 126
Earn, River **28;** 47
East Kilbride **61, 72;** 37, 43, 114, 119, 120
East Linton 88
East Neuk **36;** 59, 63
Easter Ross 169–171
Eden **36;** 59, 69
Edinburgh **45, 47, 51;** 73, 75, 80–85, 86,
 88, 89
Electrical industries 68, 84, 85, 119, 120,
 139, 169, 172, 188
Electricity **17, 18;** 29–33, 45, 66, 127
Electronics **27;** 46, 68–70, 72, 84, 86, 87,
 88, 114, 119, 188, 190
Elgin **96;** 166, 168
Elie 65
Esk
 Black 135
 North **28, 45, 52;** 47, 73, 88
 South **28, 45;** 47, 73
 White 135
Esparto grass **47, 52;** 83, 107
Ettrick, River 141
Explosives 130

Falkirk **56, 90;** 46, 93–95
Falkland **40;** 69
Fauldhouse 80
Faults **1, 2, 32, 35;** 2–8, 133, 145
Fenwick 126, 131
Fertilizer manufacture 54, 84, 88, 91, 107,
 130, 182
Fife 59–72
 agriculture 63–64
 climate 60, 83
 industries 65–72
Findhorn, River 166
Finnart oil terminal **60;** 95, 148
Fisherrow 78
Fishing **16, 35, 38, 95;** 26–29, 52–53, 56,
 64, 78, 87, 126, 139, 160, 162, 164, 165,
 168, 171, 174, 176, 178, 179, 182, 183,
 185
Flax industry 53, 56, 68–69, 100, 163
Food industries 72, 83, 105, 162
Footwear 58, 68, 129
Foreign investment 46, 143
Forest Parks **15;** 25, 170
Forestry **15;** 22, 25, 26, 27
 Commission **15**
Forfar **28, 30;** 52, 53, 57
Forres 168
Fort William **91;** 11, 156
Forth
 bridges **55;** 70, 88
 River 73 *et seq.*
 Road Bridge **54**
Forth–Clyde Canal 94, 101
Foyers **90;** 153, 154, 155
Frances Colliery **41**
Fraserburgh 160–162
Freightliners 193
Fruit farming 20–21, 52, 98, 148
Furniture 69, 130

Gaelic 14
Gala, River 141
Galashiels **81;** 143
Galloway 133–140
Galston 128–131
Gargunnock Hills 90
Garleton Hills 73
Garnock, River 122
Gartcosh **64;** 103
Garvock Hills 47
Geographical inertia 150
Geology **1, 32, 39, 41, 46, 48, 49, 50, 51, 78;**
 1–9
 see also regional chapters
Girvan 126, 130–131

Glaciation **5, 83, 86, 87;** 6, 45, 73, 97, 133–
    136, 145 *et seq.,* 175, 181
Glasgow 97–121
    as a port 99–100, 105–113
    growth of industry 99 *et seq.*
    population and overspill 115–121
    site, growth, form 99, 108–111
Glass 58, 172
Glendevon 59, 90
Glenfarg 59
Glengarnock **64;** 129
Glenkens 136
Glenrothes **43, 44;** 43, 63–64, 70–72
Glentrool **15;** 136
Gley soil 17–18
Gourdon 53, 56
Gourock 115
Grampians **1, 24, 29;** 4, 145–158
Grangemouth 59**;** 94, 95, 96
Granite 133, 135, 163
Granton **47;** 78, 85
Grantown-on-Spey 146
Great Glen **1, 2;** 3, 4–6, 180
Greenock **61, 103;** 100, 105, 107, 108, 111,
    112, 115
Guardbridge 59, 69
Gullane 88

Haddington 88
Hamilton 114, 115, 119, 120
Hardpan **9**
Harris **2;** 181 *et seq.*
Hartfell 9, 135
Hawick **81;** 143
Hebrides
    Inner 180–181
    Outer 181–183
Helensburgh 115
Hemp 69
Hercynian 3
Herring 27, 29, 64, 126, 145, 162, 165, 168,
    174, 178, 182, 183, 185
Highland Boundary Fault **1;** 3
Highland Front **29;** 47
Hillfoot towns 93, 94
Hillington **71;** 114
Hill-sheep farms **10**
Holiday industry 56, 57, 65, 72, 88, 130–
    131, 140, 146–147, 149, 157, 171, 178,
    179, 181, 183
Hosiery 57, 85, 92, 93, 100, 114, 128, 139,
    171, 184
Howe of Fife **36, 40;** 8, 59, 63, 72
Hoy 172
Hunterston **17, 76;** 33, 127

Huntly 160
Hydro-electric power **17, 84, 88, 89;** 31 *et
    seq.,* 138, 150–154

I.C.I. 130
Igneous minerals 17
Industrial estates **27, 71;** 54, 113–115, 169
Invergordon 170, 189
Inverkeithing 69
Inverness 168–169
Inverurie 160
Iron
    and steel **58–61, 65, 66;** 93–94, 101–103
    import 103
    industry, Falkirk 93–94, 100, 101–103
    ore 93–94, 101, 103
    pan 18
Ironstone 16, 93–94, 101–103, 180
    see also Blackband; Clayband
Irvine **75, 76, 80;** 43, 99, 108, 120, 128,
    129, 130, 131
Isla, River **28;** 47
Islay 150, 180–181
Isohyets **8, 17**

Jedburgh **81;** 143
Johnshaven 53
Johnstone **61;** 100, 120
Jura 180–181
Jurassic coal 16
Jute industry **30, 33;** 53–54, 56, 58

Keith **93;** 147, 152
Kelso **81;** 142, 143
Kelvin, River 97
Kilbirnie **76;** 129
Killoch Colliery **76, 78;** 126–127
Kilmarnock 123, 127, 128, 129, 130, 131
    132
Kilpatrick Hills **68;** 97
Kilsyth 93, 94, 100
    Hills 90
Kilwinning 129–130
Kincardine 66, 78, 79, 90
Kinghorn 65
Kinneil Colliery **49;** 80
Kinross **37;** 63, 69, 72
Kirkcaldy **37, 39;** 64, 66, 68, 69, 70, 72
Kirkcudbright **81;** 139
    Stewartry of 135–140
Kirkintilloch 93, 100, 104–105, 115, 120
Kirkwall 174
Knitwear 69, 84, 85, 88, 100, 128, 139, 184
Kyle 122
    of Lochalsh 179

Lace   100, 128–129
Lady Victoria Colliery   **50**
Ladybank   69
Lammermuirs   9, 73
Lanark   86, 97, 98, 117, 131
Land use   **15**
  see also regional chapters
Larbert   93
Largo   65
Largs   **76;** 130
Larkhall   114
Lasswade   88
Lauder, River   140
Laurencekirk   57
Lead   15, 17
Leith   **45, 47, 50, 104;** 27, 80, 83, 84, 85
Lerwick   183–184
Leslie   63
Leven   **36, 39;** 60, 62, 69
  Vale of   105, 114
Lewis   **100;** 175 *et seq.*
Lewisian Gneiss   **3;** 4, 5, 180
Line fishing   **101;** 27, 58, 179
Linen   68–69, 100, 129
Linlithgow   **47;** 85
Linoleum   53, 54, 69
Linwood   **64, 105;** 103, 114
Livingston   **45, 47, 55;** 43, 83–84, 85
Loanhead   78, 88
Loch Awe   **89;** 152–154
Loch Broom   **99, 101;** 178–179
Loch Sloy   **89;** 151–152
Lochaber   **90, 91;** 154–156
Lochgelly   68
Lochwinnoch   97
Lockerbie   132
Lomond Hills   **36, 39;** 8, 59, 63
Longannet   **42;** 45, 66, 78, 92
Lossiemouth   168
Lothians   73–89
Lugar valley   122
Lugton valley   131
Lunan valley   47

Macduff   **95;** 165
Maidens   126
Mallaig   **107;** 179, 181
Malting   83, 88, 142
Marine engineering   69, 84, 105–107, 129, 162–163
Markinch   **44;** 69
Mauchline   **75, 76;** 126, 127, 132
  basin   **78;** 126
Maybole   129
Mearns   **28;** 47, 52

Melrose   **81;** 143
Menstrie   94
Mentieth
  Hills   90
  Lake of   90
  Vale of   8
Merrick   9, 133
Merse   **81;** 133
Metal industries   68, 69, 75, 85, 129
  see also Iron and steel
Methil   **37;** 66, 69, 72
Middle and Lower Clyde Region   **61–74;** 97–121
Midland valley   **1**
  see also Central Lowlands
Midlothian   73–88
Migration   **19;** 36
Milk output   **77;** 126
Milngavie   115
Minerals   16–17
Mining machinery   72
Mixed farming   49
Moine schists   4
Monadhliath Mountains   **92;** 6, 145–146
Monifieth   56
Monkland Canal   101
Monktonhall Colliery   **48;** 78
Montrose   **30;** 52, 53, 56
Moorfoots   9, 73, 140
Moray   166–168
  Firth   159 *et seq.*
Mosses   90
Motherwell   **65;** 104, 114, 115, 120
Muirkirk   129, 130
Mull   3
Musselburgh   **47;** 77, 78, 88

Nairn   **6;** 168
  County   166–168
New towns   **27, 43, 44;** 37, 43, 70–72, 85, 118–121
Newbattle   78
Newburgh   **37;** 69
Newhaven   78
Newhouse   114
Newmilns   128, 131
Newton Stewart   **81;** 140
Newtongrange   78
Newtown St. Boswells   142
Nith, River   **81;** 133, 139
North Atlantic Drift   9, 10
North Berwick   **47;** 88
North Uist   181, 182
North West Highlands   **1;** 3–6, 175 *et seq.*
Norway Spruce   168

Nuclear power   **17, 18, 97;** 32–33, 127, 139, 172
Nylon   129

Oat milling   83, 171
Oats   **12, 93;** 49, 63, 77, 98, 125, 133, 136, 141, 142, 148, 160, 163, 166, 169–173, 176, 181, 183
Oban   148
Ochil Hills   **24, 36;** 8, 47
Oil
  pipeline   **60;** 95
  refining   **27, 59;** 95, 112, 130
  shale   **53;** 16, 80, 84
Old Red Sandstone   **1, 32;** 4, 6, 47
Opencast coal   65–67, 78
Ordovician   133
Ore valley   59–60
Orkneys   **106, 108;** 172–174
Overfishing   53, 162
Overspill   **69;** 37, 97, 115–121

Paisley   **6, 61;** 100
Paper industry   **52, 93, 94, 104;** 25, 69, 83, 107, 163
Papermaking machinery   83
Peas   52
Peat   **100;** 31, 32, 185
Peebles   **81;** 143
Peneplain   **2; 3** *et seq.*
Penicuik   85
Pentland Hills   9, 73
Perth   **30, 31;** 53, 57–58
Peterhead   **93;** 160–162
Petro-chemicals   **59;** 95
Pig iron   *see* Iron and steel
Pitlochry   **88;** 149
Pittenweem   64
Planning regions   **27;** 96
Plastic goods   72, 95
Plums   98
Podzol   **9;** 17
Polkemmet Colliery   80
Population   **19–23;** 34 *et seq.*
  see also regional chapters
Port Glasgow   100, 106, 107
Port trade: Scotland   **104**
  see also regional chapters
Portessie   165
Portpatrick   **81;** 139
Potatoes   **12, 32;** 49, 63, 75, 98, 126, 141, 166, 169, 171
Power stations   **17, 84, 88, 89, 91, 97;** 79, 80, 127, 139, 150–154, 172

Precipitation   **7, 8;** 11–14
  see also regional chapters
Prestonpans   88
Prestwick   **108;** 131
Printing, publishing   **52;** 54, 83, 92, 94
Pulp mill   25, 138
Pumpherston   **53;** 80

Quartz   17
Queensferry   89
Queenslie   114

Radar   54
Radio   54
Rain shadow   14, 159
Rainfall   **8;** 11, 14
  see also Precipitation *and regional chapters*
Raised beach   **36, 96;** 44, 55, 65, 85, 108, 109, 147, 153, 154, 160, 200
Ramsey Colliery   **48**
Ranching   21
Raspberries   52, 98, 133
Ravenscraig   **65, 66;** 103
Refrigerators   54
Renfrew   **61;** 105, 108, 120
  Heights   **61;** 97
Road bridges   63
Rolling stock   104
Rope   69, 88
Roslin   88
Ross and Cromarty   169–171, 175 *et seq.*
Rosyth   69
Rothes Colliery   72
Rothiemurchus   147
Rubber industry   84, 92, 95, 107, 139
Rutherglen   103, 107, 120

Sacking   53
St. Andrews   **36;** 65, 68
St. Monance   64
Saltcoats   **75;** 122, 128, 131
Saltpans   88
Sanquhar   **76;** 17, 123, 127
Scapa Flow   174
Scots   14–15
  Pine   147
Scrabster   **107;** 172
Seafield Colliery   **41;** 66
Seaweed   126, 182
Seed potatoes   49, 52, 75, 126
Seine nets   27–29, 53, 64, 165
Selkirk   **81;** 143
Settlements   **22**
Sewing-machines   **68;** 105
Sheep   *see regional chapters*

Shetland *see* Zetland
Ship repairing 107
Shipbreaking 69
Shipbuilding **63, 67, 68, 70**
  in Aberdeen 163
  in Ayrshire 129
  in Dundee 53
  in Fife 69
  in Grangemouth 95
  in Leith 84
  on the Clyde 105–107
Sidlaw Hills **28, 29, 31, 32;** 8, 47, 49, 52
Silk 68
Silurian 133
Silver 17
Sitka Spruce **81;** 25, 168
Skelmorlie 130
Ski centres **92;** 145, 146, 147, 148, 157
Skye 3, 179, 185
Slamannan plateau **53, 56, 57;** 90
Smokies 53
Snow **7;** 11
Soil survey 18
Soils **9;** 17–19
Solway Firth 9, 135
South Harris **3;** 181
South Uist 181, 185
Southern Boundary Fault **1;** 133
Southern Uplands **1, 81, 85;** 9, 133 *et seq.*
Steel *see* Iron and steel
Stenhousemuir 92
Stevenston **75;** 129, 130
Stewarton 128
Stirling **56;** 90–91
Stonehaven **30;** 47, 52, 53, 56
Stornoway **6, 107, 108;** 182–183
Stranraer **81;** 139
Strathallan 8, 59
Strathconon **5**
Strathearn **28;** 47, 52, 59
Stratheden 59
Strathmiglo 69
Strathmore **28, 29, 32;** 8, 47, 49, 52
Strathpeffer 171
Strathspey 146
Strathtay 148
Strawberries 49, 63, 77
Strip mill **66;** 103
Sugar 100
  beet **12;** 49, 63, 72, 75, 77, 141
Sutherland 169–171, 175 *et seq.*
Synthetic fibres 68, 95, 128–129, 143
Synthetic rubber 92, 95, 139

Tain 170

Talc 17
Tay
  agriculture **32;** 49–52
  climate 49
  Lower Tay Region **28–35;** 47 *et seq.*
Tay Road Bridge **33;** 55, 72
Tayside study 55
Teith, River 90
Temperature **6;** 9–11
  see also regional chapters
Tents Muir 59
Tertiary 3
Teviot River 141
Textile machinery 53, 54, 56, 68–69, 104, 105
Textiles 54, 56, 68–69, 104, 105, 128–129, 131, 139, 143, 165, 167–168, 171, 182–184
Thermal power stations 29
Thread 100, 129
Thurso **107;** 172
Tillicoultry 94
Tobacco 100, 107–108
Tomatoes 98
Torpichen Hills 73
Torridonian Sandstone 3, 4, 5, 179, 180
Tourist industry 140
  see also Holiday industry
Tranent 88
Trawling 27, 52–53, 64, 78, 160–163
Troon **76;** 127, 129, 131
Trossachs 157
Tummel-Garry 151
Tummel Valley Scheme **88;** 152
Turnberry 123, 130
Turnips **12;** 49, 63, 98, 133, 136, 141, 148, 160, 168, 173, 176
Turrif 160
Tweed 88, 143, 160, 174, 182
  basin 140–144
  River **81;** 140–141
Tyne valley **45;** 73, 75, 77
Typewriters 114

Uddingston 98
Ullapool **16;** 178–179
Unemployment **106;** 193, 194
Uphall 80
Urban population **22;** 34–37
  see also regional chapters
Urban renewal **73, 74;** 116–117
Urr **82**

Valleyfield 65

Watches   54, 114, 188
Water of Leith   84
Weighing machines   69
West Lothian   73–89
Wester Ross   175 *et seq.*
Whaling   53, 54
Wheat   **12;** 49, 63, 92, 125, 133, 141, 163, 166–168
Whisky   **104;** 58, 72, 83, 85, 131, 150, 165, 169, 171, 181
Whitburn   80
White fish   64, 160, 162, 165
Whiteadder   141
Wick   **107, 108;** 171–172

Wigtown   139
Wishaw   **65;** 104, 114, 115, 120
Woodpulp   **52;** 25, 69, 83, 107, 138
Woollen goods   69, 93–94, 100, 143, 160, 165, 169, 183–184
Woolmet Colliery   **48**
Worsteds   128

Yarrow, River   141

Zetland (Shetland)   **1, 106;** 183–184
Zinc   17